High Definition Cinematography

To

William and Annabel
who are the future

High Definition Cinematography

Third Edition
By

Paul Wheeler BSC FBKS GBCT

ELSEVIER

AMSTERDAM • BOSTON • HEIDELBERG • LONDON • NEW YORK • OXFORD
PARIS • SAN DIEGO • SAN FRANCISCO • SINGAPORE • SYDNEY • TOKYO
Focal Press is an imprint of Elsevier

Focal Press is an imprint of Elsevier
Linacre House, Jordan Hill, Oxford OX2 8DP, UK
30 Corporate Drive, Suite 400, Burlington, MA 01803, USA

First published 2003
Reprinted 2004, 2005 (twice)
Second edition 2007
Third edition 2009

British Library Cataloguing in Publication Data
Wheeler, Paul, 1945–
  High definition cinematography. – 3rd ed.
  1. Digital cinematography
  I. Title
  778.5'3

Library of Congress Control Number: 2008943003

ISBN: 978-0-240-52161-9

For information on all Focal Press publications
visit our website at www.focalpress.com

Typeset by Charon Tec Ltd (A Macmillan Company), Chennai, India

Printed and bound in the United States of America

09 10 11 12 12 11 10 9 8 7 6 5 4 3 2 1

Working together to grow
libraries in developing countries

www.elsevier.com | www.bookaid.org | www.sabre.org

ELSEVIER   BOOK AID
            International   Sabre Foundation

Contents

Preface

I joined the BBC film department in 1963 just as they were opening their second channel and moving over from 35 mm black and white to 16 mm color. I left to go freelance 25 years later, by which time I had become one of the six Senior Film Cameramen at the BBC. At the time I resigned, the BBC was just introducing portable video kits for film cinematographers; these consisted of an analog camera with a separate U-Matic recorder. I have to confess that the introduction of this kit was a contributing factor to my decision to resign – compared with the 16 mm film cameras we were using at that time they were heavier, brought back the umbilical cord between the camera and the recorder, and, to my eyes, there was a huge drop in picture quality, not what I thought the BBC was all about.

I never did take to the analog cameras but, in the years since then, I have come to appreciate Digi Beta, a much more stable format. Until recently, however, I still preferred to shoot on film, particularly 35 mm. That decision has now changed. When HDCAM came into our world 8 years ago it was, to my mind, the first digital format that could truly challenge the film image. At the time of writing we now have many recording formats, some of them with no moving parts at all, and several cameras that have sensors that will comfortably exceed the original 1920 × 1080 pixel count. I am now very happy to shoot on some of the better High Definition (HD) formats rather than film.

This third edition of HD cinematography is a substantial move forward from the previous two editions. I have deleted several chapters where their content seemed to me to now be common knowledge. I have added eight more cameras, including the RED One. There is now a comprehensive description of shooting three HD projects in the section Examples of Shoots. I have also dropped the old end chapter on Sony menus but, hopefully by the time this is published, that chapter will be on my website for those who still need it. If you do, please go to www.paulwheelerbsc.com.

About the Author

Paul Wheeler has a wealth of practical experience as both a Film and Digital Cinematographer combined with wide experience as a highly respected trainer. He is the author of *Practical Cinematography*, which is a standard work for those wishing to become Cinematographers in the traditional art of shooting film, and *Digital Cinematography*, which primarily concentrates on the Digi Beta arena. After 25 years with the BBC, by the end of which he was one of only six Senior Film Cameramen out of a total of 63 Directors of Photography employed there at that time, he left to go freelance in order to concentrate on dramatic scripts rather than factual stories.

Since leaving the BBC, Paul has had a flourishing career that has bought him many awards, including two Independent Producers Association (INDIE) awards for Digital Cinematography, two BAFTA nominations and a nomination from the Society of Lighting Directors plus numerous others. Check his website www.paulwheelerbsc.com.

Paul is equally at home shooting High Definition (HD) or film. In 2008, just prior to writing this third edition, he shot *King Lear* starring Sir Ian McKellen, directed by Sir Trevor Nunn for the Performance Company, using four HD cameras.

In between shoots he has stood in as Head of Cinematography at the National Film and Television School in the UK several times and also as Head of Cinematography at the Royal College of Art, also in the UK. He is a regular visiting tutor at the London International Film School, the New York Film Academy in London and the Metropolitan Film School in London. He has designed and run the highly respected Digital Cinematography course at the National Short Course Training Programme, part of the National Film School, as well as taking Lighting Master Classes there both for Film and Digital Cinematography. He also runs a regular Advanced Lighting course for the Galway Film Centre in Ireland, as well as visiting several other European countries as a lecturer and trainer.

In December 2000 Paul was invited to join Panavision Europe as an associate of the company in order to help introduce the Panavision HD cameras to the European film and television community. He had the luck to join Panavision just 3 days before they got their first HD camera so was in, by a whisker, just before the start! Paul spent about a third of his working life with Panavision over the next 3 years, finally parting company with Panavision, most amicably, when Europe had become familiar with HD.

Paul is a member of the British Society of Cinematographers (BSC), a Fellow of the British Kinematograph, Sound and Television Society (FBKS) and a member of the Guild of British Camera Technicians (GBCT).

Introduction

High Definition (HD) cinematography is a relatively new acquisition format which, I believe, is set to revolutionize much of the theatrical film world and, perhaps, even more, of television. It has been around now for little more than 8 years compared with film, which has been with us for considerably more than 100 years. In some areas it can compare; in some others, currently, it struggles to achieve any kind of dominance. Film, with its utterly superb image capture capabilities, is surely an anachronism in a television environment and with more and more digital effects appearing in feature films it is inevitable that, on occasion, there will be advantages in originating in the same image format as that which is to be used for the post-production.

HD picture quality can arguably be every bit as good as 35 mm film in some ways, as I hope to prove in this book, yet the pre-cutting room costs will hopefully be lower than shooting 16 mm film. Make no mistake about it, the drive to HD is fiscal, so let us Cinematographers be thankful that the picture quality, the range of cameras and lenses, and their ease of use is nearly always to our advantage. It's not just the saving in film stock and processing that is driving this engine. There is a huge value, especially to the distributors of feature films, to deliver the product to the screen without the cost of making and shipping release prints. Fortunately for Cinematographers there has been a contemporaneous advance in digital projection equipment and it is now possible to be very proud indeed of one's work even if it has never left the digital domain.

I am a great believer that people from a visual world gain as much information from pictures as they might from words. Therefore I often produce the illustrations first and then write the text to them; in this book there are some 165 illustrations.

A top-of-the-range HD camera with the finest lenses and recording either in the HDCAM format or one of the recently available equal or superior formats is now my camera of choice – nearly always, not bad for a man whose grandfather joined the British Film Industry only 2 years after the Lumière brothers showed the first on-film moving picture in Regent Street, London. Grandfather was late by the way – his brother had joined 6 months earlier!

The future is bright, very bright. If the work of future Directors of Photography can be recorded in some form of very high image quality, and it matters not on what recording format or what it is recorded on, we Cinematographers have a wonderful future to look forward to. Cinematography is a craft, and often an art form, which will be needed no matter what means science uses to record the Cinematographer's work.

Acknowledgements

My special thanks to:

Alan Piper for inviting me to become an associate of Panavision Europe a few days before they received their first High Definition (HD) camera, a moment which now seems a long time ago, an invitation which subsequently led to the first edition of this book. My only regret here is that we have both moved on to more interesting things and therefore see a little less of each other. I also have to thank him for being my technical editor on this, the third edition.

Peter Swarbrick, Head of Digital Imaging, Panavision Europe for being wonderfully supportive and a great friend and colleague who took the trouble to start teaching a film man a thing or two about HD and for giving me some great quotes.

Alan Roberts for his amazing patience in teaching me how digital cameras and television really work.

The camera suppliers and hirers, who were unstinting in their help whilst always knowing I would criticize as well as praise:

From *Sony*, Peter Sykes, Nigel Thomson and Awad Mousa for getting me access to, and permission to use the pictures of, the Sony HDW F900R and much more.

From *Arriflex*, Bill Lovell for giving me the time to explore the Arriflex D-21 and permission to use the pictures of it, including the cover picture, together with a great deal of wise counsel and encouragement.

From *Dalsa*, John Coghill for not only making sure I had my facts on the Origin correct, but also for permission to use the pictures of the camera.

Thank you to Sam Martin of Decode for my initial introduction to the RED One.

To Barry Basset of VMI for giving me access to several of the cameras, including the RED One.

And to all the other equipment manufacturers and suppliers who have given me so much of their time with the absolute understanding that I would write up my own opinions. I think it a great tribute to our industry that not a single one of them was less than enthusiastic for me to explore their product. What a wonderful industry we work in.

For allowing me access to their projection booths and cinemas and giving me a huge amount of information on HD presentation, I have to thank Mark Nice at the Odeon Leicester Square, Keith Fawcet at BAFTA, and John Houchin and Brian Naylor at The National Film and Television School.

My thanks to Mike Coleman and Chris Atkins of Stage 2 Screen for permission to use the pictures from *Birthdays*.

Thank you to Jane McGee and Christopher Billows for asking me to shoot *The Optician* and supplying the pictures from the master tape and giving me permission to use them here.

A special thank you to my old associates Richard Price and Chris Hunt from the Performance Company for asking me to shoot yet another wonderful production, this time *King Lear*, and giving me free access to use whatever I wanted from that production in this book.

And most importantly my wife Anne for her encouragement, her support and her patience with reading my drafts.

All the illustrations in this book, other than those specifically quoted above, are the copyright of the author.

Part 1
High Definition: A Quick Overview

CHAPTER 1

Why Shoot on HD?

If you want to make quality films, whether for the big screen or for television, then you should always consider High Definition (HD) as a serious option.

If you are used to shooting on 16 mm film or Digi Beta then you will see a considerable increase in picture quality.

If you are used to shooting on 35 mm film you should, with the right approach and the right technicians, see no loss in image quality. Indeed, in certain circumstances, you may see an improvement.

Again, if you are used to shooting on 35 mm, you should see a substantial drop in the cost of your recording medium.

That's it! Enough said!

1.1 What Do We Mean by High Definition (HD)?

High Definition is an electronic recording medium that takes on two challenges. First it should be able, either in a purely digital way or by printing the recorded images onto a conventional piece of film, to give the audience in a cinema, even the largest cinema, pictures with which they are familiar and that appear to have at least the technical quality, mainly assessed as definition, that they have come to expect. If it does not, or cannot, then the audience will not bother to go to buy a ticket. Secondly, in the television arena, the requirement is to provide economical recording formats that give stunning picture quality on any of the new television HD transmission formats and their associated widescreen televisions, otherwise no one will buy the new TVs.

My belief is that, handled with care and knowledge, all the above is easily achievable.

1.1.1 The Knowledge Base

Originally many people moving into HD hoped it would look like film. This is not difficult to achieve. We have been shooting film, and admiring the results, for well over a hundred years; by now we ought to know how we have been doing this. Forgive me if you find this a sacrilege, but the process of recording moving images on film is far from perfect. It is very good and, until around the year 2000, was the only medium that could successfully suspend our disbelief in a large cinema. Then HD arrived. Initially almost everybody wanted HD to emulate the film look and I was lucky enough to be, almost from the start, one of those people advising them how to achieve this. My first advice then, as it is now, was to hire a film-trained Director of Photography (DP), for with that person comes around five generations of handed-on knowledge and experience. Someone trained in film will always be able to give you those kinds of image, it's in their blood, and they can hardly help it.

Now, some 8 years on, we are beginning to see a new kind of image maker – one who is prepared to take on the images that only HD can produce. Some of these DPs come from a film background, some from television and some are so young they are finding their own way in this new and exciting medium. More power to their elbow, I say!

1.1.2 What Does It Mean to the Producer – Saving Money!

If you work in my world, or wish to, you have to accept that it is driven by a four-letter word – cash! This may not necessarily be a disadvantage, particularly if the work you have previously been known for has been recorded on film. But don't take that as a raw statement, it gets better.

If you are thinking of moving from film to HD then savings in the budget are obviously going to be an influencing factor, but more can be made of the changes than just reducing the bottom line. For example, a little of those savings can be spent on production values, thus upping the perceived quality of the product. The extraordinary international compatibility of HD should assist the producers in making money, as HD is both an origination and post-production medium. When the film is completed it can be output in almost any delivery format (cinema), any Worldwide Television format (the Net), even digital phones, and all this with an incomparable asset – no loss in quality.

1.1.3 What Does It Mean to the Director?

Confidence. With modern HD monitoring, the Director is seeing rushes (dailies) on set and in real time. Large-screen monitors can give a Director a real sense of how the picture is going to look in its final venue.

A closer working relationship with the DP, something I was nervous of when I first started using HD but have come to love. A good director does not want to be a DP, if for no other reason than they are, or should be, too busy with all the other problems, primarily their actors. A decent monitor is a wonderful communication tool.

1.1.4 What Does It Mean for the Director of Photography?

First, for me, it means I have a new and exciting toy to play with. I admit to liking toys.

Secondly, because of the cost savings involved, I may get to shoot more movies because more producers will be able to afford to get their production off the ground.

Thirdly, when shooting for television, I will be able, at a very small increase in cost, to deliver a significantly higher picture quality.

Fourthly, if the producer is sensible, and it is our job to convince them, I will be able to work with my normal film crew who, with only the slightest of training, can become HD experts almost immediately.

And last, perhaps, by embracing this new, excellent and exciting recording medium and its cameras, I can become more popular with productions and therefore busier.

1.1.5 What Does It Mean to the Other Crafts?

Very little. If they are good enough to work on 35 mm film then they are definitely good enough to work on HD. Most of the heads of departments I have worked with in high-end television would have little or no problem working on HD. For instance, I have held Make-up workshops for HD and it just isn't a problem. If the Make-up Supervisor and the DP work closely together, as in my experience they always do, then those worrying lace caps on a wig, the prosthetic nose job and all the rest present the same problems and require the same solutions. No problem!

1.1.6 Editing and Post-Production

Herein lies a very slight rub, and if there is a problem it should not necessarily be laid at the door of the DP or the post-production house. In my experience problems in this area, which are mercifully rare, nearly always follow inadequate planning, and incorrect decisions being made during the pre-production run up to principal photography. If post is going to go smoothly then you have to get the prep right. Because HD is still relatively new, it is prudent to bring together the Producer or Production Manager, the Director, the DP, the picture editor and *all* the post-production personnel, including Visual Effects (real-time effects) and the Post-Production Effect Supervisor for a significant meeting, or several meetings, before principal photography starts. They should not leave the room until agreement has been found and notes should be taken. I always do!

All of the above must be taken even more seriously now that we have cameras coming on stream that do not record a fully processed image, the data from the camera therefore requiring some manipulation before a fully formed image is ready for conventional post-production. The RAW data coming from a RED camera comes to mind, but provided this and other cameras using RAW data are treated with respect and the additional post-production layer is fully understood, this way of working can render very good pictures indeed – in the right hands, of course.

1.2 Context

When I came to lay out this book for the third time, I realized that there was no "right" or "wrong" approach. Wherever I started I would have to refer to topics to be explained later, so should I discuss the technology first, or should I consider HD from a Producer's perspective?

I decided to start with production decisions for two reasons. First, I believe that until we are all more familiar with the HD workflow, reaching correct production decisions will be an essential prerequisite to success. Secondly, if the sales and cost advantages of using HD are not understood then there is little point in worrying about the technology anyway, as no one will be using it. Getting bums on seats at a reasonable cost is the name of the game, and always has been. Nothing new there!

Part 2
Production Decisions

CHAPTER 2

Which Formats to Shoot On?

The problem, as I see it, is that there are a bewildering number of decisions to be made and they *must* be made before you start shooting or there is a very strong probability you will inherit some terrible problems when you get into post-production.

Things have changed since the introduction of HDCAM in the year 2000. Prior to that the choices were very simple – if you were going to shoot on film there was really only a choice between two formats, were you going to shoot on 35 mm or 16 mm? All the other decisions for many of the heads of departments (HODs) on the production would fall into line quite simply once that decision was announced. If you were shooting on Digi Beta were you working in an NTSC environment or a PAL environment? Again a simple and easy choice.

In an effort to be all things to all people, High Definition (HD) has many, many options to offer. This is good but it can be bewildering. It can look frighteningly daunting but, truly, it need not be. There are eight, yes eight, different frame rates to choose from. However, as you will see, the decision is likely to come down to a simple choice between only two or three frame rates, the same number of choices we had in the old days – so how difficult is that?

2.1 Progressive or Interlace?

There is the thorny question of whether to shoot in Progressive scan or interlace. Again I do hope this book will help with that decision but, usually, choosing between theatrical production and factual, cinema or television and asking yourself what the audience is accustomed to will bring the answers naturally to hand.

2.2 How Many Pixels Do You Need?

How many pixels should I shoot with? The answer is simple: as many as you can afford. The middle ground is still HDCAM with its true 1920×1080 pixel array recording on HDCAM 1/2-inch tape. It works don't knock it. Handled wisely it can easily please an audience in the largest of cinemas. It can hardly fail to make television look better than standard definition pictures be they recorded on Digi Beta or 16 mm film. Again, handled well, they should look as good as 35 mm film when shown on standard definition television, which I believe are just about the best pictures we are used to seeing. It's called the quality headroom getting through.

2.3 Recording Formats

What recording format to use? Difficult, but almost certainly the decision will be budget driven. As I said earlier, use the best you can afford. HDCAM is still the frontrunner for most productions, but if you have a really good budget there are hard drives to record on and cameras that originate their pictures at a much higher resolution than HDCAM, although they can be very expensive. One danger in going to higher formats is the amount of data you will need to record on set and the associated data delivered into post-production.

2.4 HDV – Can You Get Away With It?

No, but although I have chosen not to discuss HDV anywhere else in this book, preferring to stay with more professional formats, I have to admit a sneaking admiration for HDV. At the price it must be close to a miracle. *But* few, if any, HDV cameras actually have 1920 × 1080 pixels on their chips and the recording format – that is, the tape width or the disk or chip size – is so small that few, if any, can record a genuine HD picture. Much more worrying is the various types of compression schemes used. Many adopt the MPEG-2 recording format, where one complete frame is recorded and the next 12 images are not complete images at all, for what is recorded on the tape is only the difference in that frame from the first one – fine if not much moves in your picture or you don't wish to pan the camera very quickly. If your pictures contain either of these occurrences then the images will start to contain less and less information as the camera's processor fails to keep up with the data being sent to it. A great system, but not really up to professional cinematography. While MPEG-2 drops into an amateur's laptop reasonably easily, it is not a robust recording format and can give considerable problems later in post-production, particularly if you are going to try anything fancy. It's very cheap, though, so if this is the only way you can get your picture shot – go for it!

Hopefully, this book will make all of the above decisions very much easier.

CHAPTER 3

Picture Quality

3.1 What Does HD Look Like?

Before I go any further I must admit to a bias, with my Director of Photography (DP) hat firmly in place: I just love the images created by a High Definition (HD) camera, particularly when that camera is fronted with a decent lens. Please remember I am third-generation film industry – if I find HD appealing it must, surely, be worth your while giving it your consideration.

The images are usually very sharp with a long tonal range and the colors are lifelike and true. Whether seen on a monitor or digitally projected there is no dirt on the picture, no scratching and no picture instability such as weave or unsteadiness. Some fans of the photomechanical image miss these aberrations, but with my training having been in the BBC in London they were always artifacts we were trying to eliminate so, perhaps, this is why I welcome their elimination. If the final product is to be shown from a film print then all the possibilities of print imperfections return, of course, and if you like them have a film print and you may be very happy, especially if you have your HD image printed out onto camera negative film rather than an intermediate stock. Printing out to camera negative stock can give an even greater impression that the images were originated on film.

To be starting with such a high technical standard is a joy for a DP like me, for if one feels the image too sharp, diffusion filters allow you to reduce it to any degree or look you wish for. If the colors are too bright for the script you are working on, then with filters or by adjusting the in-camera menus this is easily attenuated. And the result of your adjustments is easily assessed on a monitor in real time. Especially when using a 24-inch HD monitor, what you see is what you get; or, to use a favorite phrase of mine, if it looks right – it is right.

If you come from a film background, as I do, then the easiest way to envisage the HD image is to think of the picture you would get shooting on 35 mm Kodak 320 ASA extended range Vision stock and printing to their Premier release print stock. The quality of lenses you deploy will change the image every bit as much as it will on a film camera and again I must admit to a bias; to my eyes and my style of shooting the Panavision and Zeiss ranges of zoom and prime lenses are unbeatable. For cinema productions I try to use no others. For television

I may relax my opinion slightly as the finite potential of the absolute resolution of the delivery medium is, inevitably, lower even if being transmitted in an HD format.

3.2 HD Images Compared with 35 mm

The most notable thing if you are watching HD projected using a state-of-the-art HD projector is the almost total lack of grain. Some people miss this effect dreadfully. If you really cannot cope with such a clean image then you can add grain, or what I like to think of as texture, in post. It is also possible to add texture in the camera: simply shoot with some gain switched in. I have very successfully shot HD with 6 dB of gain switched in and the resultant image has been much admired. If you are going to film for final delivery then it would be a wise precaution to print a short test, for the effect of gain is more noticeable on the big screen than on a monitor.

3.3 Anamorphic 35 mm

To shoot HD in the anamorphic 2.4:1 aspect ratio you simply switch the viewfinder marking to show a bright line box in that aspect ratio and compose to it; most HD cameras can do this. The image will remain unsqueezed right up to the point in post-production where you make the first film image. At that point the printer will horizontally compress the 2.4:1 section of the image to produce a conventional anamorphic photographic image. This technique has been proved many times to work very well with cameras utilizing a 2/3-inch three-chip configuration; with the latest single-chip cameras the result is simply stunning. If you are projecting the result with a digital projector then a simple switch is all that needs to be set to show the image in the 2.4:1 ratio.

As the majority of cameras, especially those using three 2/3-inch chips, record in a 16×9 aspect ratio where the image is comprised of 1080 vertical pixels, the center section used for anamorphic imaging will comprise just a little over 800 pixels vertically. There are those steeped in the film tradition who would like to deny the evidence of their eyes and say this cannot possibly produce a sharp enough image. I put it to you they are wrong and believe I can prove it. Before I do, remember that more and more of the newer single-chip cameras have more pixels than the 2.1 million per chip of the 2/3-inch cameras and they interpolate down to 1920×1080, thus further improving apparent image quality.

There are now a number of cameras utilizing a single chip the size, or near to the size, of a Super 35 mm frame and these can shoot with spherical lenses in exactly the same way as you would with 35 mm film. If you do this then you can go down the same post-production route as you would when extracting a 2.4:1 master on Super 35 for later anamorphing to a conventional squeezed 35 mm print. Or just leave it as HD and tell a digital projector to show it as 2.4:1.

The finite judgement of sharpness in the cinema is made by the human eye. The resolution of the human eye is well known and discussed elsewhere in this book, so if the picture on the cinema screen is sharper than the human eye can perceive then the brain will tell the viewer that the picture is sharp. In most cinemas 800×1920 pixels produce an image which more than meets this requirement; hence we perceive it as sharp, as anyone who has seen some of the latest features shot on HD will testify, for this is most likely how they were made.

A counter-argument goes that 35 mm film must be sharper because the image has a resolution which is referred to as a 4 K resolution, meaning 4000 horizontal pixels or samples, whereas HD only has a fraction under 2 K of resolution. This is true, but as described in Chapter 10, the 4 K film negative has to be photographically copied several times before being projected onto the screen. At every stage quality will suffer. It can be shown that the image on the cinema screen is unlikely to be better than 1.2 K.

The HD image, on the other hand, while starting at a little under 2 K resolution is transferred digitally – that is, just re-recording zeros and ones – so there is no loss of quality at any transfer point. Hence if the production has stayed within the HD domain the resolution being projected is the full 2 K – 1.92 K if you want to be exceedingly picky – image originally formed by the camera, arguably higher than can be achieved by the photochemical process.

There are more technical explanations of these matters in Part 3 – The Technology.

3.4 Comparisons with Super 16 mm

Most of the 2/3-inch chip cameras described in this book produce an image that bears direct comparison with conventional theatrical 35 mm image quality, as we have seen. All of the single-chip cameras described are capable of even greater quality.

There are HD cameras that are marketed specifically at high-end television. For instance, Sony make the HDW 700 range that have imaging chips with 1080×1920 pixels, which I would consider true HD, and these cameras use a 10- or even 12-bit processor. They are market specific in that there is a PAL standard version that will only record in the 25P or 50i format and NTSC versions recording in 28.98P, 59.97i and 60i. They can, however, be set up to give both a High Definition Serial Digital Interface (HDSDI) output, as well as a PAL in the European, or NTSC in the US, version. The HDW 750P can give a quality of image, when shown on television, which will still compare with 35 mm but the differences may become apparent when shown on a big screen in a cinema. To date there is no 24P version of the HDW 750 so direct frame rate compatibility with cinema is impossible. Compatibility is possible, however, with the newer Sony HDW 900R. Theses cameras are discussed individually, and more fully, in Part 6 – Cameras.

3.5 Comparison with Digi Beta

Frankly there is no contest. In my opinion all true HD cameras produce a better picture than a Digi Beta camera. Digi Beta cameras are considerably cheaper to either rent or buy so they will be around for use in television a while yet but, I like to think, not for all that long.

CHAPTER 4

Display Quality

4.1 HD Shown on Television

There are some who say there is no point in shooting High Definition (HD) when the finished product is only ever going to be shown on current television – I disagree. Just as a film originated on 35 mm film looks better on either PAL or NTSC than one originated on 16 mm or Digi Beta, the same is true for HD, as it is a picture of very similar quality to 35 mm. This is known as retaining the quality headroom. As HDCAM tape recorded in the 24P format was always intended to be the international exchange format we can, hopefully, expect a gradual increase in picture quality for prestige programming. It is possible to play a 24P HDCAM tape out of, say, a Sony HDW F500 video tape recorder (VTR) or similar, where the output is already converted to the PAL or NTSC formats. Even using this simplistic down-conversion the headroom is retained and clearly visible. I was present when a Sony HDW 900 was demonstrated to one of the more sceptical line producers I frequently work with. To my delight he rapidly became a fan of the system but right at the end of the demonstration asked if it were possible to see a full HD resolution monitor next to a standard PAL monitor with the picture down-converted via the HDW F500. As luck would have it there was just such a capability set up in another room for an entirely different purpose. We ran a single tape, the contents of which he had by now seen as a played-out HD image on a 24-inch HD monitor as well as the same film written to both 1:1.85 format and 1:2.4 format projected film. After staring at two 14-inch monitors right next to each other, one a full HD monitor fed from the High Definition Serial Digital Interface (HDSDI) socket on the HDW F500 and the other a high-resolution PAL 625-line monitor fed from the PAL down-converted output on the same VTR, his reaction after seeing every frame was "well the PAL looks just like 35 mm with lines!" I rest my case.

4.2 HD Written to Film and Projected Mechanically

If the transfer from HD tape to film is carried out with sufficient precision, and bear in mind the quality of image produced by different companies can vary tremendously, then to all intents and purposes the resultant print will be very similar indeed to the same image had it been acquired on 35 mm negative. There are those who will tell you different but I have met few who doubt the quality of HD when they have seen well-shot demonstration reels available at several of the top-end suppliers.

4.3 HD Shown on a State-of-the-art Digital Projector

The quality of image on a cinema screen from a high-end digital projector showing an image that has never been anything but HD is simply stunning. It looks a little less like film origination than HD written back to film, so arguments will go on for years yet as to whether that difference is an improvement or a degradation of the cinema picture quality we have come to expect. I come down firmly in the "it's better" camp. Maybe that is my training in the BBC as a Director of Photography, for I have simply been going in that direction all my working life, but I love the fact that it is very sharp, there is no dirt and dust, no picture weave and far less flicker. All good things to my way of thinking.

I have heard one explanation that purports that the blanking time of a mechanical shutter is preferable, for it lets our brain rest between the showing of each frame of image. My reply is to ask – if I blink 24 times a second will I feel less tired? Of course not. What nonsense this idea must be! If it were so I am confident God would have given me that facility. Here's to flicker-free projection, I say.

4.4 Digital Projectors

Unlike a 35 mm mechanical projector, which is roughly the same size and cost no matter what the size of the cinema, digital projectors come in many shapes and sizes – and costs. You can see a variety of them in Chapter 5 and, believe me, all those shown give a wonderful picture. Digital projection in the cinema is here and is here to stay.

High Definition Projection

5.1 Introduction

When I published my first book on High Definition (HD) in 2003, HD projection was a bit of a Cinderella at the ball. There had just come onstream some truly HD projectors but they were viewed with suspicion by those involved in acquiring the pictures whether via HD or film, especially by those using film. There were also problems arising from a lack of knowledge, understanding or availability of usable equipment. **How things have changed!**

Encoding a movie onto a hard drive and delivering this to the cinema is now so common that one of the premier screens in the UK, the Odeon Leicester Square, estimates that 75 percent of their screen time is now delivered this way and shown on their 2 K digital projector. While there are those that think we should be looking for greater than 2 K resolution in the theater I cannot agree. If you refer to Chapter 10, you will see my argument that 2 K horizontal resolution is a little more than a human eye can resolve in a cinema and considerably more than a 35 mm film release print is likely to deliver. Therefore a good 2 K projector fed with a high-quality and pure 2 K signal will deliver a picture that should be slightly better than any of the audience are capable of perceiving – if these parameters are met then that image has to be more than good enough.

Matters pertaining to projection were in such a state of flux when I published the second edition of this book early in 2007 that I decided not to update the chapter on projection and I have been criticized for this, perhaps rightly. I have decided with this third edition to take a new approach. Digital projection is now so common, so well understood and, when carried out by technicians who know their craft, delivers such superb pictures that just going into the technicalities seemed superfluous.

As this book is likely to be read by more people involved in the acquisition of pictures than in other areas of our business, I decided that, hopefully, it would be interesting for them to describe presentation venues where the equipment and resultant image quality were of the highest standard. It has to be said that the welcome I got from those running these venues was superb and the cooperation enormous.

Come on all you people who think that shooting and editing a film is the be all and end all of cinema – our work will look rubbish if those who show our pictures do not try to attain the highest standards. So next time you go to the cinema, or rushes (dailies), or see your work looking good on television, go up to the projection box and say thank you, or ring the station and ask for the duty manager and ask them to tell the telecine or image quality staff how delighted you were. It's in your interest, after all.

Please remember a phrase my father drummed into me, especially when I got my first job at the BBC, as a trainee projectionist: "Here's a thought for your reflection, a show like this needs good projection!"

5.2   Examples of Venues

5.2.1   The British Academy of Film and Television Arts (BAFTA)

5.2.1.1   The venue

The two cinemas at BAFTA are arguably the finest private viewing facilities in London. They are mainly used for screening current feature films for BAFTA members, but can also be used by the members in order to showcase their work and can be hired for industry and corporate events. There are two cinemas: the smaller, the Run Run Shaw Theater; and the main auditorium, the Princess Anne Theater (Figure 5.1, picture 1), with the BAFTA logo on the screen, this being the BAFTA mask designed by Mitzi Cunliffe.

The Princess Anne Theater can seat 227 and has a screen size of 33.3 × 14.5 feet (approximately 10.2 × 4.39 meters). The projection box contains two Cinemechanica 35/70 mm projectors and one digital projector (Figure 5.1, picture 3). The Run Run Shaw Theater has just one slightly smaller, but nevertheless 2 K, digital projector (Figure 5.1, picture 5).

5.2.1.2   The digital projectors

The Princess Anne Theater utilizes a Barco (Belgium American Radio Corporation) DP 100 projector with a 6-kilowatt lamp (Figure 5.1, picture 6). The Barco DP 100 utilizes three 1.2-inch dark metal type Texas Instruments DLP Cinema™ technology chips, each having a native resolution of 2048 × 1080 pixels. This projector also has a filter set allowing polarizing filters to be used, thus enabling BAFTA to show truly superb 3D or stereoscopic movies. The filter set is controlled by the Dolby DFC Filter Controller, which is the third installation in the processor rack shown in Figure 5.1 (picture 7).

In the Run Run Shaw Theater there is a Barco DP 1500 projector (Figure 5.1, picture 5), which uses three Texas Instruments DC2K 0.98-inch dark metal reflectors, each with a native resolution of 2048 × 1080 pixels.

Figure 5.1: The Princess Anne Theater at BAFTA, London

5.2.1.3 Digital handling

Both the Run Run Shaw and the Princess Anne Theaters can be served from the comprehensive digital handling rack (Figure 5.1, picture 7). This contains a Dolby DSS 100 Show Store server with a storage capacity of 1 terabyte, which is enough to hold approximately six feature films. Below that on the rack is the Dolby DPS 100 Show Player with full 3D capability. Again, going down the rack we come to the Dolby DMA8 Plus Digital Media Adapter and below that the Dolby DFC 100 Filter Controller, again with full 3D capabilities. As if this is not enough there is a Sony HDW 1800 HDCAM tape player (Figure 5.1, picture 2) and BAFTA often hire in a Sony HDCAM-SR player when required. Figure 5.1 (picture 4) shows Keith Fawcett, BAFTA's Head of Technical Services, setting up the Dolby Show Player for the afternoon performance.

5.2.1.4 What does it all get used for?

Most evenings there are films on display in the Princess Anne Theater to which members are invited with a guest. Both theaters can be booked by members for their own use and I have been lucky enough to have had several of my own films shown here, so can attest to the extraordinarily high quality of the image on the screen in both theaters.

Both theaters, together with the vast David Lean room on the floor below, are available for corporate hire.

5.2.2 The National Film and Television School (NFTS)

5.2.2.1 The venues

The NFTS has two cinemas. The new one, in a newly built teaching block (Figure 5.2, picture 1), has 151 seats with a screen 7 meters wide (approximately 23 feet) and is served by a Christie CP2000-X projector.

The second, and original cinema (Figure 5.2, picture 6), has 59 seats and is served by a Christie SL1-D projector.

5.2.2.2 The projectors

The Christie CP2000-X projector in the main cinema (Figure 5.2, pictures 2 and 3) utilizes Texas Instruments DLP technology just like the Barco projectors in the other two venues in this chapter and like them uses three chips. This projector has a native resolution of 2048×1080 pixels, claims a 200:1 contrast ratio and employs 15-bit image processing. The projector currently uses a 2 kW lamp and produces a very fine image.

The Christie SL1-D (Figure 5.2, pictures 7 and 8), though being of a slightly older design than the CP2000-X, has the same native resolution and again deploys a 2 kW lamp.

Figure 5.2: The theaters at the National Film and Television School in the UK

There is also a Provost 35 mm projector in this box, with reel-to-reel or "cake stand" film handling (Figure 5.2, picture 5).

5.2.2.3 Digital handling

In the main cinema a Kodak Content Player JMN3000 is used (Figure 5.2, picture 4). This player is a multiformat device, being able to handle various compression formats including MPEG- or JPEG-compressed data for 2D features, or 3D-compressed MPEG images.

In the other cinema a Sony JH-3 HDCAM tape player (Figure 5.2, picture 9) is permanently available as HDCAM tapes are the most common HD format used by the students. Other image recording formats can be brought into this cinema as needed.

5.2.2.4 What do they get used for?

The old theater is now the primary venue for students to show their work in progress, etc. The main cinema is ideal for the presentation of finished work, and the viewing of interesting or well-known feature films and major television programs. It is also a venue for industry events showcasing students' work.

5.2.3 The Odeon Leicester Square, London

5.2.3.1 The venue

The Odeon Leicester Square can claim to be one of very few "Premier" screens in the UK. It has a screen size of 52 feet wide by 26 feet high (approximately 15.85 × 12.48 meters). The main theater has 1683 seats with additional space for four wheelchairs.

The exterior is unusual (Figure 5.3, picture 1). The entire front of the theater is clad in black marble, which, while looking somber during the day, lends a special quality to the appearance of the building at night: the façade seems to disappear and the signage and posters seem to float in space – all very theatrical, as perhaps it should be.

The projection box contains two 35 mm mechanical projectors plus a high-quality digital projector, as we shall see.

5.2.3.2 The digital projector

The digital projector is a Barco (Belgian American Radio Corporation) DP 100 projector, as shown in close-up in Figure 5.3 (picture 6). As a guide to the size of the projector, Figure 5.3 (picture 3) shows Mark Nice, the Odeon's Technical Manager, readying the projector for the day's work. The Barco DP 100 utilizes three 1.2-inch dark metal-type Texas Instruments DLP Cinema™ technology chips, each having a native resolution of 2048 × 1080 pixels. This, together with a xenon lamp of 7 kW, gives 18,000 cinema lumens output and provides a contrast ratio of 2000:1 and an astonishingly good picture on the huge screen.

Figure 5.3: The Odeon, Leicester Square

5.2.3.3 Digital handling

The digital information is stored in a Dolby DSS 100 server capable of holding up to five feature films, as you can see in Figure 5.3 (picture 2). Each of these films usually arrives at the venue stored in an encrypted form on a single hard drive, one of which can be seen in its carrying case in Figure 5.3 (picture 5). Behind the case can be seen the old film storage bins; each vertical compartment would contain a 2000-foot roll of 35 mm film, which would have a screen time of 20 minutes. How things have changed! The cinema has an alternative source in a Doreme DCP 2000 unit (Figure 5.3, picture 4).

Once the data on the hard drive have been loaded into the server a separate "key" is sent to the cinema. This electronic key enables the cinema to understand the encryption of the data and run them as a picture source for the projector. This element of the process is essential to protect the film from piracy.

5.2.3.4 What does it all get used for?

The Odeon estimates that over 75 percent of the screen time in this theater is now provided by the Barco digital projector; 35 mm film prints will only usually be used when a director such as Steven Spielberg insists that his work be displayed this way.

Digital cinema projection appears to be here to stay.

5.3 How HD Cinema Projectors Work

There are many kinds of digital projector but most of the projectors designed for use in full-size cinemas, and indeed all described in this chapter, utilize the Texas Instruments DLP Cinema™ Technology chip. This chip is a quite extraordinary device for, despite being only 1 1/2 inches in size, it contains 2,211,840 pixels in an array of 2048 pixels horizontally by 1080 vertically. This means that each pixel has a width of less than one-fifth of the thickness of a human hair. Even more extraordinary, each pixel is made up of a small mirror mounted on a hinge and in addition there is an actuating device that, when a signal is received by the pixel, causes the mirror to tilt across its diagonal. Figure 5.4 represents a small portion of the chip's mirror field.

The DLP Cinema chip uses standard digital philosophy that relies on breaking up the image into very small segments, known as pixels, and distributing these tiny bits of information accurately to any piece of equipment further down the production route. With these projectors the ambition is to display from each and every mirror the exact same brightness and color that was originally seen by a pixel in the same position in the pixel array in the camera or film scanning device that generated the original digital recording. Thankfully the projectors described here do this with extraordinary accuracy, thus maintaining the highest picture quality on the screen.

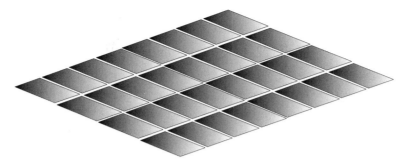

Figure 5.4: A small portion of the Texas Instruments DLP Cinema™ Technology chip

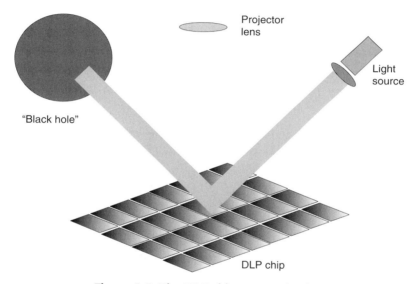

Figure 5.5: The DLP chip – no activation

The bit-stream image code entering the complete semiconductor causes each individual mirror to either stay stationary or move to its second position up to several thousand times a second. If you look at Figure 5.5 you can see how matters are arranged. With no activation the light from a lamp and condenser lens is directed away from the projector lens and on to some light-absorbing device. As each projector manufacturer uses a different light absorber, I have chosen to call this device a "black hole".

In order to simplify the explanation I have only shown light from the source hitting a single mirror, whereas in reality the light source would cover all the mirrors on the chip. So, in Figure 5.6, one mirror has been activated and has moved to its second position, where the

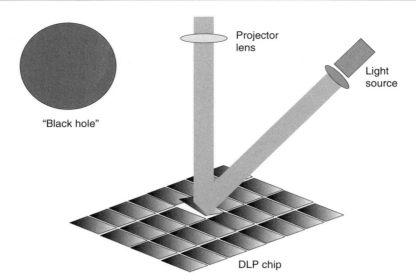

Figure 5.6: The DLP chip – activation of one mirror

light is now directed out through the projector lens. If this were all that happened, all that would be seen on the screen for this single pixel would be the option of black, no activation, or bright white, all the light going to the screen. Here is where the chip's ability to shift that mirror up to several thousand times a second comes into play. If the mirror flicks light many times a second to the cinema screen, then a bright highlight will be observed by the audience. On the other hand, if that mirror only flicks light a relatively few times in the same time period then a dark gray will be perceived by the audience. The variety of times each mirror can flick light to the screen is so variable that it is possible to convince the audience that they are seeing a range of 1024 different shades of gray.

5.4 Adding Color

5.4.1 Single-chip Projectors

In smaller venues it is economical to have a single DLP chip operating as described above with the addition of a spinning filter wheel interposed between the chip and the lens. This wheel may have only three colors – Red, Blue and Green – or more, in which case they will most likely add Cyan, Magenta and Yellow. In a projector using this configuration it is necessary to synchronize the filters on the wheel with the image being sent to the DLP chip, so that at all times the correct color signal being reflected by the chip is the same as the color of the filter currently interposed between the chip and the screen.

The disadvantage of this arrangement is that the filters on the wheel absorb an appreciable amount of light and therefore it is difficult, if not impossible, to fill a large screen with a bright enough image. The advantage is a relatively cost-effective projector that will still give a very high quality image.

5.4.2 Three-chip Projectors

All the projectors discussed earlier in this chapter have three DLP chips, for they are all required to fill a large screen with a sufficiently bright picture.

Three-chip projectors work in a manner not dissimilar to a three-chip camera – you can read about camera beam splitters in Chapter 13. The light coming from the projector lamp is split into three separate beams, each being reflected by an individual dichroic mirror so that Red light arrives at one chip, Blue at another and Green at the third. Once these separate beams of light have been reflected by their own DLP chip, in the manner required by each frame of the moving image, they are then all brought back together again in a homogeneous ray and delivered to the projector lens.

As dichroic mirrors are far more efficient than absorption filters, this arrangement produces a much brighter image on the screen for any given power of projector lamp. The downside of getting that very bright, superbly sharp image on the cinema screen is a more costly projector.

CHAPTER 6

Delivery Requirements

6.1 For Delivery on Film

There are various processes that need to follow the completion of the editing process. If you have been editing from Digi Beta copies, the original camera tapes will have to be conformed to the Edit Decision List (EDL), thus producing a continuous stream of shots that make up the movie. Just as it is with film it is prudent to keep to a minimum the number of times the High Definition (HD) information is re-recorded, so the grading process might be combined with the conform, thus taking out one copying process. If you have been editing on a platform that has been working in full HD standard and the material was played in from the camera tapes, then the material will in all probability have been stored on a disk array. This means that there will have been a zero loss of quality during the edit and a fully edited version lies in the disk array, thereby removing the need to conform. In these circumstances, and assuming they have the facilities, you might prefer to grade and add all the effects within the same post house directly from the original disk array. In some post houses you might even be able to play out from the edit suite disk array directly into the laser printer, always assuming you have never come out of the HD format, thereby maintaining a very high quality. If this is practical it is an excellent way to proceed. If this is not possible then one way or another you must arrive at a fully conformed and graded HDCAM tape, or possibly a tape format of even higher quality and stability, which contains all the effects and titles, etc. This tape will, most likely, be fed into a disk array associated with the printer, for it takes up to 2.5 seconds to print each frame. Pausing each frame on the tape is impractical, so the material must reside on some kind of drive capable of random access of individual frames. The first photographic copy that is struck can be of various types – negative film stock or intermediate film stock – just as with the traditional film process. If the printer uses a cathode ray tube (CRT), then most likely the first copy will be made onto slow-speed camera negative. If a laser scanner is being used it is more common for intermediate stock to be used – then you have the choice of writing either a negative or a positive image.

6.2 Higher Resolution in Post-Production

It is becoming more common for films wanting to maintain the highest picture quality, add greater channels of surround sound, or carry out multilayer CGI in post, to either record their material on a higher quality medium than HDCAM or at least up-res it to that higher resolution before entering the post-production arena. HDCAM-SR and -D5 come to mind. This may well be an excellent idea for cinema release but I have to question the wisdom of that added cost if the production is not going to be seen on a higher grade presentation medium than High Definition Television (HDTV) and for DVD release it seems to me to be a considerable waste of scarce production resources.

6.3 Multiformat Delivery Requirements

If you are not required to deliver a film-out print then it is likely that any international client will prefer that you deliver the product on an HDCAM tape recorded in the 24P or 25P format. The alternative is that they will require a tape converted by you to their home standard; this is relatively easy to arrange. Most post houses are both adept and experienced at this form of conversion with absolutely no, or at worst very little, loss of quality or convenience. The thing to watch out for with certain conversions, as discussed later, is that the time code has gone across successfully – you may need to stripe in new time code on the standards converted copy. If you know before shooting commences that a foreign version is required, I strongly suggest you make a small test and send it right through the post-production chain.

6.4 HD Projection

Most HD projectors are capable of taking an output directly from an HD video tape recorder (VTR). This, however, is not an ideal source if many viewings are to take place, as it involves an, admittedly minimal, mechanical wear to the tape. Alternatively, you can transfer the material to a hard disk array or transfer it to a server. There is an increasing move to persuade cinemas to accept the movie from a central point with delivery by satellite, fiber-optic or even via broadband across the Net, though at the time of writing this is technically possible but would take an inordinate amount of time. As broadband transmission rates are becoming faster and faster this may become a viable proposition. These options would only transmit the zeros and ones, not formed pictures, so there should be no loss of picture quality.

6.5 Encryption

A major consideration in shipping material around a country or even the world is the very strong possibility that somewhere out there, there will be a person not connected with the producers who would very much like to get hold of a copy of the material so that, illegally, they could make a considerable profit. The solution to preventing this looks likely to be encryption. This is a method of encoding so that only those with the key to the code are able to open the file and use the material. Perfect encryption ciphers are much sought after and are currently being seen as the holy grail of shipping physical or virtual movies around the world. Interestingly Kodak, the great yellow giant, happens to be a leader in the field of image data encryption. Kodak has not taken its eye off the digital ball.

6.6 Broadcast Delivery

With no need to convert the HD image to a piece of film the options and choices within the broadcast world are quite different. The most important thing to understand is that originating in HD does not tie the production to any of the current transmission standards. One of the most significant attractions of HD, particularly HDCAM, is that it is a stand-alone format with an incredible ability to convert, without any discernible loss in quality, to any broadcast standard.

Since writing the first edition of this book it has been wonderful to see broadcast production houses finally realize that the transparent convertibility of HD to other standards can, and I believe will, produce revenue that more than compensates for the slightly extra cost of HD origination.

At its inception HDCAM was conceived as a platform that provided an international exchange format – 24P. Unfortunately, so far, this goal has not been realized due to insular and short-sighted attitudes on the part of some producers. The "not invented here" syndrome still lives on in many parts of the world. Fortunately the HDCAM platform is able to convert, in either direction, between most of the other eight formats so that origination made in the HDCAM platform continues to move forward.

6.7 Convertibility

6.7.1 Picture

It should be noted that the misconceptions that prevail as to convertibility must be scrutinized carefully, for most of the perceived problems are easily overcome. To take the most common problem, shooting in the USA and posting in the UK or vice versa: it is hardly a problem at all. If you shoot at 24P and post in 25P you have a 4 percent run time differential. Likewise if you shoot at 25P and post at 24P again there is a 4 percent differential in run time. What does this differential mean? Very little!

6.7.2 Sound

The human eye cannot discern a 4 percent differential in the speed of movement; so as far as the pictures are concerned, 4 percent makes no difference to the final audience. Our ears, on the other hand, are a little more sensitive to changes in the speed at which a soundtrack is played back. Most sounds we hear are unfamiliar to us, so a 4 percent change in pitch is inconsequential. *But* if the audience is listening to musical instruments they are familiar with, someone with perfect, or near perfect pitch, will recognize that there is an error. Do not despair; available now, and at very small cost, are devices called pitch correctors – they work in real time and you only need to deploy them when you have your final cut, so the machine time needed will be relatively small.

6.7.3 Time Code

When swapping between 24P and 25P in either direction one must be aware of some time code problems. At the point of conversion, be it just after origination or after the master cut has been produced, it may, indeed most probably will, be necessary to stripe in a new time code at the new frame rate. This is really a very simple procedure and should not be feared. It just needs to be watched. One simply ends up with a 24P and a 25P copy, each with their appropriate time code, and the two different copies can be generated at very little cost.

CHAPTER 7

Sales Potential

7.1 Multiple Standard Sales

If you have made the master recordings on HDCAM using the 24P or 25P recording format, then it is relatively easy to produce economically many versions from this master, in many different formats. Directly from the Sony HDW 500 or similar video tape recorder (VTR), assuming it is fitted with all the conversion cards, you could play out in 24P, 25P, 30P, 23.98P, 29.97P, 59.97i, 60i and 50i. That covers most, if not all, of the television formats around the world. From the same master it is possible to print out to film in almost any aspect ratio from 1.175:1 right up to 2.4:1. Clearly, by originating in the economical and convertible formats of either 24P or 25P using the HDCAM, HDCAM-SR tape or even, nowadays, a portable hard drive to store the final version, many markets are opened up that otherwise might have been closed or for which it would have been too expensive to provide a suitable version.

7.2 Multiple Venue Sales

Therefore from a 24 or 25P HDCAM master any television station or cinema can receive a version that precisely fits their requirements. There are other venues and display points that should be considered. In-store large screen displays will benefit from the added quality and color depth of High Definition (HD). Very large screens or video walls of images are increasingly used for sales presentations; the difference in visual impact on such screens between pictures originated on conventional television formats, or even Super 16 mm, and HD, can be quite startling. When multiple screens are used the format will fulfill all likely requirements; think of an in-store situation where you might want a video wall at one point in the store but require several conventional televisions around the store. Economics may force you to use domestic televisions around the store but the big screen would be better supplied from a true HD source.

7.3 Additional Sales to HD Users

Currently, the USA, Japan and Australia have HD transmission systems and are often prepared to pay a premium for HD programs. Europe and the UK in particular are fast catching up. Most broadcasters deem an HD program to be one originated in true HD either in the 1920 × 1080 or the 720 × 1280 formats, depending on the local standard, or one shot on 35 mm and transcribed through a telecine capable of sufficient quality. With the possible exception of wildlife programs, most broadcasters will not accept more than a very small percentage of material originated on Super 16 mm or Digi Beta. As can often happen, a single additional sale to an HD station can more than finance any extra costs involved in HD origination. Clearly, a prudent producer would try to make the sale before production begins, but it is quite likely that there are reasons, some even economic, to shoot on HD even without a pre-sell in place. If this is the case then a post-production sale to one of these stations, particularly given the premium they might pay, can be very nearly all profit. The only costs involved are transcribing an extra HDCAM tape and shipping.

7.4 Future Proofing

The raw tape stock is unlikely to last physically as long as film, even given that both are stored in ideal conditions. The cost of lengthening the life of an HD tape is very low; you just make a clone every 20 years or so. The cost of preserving film is high for, even if the master negative exists in perfect order, new prints are expensive, though new copies will be required at far longer intervals.

There is always the argument that recording standards may change and they certainly will, eventually, but HD is so easily convertible between standards I cannot see why a copy in some new format could not be made simply and economically in any newly arrived format. If you want to make a new television copy at full resolution from a film the cost can be considerable, involving both telecine and processing charges.

CHAPTER 8

Cost Implications

8.1 Savings

8.1.1 Origination Costs – Different Formats

When I wrote the first edition of this book things were simple – all I had to do was compare 35 and 16 mm film with HDCAM tape. Now things are not so straightforward. Some camera manufacturers are beginning to assume that tape is the least likely recording medium and that flash drives, hard disk recorders or even commercially available Compact Flash (CF) cards will be the chosen medium.

Solid-state devices or hard drives look attractive, for, once you have lifted the data from them they are reusable, but therein lies the rub. It is essential that those precious data which represent the producer's total investment be lifted and stored with an incredible level of security. The potential for disaster at this point in the process is far greater than it used to be simply loading film from tins to camera magazines and back again, and we have all experienced at least one disaster there in our careers!

This data handling requirement can, and probably should, add a new craft on set and with this the added expense of the salary; let us call this person the Data Wrangler. No sensible production would take the data from the master recording format and store them in a single drive. They need a minimum of two backups. Once that has been done the master recording medium needs to be wiped and probably reformatted and made available again to the shooting crew in such a way that there can never be any possibility of the crew confusing newly formatted data with shot rushes. Even in the days when only tape was available, most of us at some time have managed to record over a favorite take – that becomes even easier with formats that are intended to be recorded over many times.

8.1.1.1 Stock savings – film to HDCAM

The greatest saving is in the origination medium. If we look at the pure cost of picture origination – that is, just negative stock and processing for film as against the tape cost alone – Super 16 mm costs 8.5 times as much as High Definition (HD) and four-perf 35 mm costs a staggering 32 times as much. And remember at this stage in the process the film cannot be shown, for it is still only in its negative form, but the HD tape can instantly be played at full picture quality.

8.1.1.2 Insurance savings

There are some less obvious possible savings. One producer I have met was having to put two video tape recorder (VTR) playback machines into the cutting room as a very quick delivery was required. As this equipment was already paid for, they realized that it was possible to make an exact copy of the day's work every night on wrap. This is known as cloning the tape and is simply a matter of telling the machines to transcribe the zeros and ones on the tape without processing the information, thus making an absolutely perfect copy. This very astute producer was then able to negotiate with the completion bond company to send them the camera original tapes immediately after cloning and thereby dramatically reduced the cost of negative insurance.

Another production with which I was closely involved was an American show being shot in Prague that needed to have, at the end of every shooting day, two HD copies, one to remain in Prague and the other to be sent by FedEx back to the USA every day. This show was scheduled for a 16-week shoot so the cost of making and shipping the extra HD copy looked like being considerable as, initially, the plan was to have a runner drive to Germany every night, which at the time was the nearest location where clones could be made.

After looking at the problem for a while I realized there was a much better solution. It was quite a big production and had, from the outset, budgeted for a playback crew to be on set all the time. The solution was to add an HD VTR to the playback kit so that a simultaneous copy of every shot was recorded in real time. This was particularly easy as a full quality HD signal was being sent to the playback desk and there down-converted to an SD signal that was fed into the mini DV recorder for normal action checking. The playback crew were more than happy to take on this extra task, for on the odd occasion when a full HD image was required it made their life much simpler. More importantly it saved the production a very considerable amount of money.

8.1.2 Savings in Print Costs

Were you making a very low budget movie it is possible for the production to save completely the cost of producing a print. Once you have conformed your HD masters to a single finished tape you have in your hands the highest quality version of the movie you will ever know. Assuming you have not yet found a distributor, which is very common on low-budget films, why not hire a cinema equipped with an HD projector and show them the conformed tape? It should cost no more than hiring a cinema with a mechanical projector, the picture quality will be stunning and only when a distributor has come on board do they need to make conventional prints, and this can be agreed to be at their expense.

8.1.3 Shooting for Anamorphic Release

Many first- or second-time directors find themselves in the position of wishing they could shoot in the widescreen picture ratio of 2.4:1, but are prevented from doing so by the considerably greater cost of hiring the necessary lenses, which often also increases the lighting budget as they are not necessarily as fast as conventional lenses, nor do some of them work particularly well at wide aperture where the anamorphic element within the lens is not as efficient. With HD these problems disappear. Although the camera will always record an image with an aspect ratio of 16×9 (1.777:1), if you wish to end up with a 35 mm anamorphic image from an HD original you simply switch on the 2.4:1 bright-line mask in the camera viewfinder and compose for this. You introduce similar masks onto your monitors both on set and those used in the editing room. When you come to show your finished movie there is a switch on the digital projector to enable it to project only the center section of the image, the part for which you originally composed.

Similarly, if you are heading for a film version, again it is simply a matter of telling the printing machine that you want an anamorphic 2.4:1 master and it will take the center section of the image and squeeze it to produce an image that looks exactly as if it were shot with anamorphic camera lenses.

As to lighting costs, you are using exactly the same lenses for HD origination whatever aspect ratio you choose to shoot in. Therefore it is quite possible to shoot an anamorphic picture at an aperture of T 1.8. You can therefore, if you so choose, work at far lower set brightness than with a film camera fitted with anamorphic lenses. The camera has, by the way, a limiting aperture of T 1.6 caused by the image-splitting prisms; this is described in the Technology part of this book. You will have realized that as you are not using the full height of the HD image you might well lose picture quality; you are in fact now only using around 800 pixels vertically, though horizontally you still use the full 1920 pixels. Theoretically you do lose picture quality but the quality of the image projected suggests that you don't. In fact, on some screens the appearance of the image suggests that the image is improved. This is because, provided that two pixels are closer together on the screen than the resolution of the human eye, your brain will tell you that the image is perfectly sharp. In almost all viewing conditions that is because the screen is made wider for the anamorphic viewing, so objects in the picture will be bigger and you may therefore think them sharper.

Alternatively nowadays, if you have the budget, you can shoot with a camera that has a single chip the size of a Super 35 mm film frame and then use the cheaper spherical 35 mm lenses and transfer just the 2.4:1 center section as you would from a Super 35 mm negative. This can give superlative results and, as seen elsewhere, can even reduce the lighting budget compared to using true anamorphic lenses. Both the Arriflex D-21 and the RED camera, cameras at opposite ends of the spectrum, can achieve this.

8.2 Added Costs

8.2.1 Camera Kit Rental

It is important to compare the costs of the whole camera kit and not just the camera itself. Even if you are using video assist with a film camera you will not need, say, a 24-inch HD monitor, but when shooting HD such a monitor can be an invaluable tool both to the director and to the cinematographer. They are expensive items and can push up the total kit cost dramatically. As a very rough guide, a top-end HD kit comprising, say, a Sony HDW 900R, a couple of zoom lenses and a wide-angle prime lens, together with a selection of monitors and heads and tripods, will often cost something like 130–150 percent more than a similar 35 mm kit. For television production, if comparing a Super 16 mm kit with an HDW 750P, again with Panavision lenses, the difference is 235 percent – much more expensive, but you do get a picture that looks as if it was shot on 35 mm when shown on television. Now it must be admitted that most broadcast productions will not be able to afford such high-quality lenses. This is unfortunate but top quality broadcast style lenses are still capable of showing a substantial increase in perceived quality over any digital origination previously available and can, if like for like productions are compared, still present a real challenge to a Super 16 image.

8.2.2 Editing Costs

If you are taking the most common route through the editing process, converting either film or HD to Digi Beta for the cutting room, then the expenditure is not significantly different. Most post houses charge roughly the same to telecine 1 hour of either 16 mm or 35 mm as they do to down-convert 1 hour of HD to Digi Beta. At the end of the editing session it will probably be necessary to conform the camera masters to the Edit Decision List (EDL). This comes at a not dissimilar cost to negative cutting so little is lost or gained, though it is possible to make savings by grading the HD master at the same time rather than having to have photochemical answer prints. If you can afford it, it is possible to use an off-line edit suite that can operate directly in the HD domain. In terms of picture quality this is ideal, for as finer and finer cuts are achieved the result can be played out in full HD quality without the need to conform the camera masters; indeed, some sophisticated editing packages can perform most of the grade as well. In practice, editing in full HD format is only common for movies with a very big budget or commercials where the time spent in the editing suite is much shorter and therefore becomes affordable.

8.2.3 Writing Out to Film

If you decide to write out to film it is important that you make the right decision as to producing either the equivalent of an intermediate negative or an intermediate positive.

If you only expect to make a few prints, say six or less, then the advice is usually to go to a negative. If you are making a large number of prints you would probably go to a positive so that you can make a number of internegatives, from which you then make the release prints in volume. It is most important to make the right decision as the conversion from HD master to a photochemical master can be a very expensive process. Most printers take around 2.5 seconds to print each frame, so a 120-minute movie is going to take just a little under 5 days to print. As the printing machines are very expensive you can imagine where the money goes.

There are two forms of printers, one using lasers to write lines of information to the film stock and the other forming the whole image on a cathode ray tube (CRT) and then projecting it onto the film. They produce images with a slightly different character; both can be very good but you will need to test or see demonstrations of both before you shoot and decide which you are going to use, otherwise it will be impossible to visualize the finished picture during shooting. In general, the post houses using a CRT tend to be a little cheaper, though it has to be said more people seem to prefer the image from the laser printers.

8.3 A Cost Comparison Example – *Oklahoma!*

I was asked to be the Director of Photography (DP) on a shoot transferring the National Theater stage production of *Oklahoma!* to the screen just as HD was becoming commercially available. Unfortunately, as we needed three cameras for the duration of the shoot plus a further two occasionally, using HD became an impossibility as the supplier simply could not guarantee enough equipment at that early stage of its introduction, so we shot it on 35 mm film. This, I thought, was a great shame, for there would have been many advantages with HD both for myself as DP and to the producers. For myself I would have loved to have been staring at 24-inch monitors showing the finished product, for I saw many advantages when lighting a huge set, 110 feet across and 90 feet deep, in being able to see the results of my work instantly. For the producers there would have been two main advantages: first, as they needed both a 35 mm print and a tape for international television distribution, the HD master tape would have rendered a much better image than the PAL master transfer after standards conversion to, say, NTSC; secondly, it would have saved them a lot of money. My judgement at the time was that the film version would have looked equally good originated on either medium; now I have much more experience of HD I think this particular production might even have looked better shot digitally.

8.3.1 Stock and Processing Savings

In 19 days we shot 265,000 feet of 35 mm negative. At the standard prices prevalent at the time of shooting, the cost of the raw stock, processing it and transferring it to a Digi Beta tape for the cutting room would have been about £150,000 ($215,000). The equivalent HD tape cost would have been about £3250 ($4650). So using HD, in terms of stock costs, would have saved £146,750 ($210,000). Put another way, it was over 46 times more expensive to use film.

The above dollar conversion was that at the time of shooting.

8.3.2 Camera Rental

With the camera rental prices applying at the time, I estimate that the HD camera and monitoring kit might have been £12,500 ($17,900) more expensive than the 35 mm film camera kit.

8.3.3 Additional Costs

There would have been an additional cost of making a negative from the HD master in order to provide the cinema print that was required. It must be remembered that, more often than not, there will be little need for photochemical grading as the HD to HD grade may often be done in the same photo finishing house and they will be very familiar with the in-house film-out requirements. At the time we shot *Oklahoma!*, transferring an HD tape to a film negative was far more expensive than it is now; there were very few post-production facilities that could handle it then, whereas now there is much more competition in the market, which has naturally driven costs down. Still, to be fair, let us look at the costs at the time. *Oklahoma!* had a finished screen time of 180 minutes. Transferring HD to 35 mm negative would have cost £600/minute ($858/minute), so the cost of making a negative would have been £108,000 ($154,440). You could probably nearly halve those costs at the time of writing.

8.3.3.1 Overall savings

All the photochemical costs after that would be identical except that small savings might be made in the lack of the need for answer prints, but let us ignore that. Therefore, even after making a 35 mm negative, the producers would have saved £39,800 ($50,900) on the stock and processing costs going right as far as the cut negative. Today, HD to film transfer prices are roughly half what they were when we shot *Oklahoma!* so, were they making it today, the producers could look to saving something like £79,600 ($101,800).

8.3.4 Competitive Pricing

All the above is, as I said at the beginning of the chapter, based on worst case scenarios. As HD enters the market more and as many more suppliers have much more equipment on their shelves with many more post houses also being HD equipped, the actual costs of shooting and post-producing HD are continually coming down; this makes the cost comparison with film even more attractive as those costs are remaining more or less static. It is therefore well worth shopping around but, please, don't get so beguiled with the savings available that you end up saving money by using inferior lenses. I have had a number of film-makers I have advised come back at the end of shooting and say that the quality, while good, was not quite as good as they had hoped. On every single one of those occasions it turned out that they had economized on their lenses. Many of the so-called HD lenses are not capable of producing images as good as those the cameras are capable of creating; therefore to realize fully the potential image quality of the HD system a careful choice of lenses is essential – even if they seem expensive!

CHAPTER 9

Crewing

There is an unfortunate misconception rife among some producers that if you shoot digital High Definition (HD) you can work with a much smaller crew than with film. To make the judgement simply on the recording format is, in my view, foolish and comes from looking at the history of the HD medium from the wrong perspective.

Historically, video shoots have used smaller crews. This is because they have been conceived from their beginnings as low-budget productions and, had the decision been made to shoot them on film, it too would have been done with the smallest crew possible.

There is another significant and unfortunate result of these misconceptions. With some rare exceptions tape has not, in the past, been scheduled for many productions that would have had even the slightest chance of affording film. As a result, even Digi Beta has rarely been given the chance to show its true potential as, with the lower budgets it is usually confined to, the quality of the design input is often so poor, the daily minutes of screen time shot so high and the crew so small that it becomes impossible to produce a high-quality product no matter what you are recording on.

If you subscribe to any of the above opinions of low-budget tape productions you must change them when shooting HD. With HD the recording medium is irrelevant to these arguments, for it is the *picture quality* that is the key technical contributor to the crewing decisions. The quality is as high as that of 35 mm and therefore all crewing must relate to previously gained 35 mm experience. The kit is usually bigger and heavier than a Digi Beta, though the HDW 750P and the newer HDW F900R and Panasonic Varicam camera kits come in much nearer to the same weight. Single-chip cameras currently weigh roughly the same as 35 mm film cameras and you must include in this all the on-board accessories the Director and the camera crew will expect mounted on the camera in order to produce a truly professional job.

9.1 Should the DP Operate?

In my opinion, not if you want your digital output to look as good as possible. The viewfinder on the cameras is usually poor compared with a film camera and therefore I believe that it is essential that the Director of Photography (DP) stays back at a correctly set-up HD monitor in order to judge both their lighting and what is being recorded. There are better HD viewfinders coming on stream so this may soon change.

9.2 Do You Need a Focus Puller?

Operators with a television studio background are used to pulling focus for themselves. Allowing them to continue to do this on an HD shoot can be a very dangerous decision indeed. Those of us who are trying to produce really good images from 2/3-inch HD cameras are usually trying to work at very wide apertures in order to reduce the depth of field to something that looks similar to that expected on film. Once this shorter depth of field is achieved, the focus pulling difficulties become the same as for 35 mm film and a fully trained and experienced focus puller becomes essential. More often than not this desire to reduce the depth of field, and have softer backgrounds, comes not only from the DP, but is also a requirement of the Director.

If you are planning to shoot with a single-chip camera with a chip roughly the size of the 35 mm film frame, then it is essential that you have a fully trained focus puller familiar with working on the 35 mm format. This is also true if you are putting lens adapters on 2/3-inch chip cameras in order to use lenses from the 35 mm world. If you go for, say, the MoviTube or Pro 35 then although this may look like an economical solution, unless you spend the money on a fully trained and experienced focus puller, there is a very high probability that a significant number of shots will be soft.

Focus pulling is about talent and mathematics. The first you have to pay for; the second, depth of field, is totally unavoidable. You heard it here!

9.3 Do You Need a Loader?

There is no job for a traditional loader but there is a vital job for a slightly differently trained camera assistant. Fortunately many very good film loaders are just as skilled and useful on an HD shoot. While, admittedly, there are no camera magazines to load, tapes still have to be changed and labeled, and report sheets prepared for the cutting room. Still more importantly, the color monitor will have to be set up, organized and lined up, a task I usually give to this camera assistant. Most of my camera assistants who perform these tasks are more than able to line up the monitor and I have come to rely on them to do so. As I would not necessarily have the time to do it, my camera assistants will check the line-up every time the monitor is moved and after every break. If you are on a multicamera shoot then the logging of the tapes becomes vital and a camera assistant can end up the busiest person on the set.

9.4 Naming the Camera Assistants

Within a year of the introduction of the Sony HDW F900, the first HDCAM camera available, the Guild of British Camera Technicians (GBCT) suggested to its members that the current naming of the camera assistants as Focus Puller and Clapper Loader should revert to the older names of First Assistant Cameraperson (AC1) and Second Assistant Cameraperson (AC2). This, I believe, was both sensible and significant. The GBCT saw that HD was a reality and that many of its members would be working in this area, and renaming their grades would help them to gain work within the new parts of their industry. It is not often that one sees an established industry guild look forwards rather than hang on to the past as furiously as possible and I, for one, commend them for an almost unique foresight.

9.5 Do You Need a Clapperboard?

My answer is definitely yes. It only takes the slightest error in the camera, the play-out machine feeding the editing suite, the edit suite itself, the conform suite or in the creating and reading out of the Edit Decision List (EDL) for a shot, or whole scene, to go completely out of sync or, even worse, end up cut into the wrong place. If a film-style clapperboard is used there is always the visible shot number to refer back to, and the physical clapper for synchronizing the shot. I have to admit that I doubt any machine's ability to count reliably. This lack of faith has saved many a production considerable amounts of money by them being able to go back to the clapper to regain sync. Some old ways are still the best!

There is another reason to use a clapperboard that is just as important. Most technicians are so tuned to knowing a take starts with calling the number and banging two bits of wood together that they don't really go quiet or, more importantly, really start to concentrate until they hear the board. It pumps up the adrenaline and you will find you are going for far fewer takes if you use a clapperboard than if you do not. That can be a big saving. Actors find the same to be true; to a film-trained or experienced actor the moment to perform simply has not come until the board has gone on.

9.6 Do You Need a Dolly Grip?

Definitely. The modern style of shooting usually involves a very mobile camera and the grip, or dolly grip in the USA, is the person to provide this quickly and smoothly. They also provide all the usual toys and accessories one expects on any shoot. A good grip's van is an Aladdin's cave and a treasure trove of solutions to problems. They also do all the usual and useful things like having the required camera support needed for the next shot already set up and that can really speed things up.

9.7 Sound

The manning requirements for sound hardly vary at all between film and HD. The route chosen for post-production will dictate whether or not the sound is recorded on the HD camera tracks alone or if a second recording is to be made, in which case this is usually recorded on a portable Digital Audio Tape (DAT) recorder. When shooting HD it is usual for the DAT recording to be the master with the camera tracks as backup, so there will usually be a cable between the camera and the recordist. Clearly the recordist, more properly referred to as the mixer in the UK, will not be able to operate the mixing desk, the DAT recorder and the microphone, so the absolute minimum sound crew will nearly always consist of a mixer and a boom swinger. A third person on sound, often known as the sound engineer, can be a great boon as they can swing a second boom and greatly speed up the turn-round to a new set-up.

9.8 Electricians

As I have said, it is a popularly held misconception that HD cameras need less light. This is a fallacy. The baseline equivalent film speed of an HD camera is usually 320 or 400 ASA to tungsten light, sometimes a little more, and this is roughly the same as for some of my favorite film stocks. The DP will frequently be lighting to balance with existing sources such as daylight or practical lamps within the set, what I think of as the "given", and then exactly the same amount of light will be required no matter how you photograph the image. This said I am often using a lens setting around one stop wider on 2/3-inch HD cameras than I might for Super 16 and two-and-a-half stops wider than for 35 mm. This is to obtain roughly the same depth of field purely for artistic reasons. The differences will be obtained by the choice of film speed in the film camera and by the sensitivity setting on the HD camera, and with neutral density filters, behind the lens with HD, and in front of the lens in both media.

When all these considerations are taken into account, it becomes clear that the same number of electricians are likely to be needed and that their number will be dictated more by the script, the "given", and the way you intend to shoot it than by what you are recording the image on.

9.9 A New Member of the Crew – the Data Wrangler or Downloader

If you are recording to tape all that has gone before is just fine but if you are recording to any kind of hard drive, flash card or similar you have another problem to contend with – the fact that during the shooting day your all-important images have to be copied from that very expensive capture medium, that medium wiped or reformatted, and that data storage device returned to the set for further recording. I cannot state strongly enough how important a job this is. Anybody who has shot using these kinds of storage media has, almost certainly, lost data at some time. That is a very expensive mistake! If you think of a reasonable television drama the producer is spending upwards of £100,000 ($200,000) a day. Imagine what might be the consequences if all the morning's work was accidentally erased during lunch.

Many producers have tried to suggest that the camera trainee can easily handle the data transfer in their spare time. This is a ridiculous premise for several reasons. First, it has always been next to impossible to get the picture insurance company to allow the trainee to load film magazines and the likelihood of a mishap during data transfer and the recycling of storage medium is far higher than accidents in the changing bag. Therefore the insurance company will not countenance the idea. Further, it is unwise to transfer all those important data to just one new home; at least two copies must be made, though I grant that these may well be made simultaneously if the budget allows for sufficient equipment.

After the transfer of those expensive data the storage medium has to be erased and/or reformatted. The next step is, in my experience, the most likely moment for an accident to occur, when a crew member comes to collect what they assume is a fully backed up and ready to record data unit. Is everyone *absolutely* sure that it is safe to use? For your sake I do hope so.

The Data Wrangler (I do like this very American job title; it sums up the craft so well) should have a quiet space to themselves and most importantly establish an area away from the rest of their kit where only fresh data storage is collected by crew members so that no mistakes can possibly occur.

The Data Wrangler is not a job created by imaginative crews to get another person a salary, but an absolutely essential and very skilled person who is vital to the protection of what used to be the rushes and brings peace of mind to everyone. The insurance company will, most likely, not insure the picture without one if you are going tapeless so you might as well get a good one, whatever the daily rate.

Part 3
The Technology

CHAPTER 10

Digital Imaging

10.1 The History of Digits

It is widely thought that one Claude Elwood Shannon, who died at the age of 84 in 2001, single-handedly laid the foundation for what became known as information theory, that branch of mathematics concerning the transmission of data in a digital form.

In what has been called the most important Masters Thesis of the twentieth century, *A Symbolic Analysis of Relay and Switching Circuits*, published in 1938, he first put forward the notion that it was possible to solve problems simply by manipulating two symbols – one and zero – in an automated electrical circuit.

Later in his work *A Mathematical Theory of Communication* he first coined the term "bit" as the fundamental unit of information that encapsulates digital certainty as in true or false, on or off, yes or no. He also was the first to show how to design circuits to store and manipulate bits. It was Shannon who set in motion the route to the compact disk, cyberspace, digital television and the digital movie camera.

I think I should have rather liked Claude Shannon, for although preferring to work alone he was friendly and liked to start his day at noon with a game of chess against the director of the Mathematics Center at MIT, then working on late into the evening. He had a fascination for juggling and produced a paper on the underlying mathematics of juggling. While working at the Bell Labs he could occasionally be seen juggling while riding a unicycle down the halls.

10.2 Digital Tonal Range

In a digital camera the whole tonal range is divided into a large number of individual values, or samples, and each sample is assigned a given value. The number of samples that constitute the complete tonal range of the output of each individual pixel determines the smoothness of the overall tonal range. The more samples that are used to record the complete tonal range of the picture, the smoother will be the transition from one tone to another and the subtler will be the final image.

If, for instance, you decided to divide the complete tonal range of the image into 1000 parts from each pixel's output and should you record them mathematically you would have to read any number between 0 and 1000. This would be complicated, as your recording and playback process would have to be capable of recognizing 1000 different units of measurement.

In order to overcome this the digital camera records information using a binary code. A binary code uses a combination of zeros and ones, as Shannon had suggested, to write any value and the number of zeros and ones you use in the code determines the number of different values you can record.

If you are only going to use two units of zeros and ones, a 2-bit code, you can write four combinations, which are:

00, 01, 10 and 11.

You already have two advantages: you only have to use two numbers in order to write, in code, any of four values; secondly, and just as important, your recording and playback machines only have to recognize either a zero or a one, the equivalent of "on" or "off", and even a pretty stupid machine can tell if it is on or off and this leads to a high level of repeatability when writing and reading this form of code. It also needs to understand the code in order to write or reconstitute the zeros and ones into a picture; fortunately with modern electronics this is relatively easy.

If we increase our code length from 2 bits to 4 bits we can record 16 values as there are that many combinations available:

0000, 0001, 0010, 0011, 0100, 0101, 0110, 0111, 1000, 1001, 1010, 1011, 1100, 1101, 1110 and 1111.

The mathematical function works like this: if you had a 1-bit code you could only record two values, the first represented by zero and a second represented by one. Increasing the code to 2 bits multiplies the number of codes you can write by a factor of two. In fact, every time you add a digit to the code you will increase the number of values you can record by a multiplication of two. Adding two more values multiplies the number of available samples by a factor of four. Figure 10.1 shows the progression up to the remarkable 8192 values recorded by a 14-bit code now being used in some of the more advanced digital cameras.

If you were to read the specification of a camera you might not think there was a huge difference between one where the camera's processor uses a 10-bit code and one using a 12-bit code, but as we have seen the difference is between the tonal range being broken down into 1024 values and 4096 values. This might make a difference to the perceived picture quality depending mainly on how you would be viewing the final image; on a television screen it may be next to impossible to see any difference.

```
1 bit     0    ( or 1 )
          2 = 2 values

2 bit     0    1
          2 × 2 = 4 values

4 bit     0    1    0    1
          2 × 2 × 2 × 2 = 16 values

6 bit     0    1    0    1    0    1
          2 × 2 × 2 × 2 × 2 × 2 = 64 values

8 bit     0    1    0    1    0    1    0    1
          2 × 2 × 2 × 2 × 2 × 2 × 2 × 2 = 256 values

10 bit    0    1    0    1    0    1    0    1    0    1
          2 × 2 × 2 × 2 × 2 × 2 × 2 × 2 × 2 × 2 = 1024 values

12 bit    0    1    0    1    0    1    0    1    0    1    0    1
          2 × 2 × 2 × 2 × 2 × 2 × 2 × 2 × 2 × 2 × 2 × 2 = 4096 values

14 bit    0    1    0    1    0    1    0    1    0    1    0    1    0    1
          2 × 2 × 2 × 2 × 2 × 2 × 2 × 2 × 2 × 2 × 2 × 2 × 2 × 2 = 16,384 values
```

Figure 10.1: The effect of adding more bits to the binary code

10.3 Linear and Logarithmic Sampling

There is a way of encoding the original scanned image of the camera that can make the picture more appealing to the eye, make it appear more like a film image and at the same time reduce the size of the digital files used to store the images. It involves the use of logarithmic sampling rather than the traditional linear sampling.

With linear sampling the steps between each brightness sampled are exactly the same throughout the tonal range of the image, as in Figure 10.2. Some high-end High Definition (HD) cameras set out to emulate a film image as closely as possible; a modern film emulsion can comfortably handle a brightness range of 11 stops and so can many HD cameras. A full 11 stops of tonal range recorded linearly to the current industry standard will need a 13-bit file to hold all the data if the image is going to be of sufficient quality to be printed to film without any noticeable loss in quality compared with a film original.

Our eye/brain combination is more interested in shadow detail than highlight detail and therefore the quality of image in the shadows needs to be better than in the highlights for us to think of the recorded picture as real. In order to get sufficient data for the shadows to look real, and like 35 mm film, there must be 8192 options of recordable brightness for each pixel of the image.

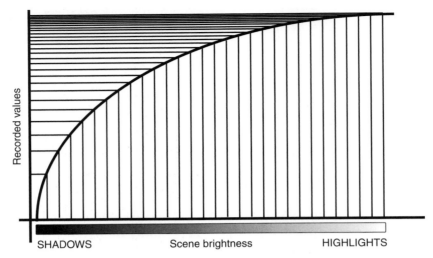

Figure 10.2: Screen brightness using linear sampling

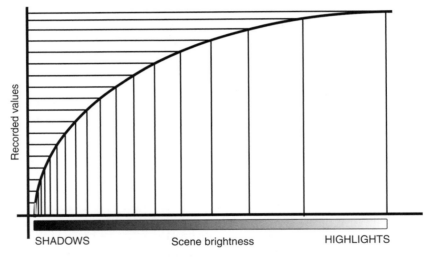

Figure 10.3: Screen brightness using logarithmic sampling

Because of the shape of the brightness response curve a finer gradation between recorded values will occur in the highlights than in the shadows when the image is sampled linearly. With logarithmic sampling, as shown in Figure 10.3, there are more steps in the area of the shadowed part of the scene than in the highlights and this results in the recorded values being evenly spaced across the tonal range.

If a tonal range of 11 stops is sampled in a logarithmic way and to the same subtlety of tonal range, then the same amount of information can be recorded on a 10-bit file, which has only

Figure 10.4: The effect of pixilation: original scene

1024 options. This means much smaller files are needed and the audience will still believe they are seeing an image of equivalent quality.

10.4 Image Resolution: Why So Many Pixels?

Figure 10.4 shows a black and white image that has been chosen for its very smooth gradation of tones. Nevertheless, if you take a magnifying glass to the picture you will see that it is made up of a huge number of tiny dots, which at normal reading distance are totally invisible to the eye. This is the way images are printed in books and newspapers. In this application the size of the dot changes, and it is always black, so lots of small dots at the same spacing appear pale gray and large dots, again at the same spacing, will appear as dark gray. With digital imaging we vary the actual brightness of each dot, not its size.

Figure 10.5 shows the original smooth tone image broken up into a reasonably mild pixilated image; the image is still recognizable but the individual pixels are clearly defined. Figure 10.6 shows a much coarser pixelated image and in Figure 10.7 the pixilation is so coarse that had we not seen the original picture we wouldn't have the faintest idea what the image contained. The important lesson from this is that for the digital camera to deliver a really fine image each chip is going to have a very large number of pixels.

10.5 Required Resolution for HD

One often hears arguments as to the image resolution needed to satisfy the human eye on a large cinema screen. Many, predominantly from the post-production community, will claim

Figure 10.5: Scene with mild pixilation

Figure 10.6: Scene with coarse pixilation

that a "4K" resolution is required and that a 1920×1080 pixel camera is inadequate for it only has a "2K" resolution, the "K" in this instance referring to the number of horizontal pixels used. "K" in this context represents 1000. The argument for a 4K image only holds true when a 35 mm piece of film is scanned, manipulated digitally in some way and cut back into the original roll of film for printing. This is because original 35 mm camera negative is capable of holding an image equivalent to a horizontal resolution of 4000 units.

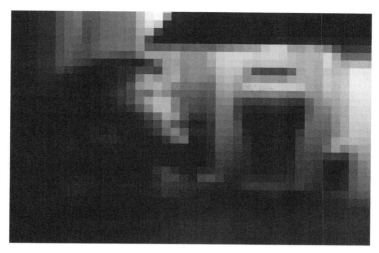

Figure 10.7: Scene with very coarse pixilation

You do not necessarily need 4K resolution when originating an image to get an image onto a cinema screen as good as one expects from 35 mm film. Let us look at a film's route from camera to cinema screen. In order to duplicate the original negative many, many times so that it may be shown simultaneously in many cinemas, the picture will have to be copied, photographically, several times, as shown below.

The original camera master is copied to:

    an inter-positive print film which is then copied to:

    an inter-negative film which is printed to:

    the release print which is then shown through:

    the projector lens on to:

    the cinema screen.

This lengthy process is necessary because film is mechanically vulnerable and the Producer, wisely, will only allow the camera master to go through a printing machine a limited number of times. By the end of post-production that Producer's whole investment lies in the camera master and they do not want it damaged. Each intermediate copy has a limited mechanical life so each inter-positive will produce a finite number of inter-negatives and the inter-negatives a finite number of release prints. Hence the cascading of the printing process is essential to arriving at hundreds of prints for eventual showing in cinemas.

Unfortunately even the finest photographic copying process slightly degrades the quality of the image. By the time that a 4K master negative image reaches the screen, most experts agree that the image on the screen is unlikely to be better than 1.2K; even the most optimistic don't claim better than 1.4K. Compare this with a 1920 × 1080 HD image that in an ideal world will have stayed in that format right through post-production and will be projected by the finest digital projector currently available. In this instance the only degradation the image will have suffered will have come from the projector lens. This image is going to be considerably better than 1.4K. In fact, it will be very close to 2K!

If that HD image has to be printed out to film for exhibition, careful planning of the post-production workflow can considerably reduce the number of photographic copies needed and therefore ensure the image is finally seen with at least 1.4K horizontal resolution.

Whatever the argument the picture on a cinema screen has to please the human eye and the finite resolution of the eye is generally agreed to be an angle subtending to the eye of one minute of arc. There are 360 degrees in a circle and each of those degrees, for measuring purposes, is divided up into 60 minutes, so one minute is a very small angle indeed. This way of defining the eye's resolution relies on the idea that if two dots are placed next to each other and, when looked at they are inside an angle to the eye of one minute of arc, then they will appear as a single dot. If together they are outside the angle of one minute then we will be able to see them as two dots.

Here are two dots:

••

Try moving the book away from you until they merge into one dot. At that distance the angle subtended from the outside of the two dots to your eye will be roughly one minute of arc. The actual distance will to some extent depend on the quality of your vision.

The above criterion is used to determine if an image will appear acceptably sharp to an audience. If we take HD's most taxing method of display, a large cinema screen, and then compare the accepted resolution for 35 mm film presentation with HD we can tell whether an HD image will look better, worse or the same as the 35 mm image. If you look at Figure 10.8 you will see how the mathematics work. Standard practice is to assume the optimum viewing position in a cinema is one-third of the way back from the screen. The angle of one minute of arc is drawn out to the screen from this position and back to the 35 mm film in the projector gate. One minute of arc translates as one-thousandth of an inch at the film gate.

The image on a piece of 35 mm film is two and a half times bigger than the 2/3-inch chip used in most current professional HD cameras so in order to give the same apparent resolution the smallest dot recordable on an HD chip, one pixel, must be 1/2500 inch. A 2/3-inch chip with

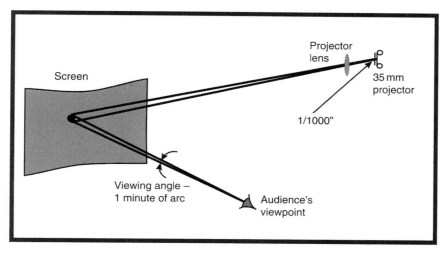

Figure 10.8: The resolution of the human eye

1080 × 1920 pixels on it has a single pixel size of exactly this value, so we can expect the same resolution as 35 mm film.

The evidence clearly shows that pictures originated by a 1080 × 1920 HD camera are, theoretically, as sharp and can have the same tonal range in the cinema as conventional 35 mm film.

One should not always be swayed by any other argument than the evidence of your own eyes in these matters. As I said earlier – if it looks right, it is right.

10.6 Data Quantity

It is interesting to note the quantity of data being processed just behind the three chips in the camera. First let us look at the information we are trying to record. We have seen that in a three-chip camera using the 1920 × 1080 format there are 6,220,800 pixels being deployed to capture the whole image and that each pixel's digital output in a typical camera using a 12-bit processor can have the choice of 4096 different values. Therefore the total number of options is 6,220,800 × 4096 = 25,480,396,800. This, of course, is not necessarily the number of units being recorded, just the number of options.

What the camera has to record is the 12-bit binary code from every pixel and this sum goes as follows: 1080 vertical pixels × 1920 horizontal pixels × 3 chips × 12 bits of binary code per pixel, which equals 74,649,600 bits of information per picture.

That is all very well, but we are recording a moving image and even at the camera's slowest frame rate of 24 frames per second (fps), a single second of moving image will require 74,649,600 × 24 = 1,791,590,400 bits of information to be recorded each second.

Just for fun let's look at a complete recording tape lasting 50 minutes at 24 fps. It will store 1,791,590,400 bits × 60 seconds × 50 minutes = 5,374,771,200,000 bits of information per tape. Quite astounding!

CHAPTER 11

Scanning the Image

11.1 A Little of the History of Television

Television was developed in the mid-1930s and two very different systems came to the fore: one was based entirely on an electronic platform using cathode ray tube technology that had been developed by the Marconi company; the other was an amalgam of electronics and mechanical shuttering to divide up the picture, developed in England by John Logie Baird, who was almost certainly the first man to transmit a moving picture over the airwaves.

Extraordinarily the Marconi system utilized interlace scanning and Baird's method used, in effect, progressive scanning. It has taken 70 years for the world to realize that, in this respect, Baird was ahead of his time. Not only in that respect, for he arguably invented color television and 3D television and demonstrated both to the public; all this is well known and well documented, but sadly forgotten by many. There were many other differences. The Marconi company thought the ideal format would be landscape (that is, a rectangle that is wider than its height) and they scanned it horizontally, and Baird initially thought much of television would be illustrated radio so initially his first format was portrait (a rectangle that is higher than it is wide), this being more suited to talking heads, so he started by scanning his frame vertically, with a little curvature to the lines it has to be said. Later, when he moved to a 240-line format he also incorporated a 5×4 landscape aspect ratio.

Initially the basic principle of Baird's camera was a lens focusing an image on a spinning disk, which had a series of holes in it (arranged as in Figure 11.1), behind which was a single photoelectric cell. In this illustration I have much exaggerated one of the problems with this system: the scans are circular in nature, resulting in an image made up of lines of information, shown in Figure 11.2. A very much bigger shutter with the holes all grouped near to the outer edge more or less solved this problem. Baird moved to larger shutters and finer holes grouped closer together, thus improving picture definition, but he did not have the resources of the Marconi company and this, together with other problems, resulted in the Marconi system being adopted for the first public broadcasting system by the BBC (British Broadcasting Company, later Corporation) in London.

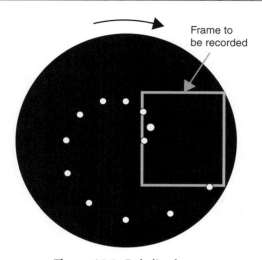

Frame to
be recorded

Figure 11.1: Baird's shutter

Figure 11.2: Baird's scan (curvature much exaggerated)

Nevertheless Baird's model did scan in the way we now describe as progressive, for the lines were scanned one after the other in a sequential way. The Marconi system scanned all the odd numbered lines of a single picture first and then went back and scanned all the even numbered lines, just as standard definition television does today. The considerable advantage of this scanning format is that it results in a small amount of data being scanned continuously and fools the eye/brain combination of the viewer into thinking it is seeing twice as many pictures, thus considerably reducing flicker, which is especially apparent in the highlights of a picture. As human vision is blessed, or cursed, with a phenomenon known as the persistence of vision the audience, more or less, happily adds together both scans and believes it is seeing all the image at the same time.

Persistence of vision means that any image we see at a given moment takes some time to die or fade away; it persists in the retina of the eye and within the brain. The image will still contain the remnants of an earlier moment and we add together a little bit of past images to the immediate and current image. If the human eye/brain combination did not have

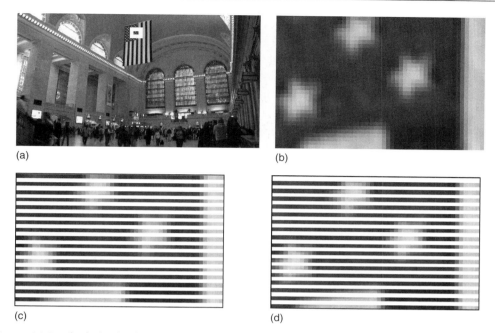

(a)

(b)

(c)

(d)

Figure 11.3: Pixels in the lace and interlace scans: (a) scan of original scene; (b) blow up of selected section showing both lace and interlace scans added together; (c) lace scan; (d) interlace scan

this anomaly then cinema images would not work and television images would be quite unacceptable in their current form.

11.2 Interlace Scanning

As we have seen, interlace scanning is simply the dividing up of an image into horizontal lines and sampling the data along the odd numbered lines, then returning to the top of the picture to begin scanning the lines that were previously ignored – the even numbered lines – in the same way.

The definition, or perceived sharpness, of the resultant image will effectively be determined by two factors – how many lines the picture is divided up into vertically and how often a sample is taken as each line is scanned. The two most popular High Definition (HD) standards in use at present either scan 1080 lines and sample each line 1920 times or scan 720 lines and sample each line 1280 times.

Figure 11.3 shows how the scanning takes place. We can see that when both the lace and the interlace scans are performed, small blocks of information are produced. Each block is an even density; each block is representing the output of one pixel on the camera's chip. You will also see that if the small area on the flag is blown up then the blocks, or pixels, make little sense even when both scans are shown together, for it requires a large number of lines and very frequent sampling to make our eyes believe we are seeing a completely smooth tonal range with sufficient sharpness for us to believe we are looking at real life. Figure 11.3 has been prepared so that the original picture of Grand Central Station and all the derivative pictures actually come from a master photograph scanned at a resolution giving 1080 vertical lines each sampled 1920 times.

Think about this: the master picture looks to be of very high quality but the blow-up of the section of the flag proves it is not. This is how digital imaging works. With enough pixels we can produce an image that the human eye thinks is perfect; hence the need for HD images – the pictures are so much more realistic.

11.3 Progressive Scanning

With the introduction of the 1920 × 1080 HD pixel array it became possible to fill a cinema screen with a digital image arguably as good as a film image, as we have seen in Chapter 10. Unfortunately if the HD image was captured in interlace scanning the way things moved across the screen was not acceptable to a cinema audience. This is probably for two main reasons: first, when blown up to the huge size of a cinema screen the interlaced image was not completely convincing as real life and, perhaps more importantly, did not display the kind of movement on the screen the audience had come to expect in the cinema – this we call conditioning. Personally I am not convinced we look at the best pictures possible in a cinema but they are the pictures we have become used to.

There are two issues when viewing pictures in the cinema: the screen is very dim compared with a television picture so flicker at 24 frames per second (fps), shown twice (i.e. 48 times a second), is not too big a problem and the display size is large, particularly when you consider the viewing angle from the audience's eye. As an example it is common to view a standard definition picture in the home from a distance of around 6–10 times the height of the picture. As HD screens, which are usually bigger, come into the home the viewing distance is reduced to 3–5 times the height of the picture *but*, in a decent cinema, the viewing distance becomes 0.7–2.5 times the picture height.

So what did a cinema audience expect and how was it created? To answer this question we need to investigate two matters, image flicker and motion blur.

11.4 Traditional Cinema Flicker

Much as purists would like to deny it, all film images flicker to some degree.

The current standard for the mechanical projection of 35 mm film is 24 fps, with each frame shown twice. This gives rise to a certain amount of flicker on the cinema screen, particularly noticeable in the brighter parts of the image. The audience are, happily, conditioned to this as just enough images are shown per second to be acceptable but even to begin to remove this flicker the display rate (fps) would have to be doubled. As we have seen, it is also true that the relatively dimmer picture in the cinema, compared to television in the home, makes flicker far less apparent. Things are just a little less simple than that; they are also a little more elegant. Figure 11.4 shows how a camera shutter is orientated to leave the aperture open during 180 degrees of its rotation and blank the aperture for the other 180 degrees. This is very simple and effective, for at 24 fps it results in an exposure of 1/48th of a second. When the shutter is closed the film is being moved to the next frame and when the shutter is open the time is given over to exposing the film to the image.

In the camera, which is usually close to the microphone picking up the sound, the film transport mechanism has to be very quiet. A claw mechanism is usually deployed, which might not be terribly fast at pulling down the film but is accurate and quiet. It does not necessarily have to be very kind to the film's perforations as they will only pass through the camera once.

In the cinema projector things are a little different. In designing the projector a prime consideration is to maximize the amount of light reaching the screen. As the projector will

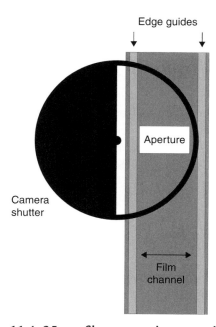

Figure 11.4: 35 mm film gate and camera shutter

almost certainly be in a room separate from the audience, known as the projection box, how much noise it makes is not a consideration. What is a consideration, though, is how kind the transport mechanism is to the film and its perforations, for whereas the camera only passes the film once, a film print may pass through a projector many hundreds of times.

Most cinema projectors use a transport mechanism driven by a device known as a Maltese Cross. The mechanism consists of sprocket wheel attached to a drive shaped a little like a Maltese Cross, which is driven by a rotating pin. This arrangement causes the sprocket to rotate intermittently, usually a quarter turn each time the pin hits one of the four slots in the cross. The advantages of this transport mechanism are that it is very kind to the film, as at least four perforations on each side of the film are engaged with the sprocket teeth at any one time, thus greatly reducing the load on each perforation, and it can therefore safely pull the film down much more rapidly, usually in one-quarter of the full frame rate, without damaging any of the perforations. It is, however, very noisy.

As the projector mechanism only needs one-quarter of total time to transport the film, the shutter can now be opened for 270 degrees and closed for 90 degrees. This increases the screen brightness by 50 percent relative to a 180-degree shutter. The disadvantage of this arrangement is that having a greater opening time than closed time brings us back to our old problem, flicker. Extending the shutter opening time will considerably increase the apparent flicker.

This is overcome by introducing a very small extra shutter blade, as shown in Figure 11.5, which effectively fools the eye into thinking it is seeing 48 fps despite every two consecutive frames being identical, as the same frame is still in the projector gate. This extra blade is known as the "phantom shutter".

All this may seem less than relevant to HD cinematography; it is not, for it is important to understand what many film makers are asking the HD 24P format to try to replicate – the look and appearance of film when shown in a cinema or on television, warts and all! While I have happily shot several HD productions giving this look, I feel we might be missing something important. HD can have its own look; it may not be familiar to the lay audience but I, for one, like it very much and look forward to the day when, hopefully, I am asked to give my all to a pure HD image. That, perhaps, was the sponsor's message!

11.5 How are Images Captured by the Two Scanning Formats?

Let us use a simple example of a disk moving left to right across the frame to be photographed as in Figure 11.6(a). If we photograph this moving disk using interlaced scanning, then we will record a picture, known as a field, and each field will be photographed in a slightly different moment in time. Each field contains half the vertical information twice

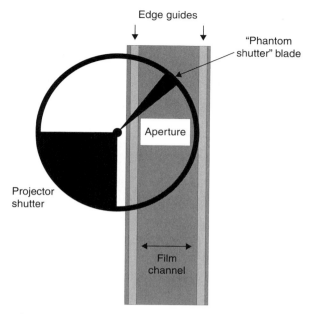

Figure 11.5: 3 mm film gate and projector shutter

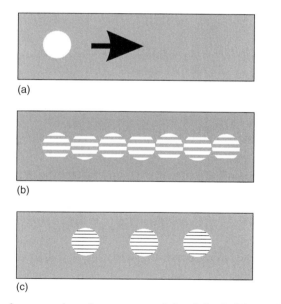

(a)

(b)

(c)

Figure 11.6: Sequential photography of movement: (a) original object; (b) photographed with interlace scanning; (c) photographed with progressive scanning

for every complete picture, the complete picture being known as a frame. As two fields are required to complete each frame, in US television 60 fields are required to complete the required 30 frames in every second of recording and in the UK 50 fields are required to complete 25 frames every second of recording.

Each field is displayed sequentially on the screen so the progression of the disk across the picture will be displayed as in Figure 11.6(b).

With progressive scan each frame is captured in its entirety in a single moment in time and will be recorded as in Figure 11.6(c). If it were then to be written out to film there would be one complete disk recorded on each frame of film and this would very closely emulate an image recorded by a film camera. Unfortunately not all HD formats work this way.

Sony call the frame recording standard for HDCAM progressive segmented field (PSF). This means that although in our illustration the disk moving across the screen will be *captured* in its entirety at the given frame rate, it will currently be *displayed* electronically on a cathode ray tube (CRT) television in the same way as an interlace picture *but* with each lace and interlace field being from the same moment in time. This is not all bad, for it is exactly the way film is displayed when shown on television. On a CRT television screen, however, it will not appear as smooth a movement as an image captured using an interlace scan, where twice as many half-resolution fields are usually displayed per second, but it will be a much more acceptable image when shown in a cinema. That acceptability comes partly from the technical reasons described and partly from the fact that the audience is conditioned to expect a different kind of picture when watching television at home and a film in the cinema. Interestingly these differences may start to become less apparent as home screens for High Definition Television (HDTV) become larger and larger.

Another factor is coming into play in the domestic marketplace for televisions. There is a dramatic move from the purchase of CRT televisions to larger flat-screen televisions. Indeed, after 2006 one major British retailer stopped selling CRT televisions altogether. These larger televisions cannot be made using CRTs and the new flat-screen technology requires that the display is configured in the progressive scan format, thus solving many of the problems.

To take this a step further let us consider how interlace fields actually arrive at our television screen. In Figure 11.7 each box contains the image of one field containing half the vertical information of the moving disk but, importantly, each field has been captured in a different moment in time. When the audience looks at their television their persistence of vision adds the subsequent fields together and they believe they are seeing smooth movement. Up until recently this is how television has traditionally worked, both in the standard and HD arenas.

There is another, and possibly more important, human factor at work here – saccadic eye-tracking. In essence this describes the fact that our eyes inherently follow a moving object; we

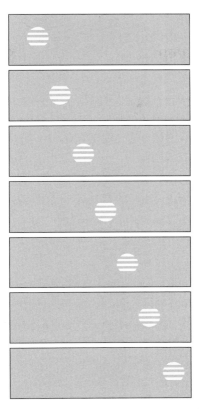

Figure 11.7: Interlace fields as displayed on a cathode ray tube

inherited this from our ancient ancestors, where the ability to follow food or a predator was crucially important.

Figure 11.8, on the other hand, shows how a series of pictures shot in progressive scan television, and film, appear when shown on an interlace display device. Half the vertical information is shown on each field but between the first and the second fields the disk has not moved. While the viewers' persistence of vision happily adds the fields together and sees the true resolution, they still only think they are seeing half the number of samples as the disk crosses the screen. This produces a juddering movement but, because saccadic eye motion is interrupted, the eye suddenly can't follow the track accurately so splits the two fields into two separate objects moving across the screen. If the spacing of the objects on the two separate fields is small it appears as judder, but if it is large the eye starts to think of it as two separate objects. Fortunately, once the audience is conditioned to it this is hardly apparent to them, provided the distance between objects on the two fields is small.

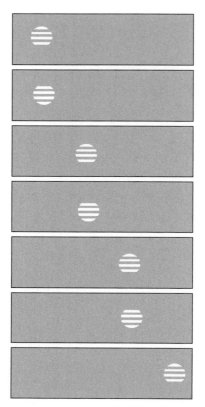

Figure 11.8: Pictures photographed with progressive scanning displayed on a cathode ray tube using interlace scanning

Many years of experience have enabled cinematographers trained in film to minimize the perceived effect. Remember we have been looking at film on television displayed just this way for many years and many of the audience have been perfectly happy with the results. Some technicians are less than happy, which is one reason why so much work is being done on the new HD standards in the hope that in the near future a much higher technical, artistic and emotionally involving picture presentation format will result.

Why are we just as happy with the two very different ways of delivering the whole of the information? The two effects work best with different genres. Here are two examples. A feature film, being fiction, usually though not always contains slowly moving objects and the film exposure and progressively scanned HD are best suited to the recording of slow-moving objects. Interlace scanning is much more suited to fast-moving objects. Witness the fact that most sports fans hate seeing their favorite game shot on film – they much prefer it on television, in interlace.

Our eyes can be fooled in several different ways into believing that sequentially displayed still pictures are a true representation of a moving object, thank goodness, or cinema and television would be in dire trouble!

Each interlace field is photographed in half the time taken for a complete frame and each of those fields will therefore have been photographed in half the time a complete progressive scan will have taken place. Therefore the effective shutter speed for a field of interlace will be half the shutter speed for a complete frame. The shorter the exposure time that is used to capture a picture of a moving object, the sharper will be the leading and trailing edge of that object on the picture. Think of trying to photograph a car passing the camera using a relatively slow shutter speed: the background will be sharp since the camera did not move relative to it, but there will be a noticeable blur surrounding the car as that is moving relative to the camera.

The core difference is that although the interlace fields are sharper we are given twice as many of them per second so our brain, seeing so many, assimilates them as a true rendition of a moving image. With progressive scan, and film, we are tricked into believing we are seeing a true moving image, because although we are seeing half as many pictures they have twice the resolution but, more importantly, they have a blurred edge, because the exposure is twice as long, and blurred, just as persistence of vision gives us in real life. Which is all fine, so long as the movement in the frame is relatively slow. To an experienced eye rapid movement within the frame shot on film at 24 fps is not satisfactory at all – the judder can be most disturbing. If a good Director of Photography (DP) is asked to photograph rapid movement like this they will nearly always try to work with a small depth of field, thus putting the background out of focus and removing the relative movement between the moving object and its surroundings – that horrible judder is now no longer apparent. It is interesting that this is one of the primary reasons good DPs and camera operators hate unmotivated pans.

The conclusion must be that either you need to give the eye a sufficient number of sharp pictures that they appear to blur together in our brain or you need to record some kind of blur on each frame so that the brain is satisfied it is looking at real life. In order to give a little light relief to the simple moving disk, Figure 11.9 shows first a hot air balloon stationary in the sky and then a representation of a single frame of progressive scan or film as captured when the balloon starts to move. Looked at in isolation this blurred frame looks odd, but when 20 or more pictures of its subsequent movement are shown every second the viewer will be completely convinced they are watching natural movement.

11.6 Printing Out to Film

As yet cinemas that can project a digital image via an HD electronic projector are in the minority and therefore in most cases it is necessary to take our digital image and transcribe it to a film print for display in a cinema.

(a)

(b)

Figure 11.9: The effect of motion blur: (a) scene with no movement; (b) background still – balloon moving showing motion blur

First let us consider how a picture captured using interlace scanning will look on that piece of film. Remember the two fields have been captured at slightly different moments in time. Figure 11.10 shows how subsequent frames of our moving disk will look if the two fields making up a complete frame are both printed to a single frame of film – odd, to say the least. Fortunately this transfer technique, though used extensively in the past, particularly with CRT display devices in the transfer equipment, is not common now, though can still be found in some post-production houses – beware of them!

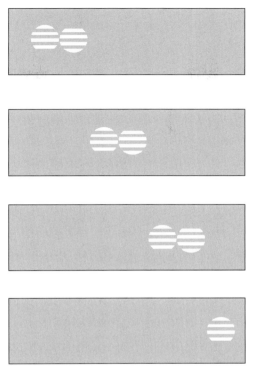

Figure 11.10: Interlace scanning printed to film

It is now possible to combine the two fields, superimposing them in the same space on the film print, and this is currently much more common; this will provide a single complete disk on each frame having full resolution, but that disk will be made up of alternate lines taken at different moments in time – believe me, this looks equally odd, at least to me, and though different, perhaps not quite so bad. It is possible to pass the image through a good adaptive interpolator that will improve things enormously and, thank goodness, this is much the most common procedure today.

Were we to print a complete frame of picture acquired using progressive scan we would get a series of complete disks, where all the information contained in each frame had been acquired at the same moment in time, very much as in Figure 11.11, and also very much as if it had been recorded on film.

At present, progressive scanned images when used in the television environment may not have quite as many advantages as some people would have us believe. There are many subjects, notably sport, where interlace scanned pictures are more acceptable if shown on a television at the present time; they are also what the audience is used to. However, ABC in

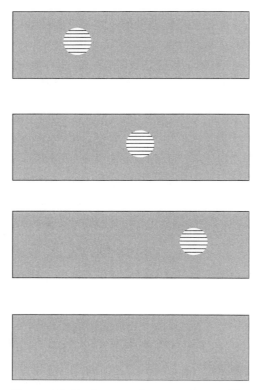

Figure 11.11: Progressive scanning to film

America and some Scandinavian countries show sport in a 720P with 60 fps or 720P with 50 fps, both of which give a wonderfully smooth motion; indeed, this has been the ATSC specification since 1990. The difference here is that although the pictures are captured in progressive scan the frame rate is much higher, 50 or 60 full frames per second, and it is this that removes most of the problem.

I strongly favor this move as it undoubtedly makes movement appear much more natural no matter what the subject, be it fiction, documentary or sport.

Having said all the above, if you wish to acquire your images digitally and then want to show them in a cinema, via either a digital projector or from a film print, my belief is that capturing them with progressive scan is *essential* to give the audience the experience they expect of cinema presentation.

There are a number of other issues that affect the perceived quality of a digitally acquired picture and most of these are discussed in the next chapter, covering line standards.

CHAPTER 12

Line Standards and Definition

There are two main structural standards for High Definition (HD), one based on a pixel layout of 1920 × 1080 pixels and the other of 1280 × 720 pixels. In addition to the number of pixels there are other factors that contribute to the perceived quality of the picture; these include the choice between the image being scanned in an interlace or progressive manner and, if it is scanned in interlace, a factor best described as line summation that can affect that perceived picture quality. While both the standards can support up to 60 frames per second (fps) it is more common, with professional cameras, to find a 1080 camera limited to 30 fps with several 720 cameras going up to 60 fps.

The 1080 format has the choice of the original image being scanned in either interlace or progressive while the 720 format is always scanned in progressive. Let us consider the 1080 format first. When Progressive scanning is used with 1080 lines, especially when shown in the cinema, it undoubtedly gives the highest perceived, and indeed technical, quality. Unfortunately for the picture quality interlace scanning, in any format, comes with the function called line summation.

12.1 Line Summation

In the early days of standard definition television, cameras utilized tubes as their pick-up device and they scanned the target with a 287.5-line raster, phase shifted by a half-line each field, two fields making a complete frame. The scanning spot was Gaussian in shape and spilled over into adjacent lines, thus cleaning the target of all charge each time a field was scanned. The phase shift produced the spatial information for the interleaving lines. With the introduction of chip cameras it was necessary to mimic the picture produced by a tube camera in order to continue to be able to deliver the output that the transmission systems existing at the time expected and required.

In order to do this every line of pixels is scanned independently and therefore the effective spot size is defined by the size of an individual pixel. What is recorded to tape as line 1 is the summation of the electrical output of lines 1 and 2 added together and then recorded as if it were just line 1. Line 3, the second scanned line in an interlace format, is then recorded as the electrical output of lines 3 and 4, again added together. This continues to the bottom of the picture until the scanning returns to the top of the picture in order to record the even numbered lines and line 2 is then added to line 3 and recorded as just line 2. Again this continues to the bottom of the frame and then things move on to the next complete frame and the whole event happens all over again. This summation of the output of adjacent lines of pixels replicates the way a tube camera will have a scanning spot that overlaps the adjacent lines and, happily, doubles the voltage recorded which, effectively, makes the camera twice as sensitive, or one stop faster.

You might think that the loss in image quality caused by adding two lines together in this way would halve the vertical resolution but this is not so; there is another factor at play that helps to bring back some of the apparent loss in quality. Each field has half the total resolution of the entire picture for it only contains half the information – half the lines. The "interlace factor" increases the apparent vertical resolution of the picture. This is because the persistence of vision of the human eye helps to blend the two fields together into a single, complete, picture. As a rule of thumb the effect of persistence of vision increases the apparent resolution from 50 percent to about 70 percent of that which would be perceived on a picture where all the lines were shown at once. Thus losses on one hand are, partly, replaced by gains on the other.

The 1080 format is mainly recorded in either interlace (i) or progressive segmented field (PSF), where the camera is working in a progressive mode but the picture is delivered in an interlace structure. It should be noted that there are few very high-end cameras that are dedicated primarily to feature film production, working in a true 1080 Progressive scan (P) mode. 1080P will undoubtedly give the highest quality picture in every respect, especially when shown in the cinema, with 1080PSF being indiscernible from 1080P in this application. Unfortunately, 1080PSF does not always look quite as good as 1080P when broadcast.

So, in the television arena, how does a 1080 interlace picture compare with a 720 progressive picture when judged side by side, especially subjectively, and by eye? These after all are the most commonly encountered and currently the most argued over.

12.2 Apparent Picture Quality

I have prepared some illustrations to demonstrate the differences in apparent picture quality, which, I hope, will show what happens despite their having had to be rescanned for publication. In producing these pictures I have imported them into my Corel Draw 12 program in which I have scanned them in, defining the bits to be used both in the horizontal and vertical dimensions. This gives a very close representation of any given digital picture if the number of bits in the illustration exactly matches the number of pixels that would be used in the digital camera.

If you look at Figure 12.1(a) the picture has the full 1920×1080 pixels, while in Figure 12.1(b) the picture has had the lines added together and is therefore showing, in effect, 1920×540 pixels or bits; this is very much a worst case scenario. I would expect you to see very little difference; this is as it should be, for in a relatively small picture the loss is not very

(a)

(b)

Figure 12.1: The effect of line summation: (a) 1920×1080 pixels – Progressive scan; (b) 1920×1080 pixels with line summation

apparent to the eye. Here the width of the illustration in this book represents something like the same angle of view to your eye as a fairly large television screen would when viewed in a normal size room. The image quality loss would only become apparent if we were to blow that second picture up to the angle of view you would encounter in a cinema. This is why television has been getting away with the trick all these years.

One thing you might notice if you consider the two pictures in Figure 12.1 very carefully, and here look at the window at the end of the station, is that at first glance the window in the lower picture might look sharper – not what you would expect. If you look more carefully still, you will see that the window is not quite as sharp in the vertical dimension but the difference between the black bars and the brighter glass behind seems greater. This is because as we coarsen the definition, and use bigger pixels, the *apparent* contrast goes up and, as explain fully in Chapter 20, when apparent contrast increases the perceived definition can increase although, technically, it has definitely reduced. This is because the *impression* of sharpness is the product of detail *and* contrast.

Let us look at the actual resolution of the two pictures in more detail. In Figure 12.2 the top left-hand portion of the flag from Figure 12.1 has been magnified 10 times. At first glance you may think the lower picture sharper; this is because the blocks making up the picture are bigger – twice as big vertically. Now move the book away from you until you can no longer resolve the blocks in the lower picture. The upper picture should now look sharper; this is because the information content of the upper picture is greater and this becomes apparent when the eye can no longer see the blocks making up the picture. Bring the book back to your normal reading position and compare the lower edge of the dark portion of the flag, the portion that contains the stars. The coarser vertical resolution of the lower picture creates a very jagged edge to the nearly horizontal line, whereas in the upper picture this is hardly apparent. If both pictures were to be blown up to a cinema size screen then the upper picture would remain perfectly acceptable while the lower would be most unpleasant to look at, particularly where any lines somewhat off horizontal are present.

12.3 1080 Versus 720 in Television

If we confine the argument to the current HD television world, where 1080i has often competed with 720P as an acquisition format, though 1080PSF is increasingly taking over from 1080i, the outcome of the comparison is surprisingly similar. 1080PSF would look better still but let us, for now, confine ourselves to the worst case scenario. Figure 12.3 shows the same scene as before with the upper picture (a) representing 1080i with line summation and the lower picture (b) a 720P frame where every line is independently recorded. As we established earlier, if we compare a 1080i picture with a 1080P picture the interlace version will have apparently lost around 30–50 percent of its vertical resolution.

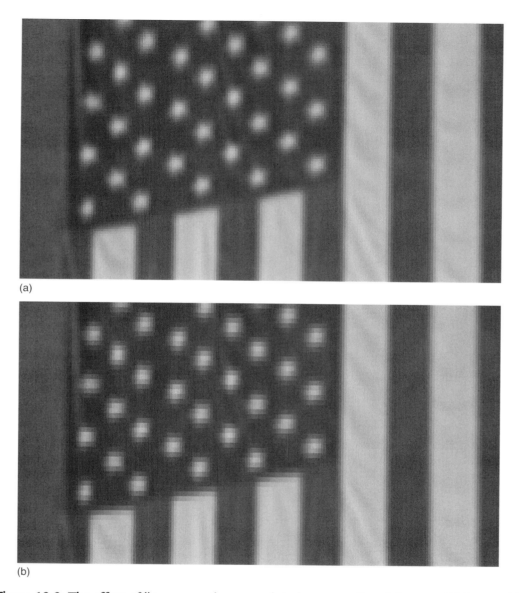

Figure 12.2: The effect of line summation on an interlace recording: (a) a true 1920 $\times$ 1080 pixel image enlarged 10 times; (b) a 1920 $\times$ 1080 interlace picture with line summation enlarged 10 times

(a)

(b)

Figure 12.3: 1080i with line summation compared with 720P: (a) 1920 × 1080 interlace scan with line summation; (b) 1280 × 720 Progressive scan line standard

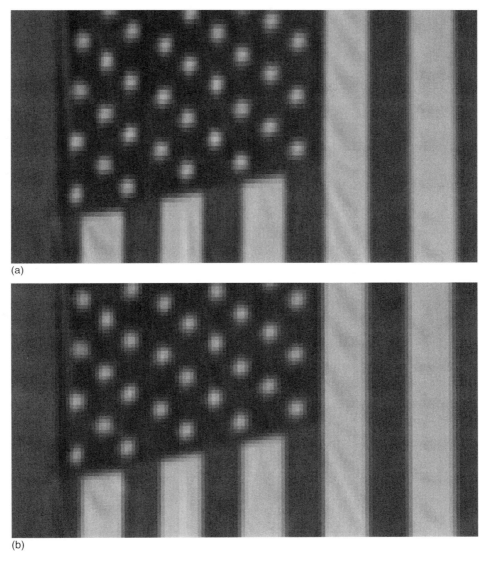

(a)

(b)

Figure 12.4: 720P × 10 compared with 1080i with line summation × 10: (a) a 1920 × 1080 interlace picture with line summation magnified 10 times; (b) 1280 × 720 Progressive scan image magnified 10 times

As 720 is approximately 70 percent of 1080 it follows that the pictures may look very similar – in Figure 12.3 this is so. Now, just to be sure, let us compare the 10 times magnified portion of the flag again; this can be seen in Figure 12.4 where, not surprisingly given the arguments above, both pictures show remarkably similar attributes regarding both definition and diagonal edge resolution. If you again take the book away from you until you cannot resolve the blocks, or pixels, you would almost certainly judge both pictures to be equally sharp.

12.4 Conclusions

Here I am going to be brave and give you my straightforward opinion.

With regard to picture definition, if you are shooting for television, you will not notice much difference between 1080i and 720P given a good enough, and identical, delivery system, be it cathode ray tube (CRT), plasma screen, TFT screen or projection. But 1080P, or 1080PSF to a lesser extent when shown on television but not in the cinema, will always look superior to either of the two former standards. Motion artifacts, or motion blur, are another matter and your decision will be partly based on personal preference and partly on your need to closely replicate a film look; these matters were discussed in Chapter 11.

If the images are definitely going to be shown in the cinema, no matter if they are to be shown from film or a full resolution digital projector, I would not hesitate to choose 1080P with 1080PSF a very close second. This decision is based on two criteria: first they provide the best resolution of any of the available formats and secondly the audience will have the preconceived idea that they are about to enjoy the film experience, and Progressive scan most nearly replicates this.

12.5 Is HD Worth the Trouble?

Most certainly "yes" has to be the answer. As discussed in Chapter 10, the 1920 × 1080 pixel resolution at least fulfills the resolution requirements of an audience in a commercial cinema so far as theatrical presentation is concerned. In most cases there will be little discernible difference in perceived quality between 1080PSF and 1080P but if budget and the convenience of the camera's layout were not considerations then 1080P has to be the first choice. If there is a need to acquire pictures digitally and those pictures must seem to the audience as good as 35 mm film then this standard, or something at least as good, is essential.

For television the argument is a little different. Let us not beat about the bush: the driving factors for a push to introduce broadcast HD television is the war between the broadcasters themselves and the industry's wish to sell more televisions. An almost incidental factor is a very noticeable increase in picture quality, something the film-makers – that is, the technicians – are very keen on.

How great is the improvement? If you look at Figure 12.5 you will see a picture of Grand Central Station that has been scanned with the same number of image elements as the HD, NTSC and PAL television formats. The whole picture at this size and printed in a book is not

Figure 12.5: Comparative resolution between HD, NTSC & PAL: (a) HD – 1920 × 1080;
(b) NTSC – 720 × 487; (c) PAL – 720 × 576

going to look significantly different, so against each picture there is an enlarged section of the flag. In the enlarged HD example the picture elements, or pixels, can hardly be seen and all the edges, even of the stars on the flag, are smooth. In both the NTSC and PAL versions there is a noticeable pixilation – each element is quite clear.

With the move to larger and larger television sets, even in the home, this improvement will increasingly be welcome.

CHAPTER 13

Three-chip Technology

13.1 Additive Color Imagery

On a television screen, for a single dot to appear as white it will have to be made up from three smaller dots. The dots, in the case of a cathode ray tube, are phosphors and phosphor will glow when hit by a beam of electrons and it will glow with a different brightness depending on the strength of the beam. The three small dots of phosphor that make up a larger dot that can appear to glow white have phosphors capable of glowing red, green or blue. A nearly infinite number of colors can be obtained from varying the brightness of each of the colored dots. If all three dots are glowing at 100 percent brightness then this will appear as pure white and if they are all switched off this will represent as near to black as the screen can produce.

Color plate 1 shows how additive color mixing works. Three beams of light, respectively red, green and blue, are projected on to a white background and where all three overlap the color will appear to be white. Where red and green alone overlap, the light appears to be yellow. Where blue and green overlap we get cyan and where blue and red overlap we see magenta. The three original colors red, green and blue are known as the primary colors and the three colors obtained by mixing equal amounts of only two of the light beams, i.e. yellow, cyan and magenta, are known as the secondary colors.

The glowing phosphors on the television screen work in exactly the same way, for if the dots are small enough and close enough together they appear as continuous tones and work just as if colored beams of light were being added together. Those of you with a background in art will already have realized that adding pigments of red, green and blue together creates a very different effect from adding light together.

13.2 The Three-chip Camera's Beam Splitter

To anyone coming from a film background the description that is about to follow will seem like a nightmare, for they expect nothing but air between the back of the lens and the image plane at the time of exposure.

In order for a modern three-chip video camera to function, the image from the lens must be split up into its red, green and blue components and each of the resultant images must then be delivered to a receptor, or chip, dedicated to that color. This is necessary because the sensors on the chips, the pixels, are only sensitive to brightness; they cannot discern color and therefore the three primary colors, red, green and blue, must be separated optically before the three component colors are each sent to a dedicated chip. As only one color reaches each chip the electronic output from that chip will only be an analysis of that single, primary color's component part of the whole image.

While all this separation is happening it is vital that each color image travels through a light path that contains identical amounts of both air and glass. In order for this to be achieved three prisms are cemented together as in Color plate 2. Between the joined surfaces of the prisms are two dichroic mirrors, one reflecting blue light only and the other red only. Dichroic mirrors are used because they enable far brighter images to be separated than would be possible with absorption filters.

A dichroic mirror works on the principle of coating a sheet of glass with interference layers which have both a low and a high refractive index. These layers have a thickness of approximately one-quarter of the wavelength of the light that is to be separated. For instance, a mirror that has a maximum output of 700 nanometers (nm) and a minimum output of 350 nm will therefore be a red reflecting mirror. If the sheet of glass upon which the mirror is coated has a higher refractive index than the coated layer then the maximum output will be 350 nm and it will therefore be a blue reflecting mirror.

Looking at Color plate 2 you will see that a full, three-color image enters the block and arrives at the interface between the first and second prisms; on the back of the first prism there is a blue dichroic mirror. All the blue portion of the image is then reflected away, and is then reflected a second time by the outer surface of this, the first prism, finally exiting this prism and arriving at the chip that is to give the blue signal.

Both the red and green elements of the image pass cleanly through the blue dichroic mirror and on to the second prism in the block. At the back of the second prism is the red dichroic mirror, which separates off the red portion of the image, sending it to the far side of that prism where it is reflected yet again and exits this prism to arrive at the red chip.

The green image, having passed cleanly through both the blue and the red mirrors, travels through a simple block of glass to arrive at the green chip.

The block of glass in front of the green chip may appear unnecessarily thick but it is essential to add sufficient glass to the light path of the green image for it to exactly match the distance traveled by both the red and blue light paths. This is vital, for the taking lens will have formed an image in which all colors arrive at their point of focus precisely the same distance from the back of the lens. Therefore with all the three light paths now identical, all three receptors will receive a sharp image.

While this splitter block is very effective it has one significant drawback created by all the glass the images have to travel through. Any image traveling through anything other than an absolutely clean and perfect vacuum will disperse some of its energy away from the desired light path; this we call flare. One can imagine that an image that is required to pass through three glass prisms and encounter two dichroic reflectors will disperse quite a lot of light on its way through this complex optical device. The video camera overcomes this by placing circuits downstream from the image sensors to electronically enhance the picture by improving the blacks and restoring the image to a higher gamma, for that too will have decreased as a result of the overall flare.

While all this electronic image correction and enhancement is very successful it does, in my opinion, contribute to the "video look" so disliked by film cinematographers. If one shot a piece of film which had, perhaps by accident, an overall flare on the front surface of the lens, then one can imagine the result. There would be a dramatic loss of contrast and the blacks would have become what is referred to as "milky". To correct this at the printing stage would be next to impossible and even if the image was carefully transferred to tape using a modern telecine transfer suite, then while the blacks could be improved and the gamma altered, the image would never be as pleasing as had the lens been adequately shaded in the first place. This electronic grading is very much what is happening in the video camera and, as I say, I feel it is one of the primary causes of the video look.

The settings of these circuits are optimized at the factory and, despite sometimes appearing in the camera's menus, should be left well alone when shooting in the field.

13.3 The Image Sensors

As we have seen, the beam splitter separates the red, green and blue elements of the image and presents them to the individual, dedicated, sensor chips. Each sensor is, as we know, in effect a brightness-only device that has a single color presented to it. The output of each sensor can be thought of as representing a red, green or blue component of the original image. If all three components are simultaneously shown on the screen it might look as in Color plate 3, a perfectly normal color image. Should only the red component be sent to the screen then it would look much like Color plate 4; correspondingly the green and blue components would look as in Color plate 5 for the green component and Color plate 6 for the blue component.

The image sensor's job is to break up an optical image into bits of information that can be handled electronically and finally recorded on a magnetic tape. The sensors are in effect an array of very tiny single sensors each assessing the brightness of the equivalent of the dot earlier described as making up a printed image in this book. In this application each tiny segment of the image is known as a pixel. The greater number of pixels each color image is broken up into, the finer will be the resultant definition of the image. The principle is exactly the same as that described in Chapter 10. In paper printing terms we define resolution as the number of dots per inch (DPI) but in electronic imaging we refer to the pixels on the chip, i.e. for the most common HD format 1920 × 1080 – the vertical number of pixels and then the horizontal number.

13.4 The Sensor Chip

The sensor chip itself is a printed circuit board (PCB) divided into a grid with horizontal and vertical squares relating to the number of pixels chosen by the camera manufacturer, most often for HD 1920 pixels across the chip and 1080 from top to bottom. The whole of each square of the grid cannot be made sensitive for various reasons, including the need for wiring space. Each sensor square therefore comes out slightly smaller than the grid size and the actual sensitive spot is smaller still. Figure 13.1 shows a grid layout in plan and Figure 13.2 a cross-section where the relatively small size of the sensitive area relative to the grid pattern can clearly be seen.

The biggest problem with this manner of construction is that only a small percentage of the light energy available for the whole of the grid area will reach the sensitive areas. This leads

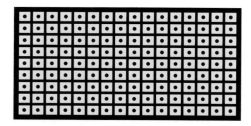

Figure 13.1: Pixel receptors

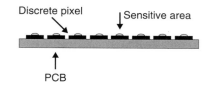

Figure 13.2: Pixel array showing area covered by the sensitive units

Figure 13.3: Lens-enhanced pixel array

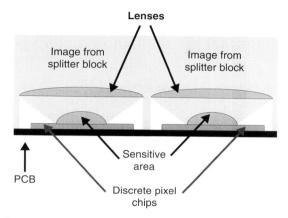

Figure 13.4: Enlarged section of a sensor array with the lenses showing just two pixel areas

to a serious loss of sensitivity; perhaps only 50 percent or less of the energy available within each grid square actually arrives at the sensitive area. To overcome this, some manufacturers overlay the grid with a mesh of small lenses each having nearly the diameter of the grid's width, and these lenses focus a far higher proportion of the grid squares' available energy on to the sensitive area.

Figure 13.3 shows the cross-section of a sensor array with the lenses in place, from which can be seen how the lens covers a considerably greater area than the sensitive area. Figure 13.4 is a much enlarged section showing just two pixel areas. Very little of the light energy of the optical image is now wasted as all the energy falling on the lens is directed on to the sensitive area of each pixel element.

CHAPTER 14

Single-chip Technology

14.1 What is Available?

Currently there are two types of sensor available that, between them, dominate the High Definition (HD) arena: charge-coupled devices (CCDs) and complementary metal-oxide semiconductor (CMOS). Both have advantages and disadvantages. The purpose of any sensor is to convert small parts of the image formed by the lens, and therefore being made up of varying amounts of light energy according to the brightness of the original scene in that particular area, into amounts of electricity corresponding to the light energy. Each of these discrete portions of the image is usually referred to as a pixel. It is important that the number of electrons coming out of each pixel can be assessed and recorded. CCD and CMOS sensors do this in slightly different ways; the way they do it and, more importantly, the way they divide up the primary colors Red, Green and Blue is crucial. Let us take a look at each type.

14.2 CCD Sensors

In a CCD sensor the electronic charge accumulated in each pixel during a single exposure is, after the exposure is complete, transported across the sensor to one corner of the chip where the individual charges can be read sequentially. An analog-to-digital converter (the A-to-D converter) then turns each pixel's electrical output into a value expressed as a binary code.

CCDs require a specialized manufacturing process dedicated to their production. This leads to high manufacturing costs but does arrive at a situation where the CCD sensors usually have a very high quality output, are very sensitive and the output will have a very low noise content, especially in the part of the image dealing with shadow detail.

By the nature of the beast, CCDs tend to be relatively power hungry.

14.3 CMOS Sensors

CMOS sensors are much cheaper to produce than CCDs as they can be manufactured on a production line very similar to, or the same as, normal microprocessors that are used in most computers. The primary difference is that while CCDs transport the charge from each pixel to a common output, a CMOS sensor can allow each pixel's output to be individually read and therefore recorded independently. In certain applications this may seem a considerable advantage but it does come with some drawbacks.

In order that a CMOS sensor can do its clever trick of offering the output of each and every pixel to be individually assessed, every pixel on the chip has to have its own very tiny amplifier to boost the signal from that pixel and herein lies its disadvantage. First, amplifiers take up space and if that amplifier has to live on the surface of the chip, as it does, then this must reduce the area occupied by each pixel that can be apportioned to the light-sensitive device, and as that device gets smaller so its potential output will also be reduced. CMOS sensors do not tend, therefore, to have very high equivalent sensitivity or ISO ratings compared with CCD sensors.

Secondly, amplification tends to bring noise and noise tends to be more noticeable where the signal started off very low. In this context we are talking about shadow detail. CMOS sensors do suffer from noise in the shadow parts of the image, though they have improved in recent years. To a film person noise in these circumstances is very similar to film grain, so CMOS sensors tend to produce the equivalent of grainy shadow.

CMOS sensors require relatively little power.

14.4 CCDs versus CMOS Chips

Here is a quick checklist:

1. CCD sensors usually have high-quality, low-noise images. CMOS sensors are more susceptible to noise, which is more noticeable in the shadow detail.

2. CMOS sensors tend to be less sensitive – that is, have a lower relative ISO speed – as part of the pixel area must be taken up with an amplifier, whereas in a CCD far more of the pixel area is light sensitive.

3. CCD sensors consume more power than CMOS sensors. CCDs can consume as much as 100 times as much power as CMOS sensors.

4. CMOS sensors tend to be cheap; they can be fabricated on a normal silicon production line whereas CCD sensors require a dedicated production line, making them much more expensive.

5. Because CCD sensors have been around much longer, the knowledge base and experience in their production is much greater though, in this respect, CMOS sensors are undoubtedly catching up.

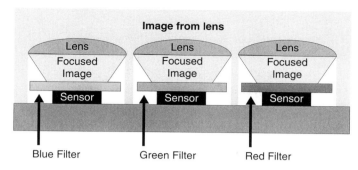

Figure 14.1: Single-chip individual pixel filtering

14.5 Color Filtering in Single Sensors

With single-sensor cameras each individual pixel has to have its own absorption filter, thus allowing only one of the colors Red, Green or Blue to reach the sensitive part of the pixel. The layout of three pixels arranged in this way is shown in Figure 14.1.

Before single sensors started having the very high number of pixels that have recently been introduced, and currently some have over 12 million pixels on a single sensor, there was a major issue with sensor cameras in an area known as aliasing. If you can look back well over 10 years or more and think of a TV presenter wearing a check jacket then sometimes the jacket would display a completely unconvincing pattern over it. This was probably a moiré pattern caused by an interference between the frequency of the checks in the jacket and the number of pixels on the cameras sensors. If, at the image plane, the frequency of the checks was similar to the frequency of the pixels, or a multiple thereof, then strange and unwanted images occurred. As the number of pixels that can be put on a chip is increased, this problem is reduced.

Film does not have these particular aliasing problems because on a single frame of film the sizes of silver grains, from very large to very small, are distributed in a somewhat random pattern and therefore will not form regular interference patterns with a constant and repeated pattern within the scene. Furthermore, each frame will have a distribution pattern utterly dissimilar to the frame preceding it or following it, and hence the repeat pattern problem does not exist.

14.6 Bayer Pattern Filtering

In order to overcome some of the problems with aliasing, Kodak invented a pattern of distribution of the Red, Green and Blue filters covering each pixel in a single-sensor camera and this patterning is referred to as Bayer pattern filtering. While it would be impossible to read out the signal from a chip with a truly random distribution of Red, Green and Blue filters, the Bayer pattern goes a long way towards it. The idea is to have an orderly distribution of filters in such a way that each line of filters will have its colors in a different distribution to both the line of pixels above it and the line of pixels below it. To achieve this, twice as many Green filters are used as are used for both Red and Blue.

Each row of pixels contains only two colors and one of those colors will always be Green. So the first line, say, will alternate Green and Red, the second line Green and Blue, and the third back to Green and Red, as in Color plate 7. Now while this is not exactly random it does approach that state. One of the effects of Bayer patterning is that the output from all the Green pixels, assuming all the pixels receive the same amount of light, will be twice that of either the Red or Blue pixels. The resolution of the Green image will also be twice that of the Red or Blue images. The RAW output from a chip using Bayer pattern filtering is usually rather low in contrast and very green, as one would expect.

Interpolation circuitry can sort out a RAW Bayer image. Clearly it is easy to either amplify the Red and Blue outputs or attenuate the Green. This has to be done carefully or one of two problems, or both, will result. Amplifying the Red and Blue outputs will bring up the noise content of the signal, far from an ideal situation, and attenuating the Green signal may significantly reduce the sensitivity of the camera.

The solution is to apply very sophisticated algorithms to the signal to come up with a complete signal where Red, Green and Blue all match in exactly the proportions of the original scene – this can be done but it requires considerable computing power and time. This is why many cameras employing Bayer patterned sensors leave this conversion from the RAW data to the mains powered computer in the cutting room, for to do it in-camera would dramatically shorten battery life and make the camera much heavier and hotter – not a good thing.

All this said, I have seen some very pleasing pictures from cameras using Bayer filtering, though it has to be said not all the cameras can easily be monitored and some only really produce an ideal picture after post-production.

14.7 Sequential Filtering

As described earlier, until the advent of chips with very high pixel counts single chips using sequential filtering showed signs of the aliasing described above and sometimes vertical colored stripes could be discerned in certain circumstances. A single sequentially filtered sequence is shown in Color plate 8. If a sensor has so many pixels that the sampling rate is higher than any pattern frequency likely to be found in any given scene then the problems disappear; it has only recently been possible to produce sensors of this kind. Currently one of the best of this kind of sensor is to be found in the Panavision Genesis, which has 12.4 million pixels. At this sampling rate Panavision can safely employ sequential sampling, and therefore the level of output and degree of resolution will be identical for all the Red, Green and Blue signals. Compared with Color plate 8, Color plate 9 has three times as many pixels horizontally and twice as many vertically, which represents the six times subsampling on a Genesis sensor. By comparing the two plates you can see how, with so many more pixels in the same area, the impression of stripes is considerably reduced.

14.8 Comparative Resolution

If you compare Color plate 7, showing Bayer pattern filtering, with Color plate 8, showing sequential filtering, and count the number of color patches something interesting and significant is revealed.

Remember each of the plates contains the same number of pixels or colored blocks and they are the same size. In Color plate 7 with Bayer patterning there are 72 Red pixels, 144 Green pixels and 72 Blue pixels. In Color plate 8, which uses sequential patterning, there are 96 Red pixels, 96 Green pixels and 96 Blue pixels. What are we to make of these differences?

At the end of the day, digital color imagery requires that the complete signal, known as RGB, should have the same amount of available information in each of the color signals. So with a Bayer patterned image the starting point must be the maximum number of pixels available in the Red and Blue image and, somehow, the excess of Green pixels must be reduced to match. If you were to take the opposite approach and artificially increase the proportion of Red and Blue, the image would no longer look true. The results from putting the Bayer pattern image through its algorithm will therefore be 72 Red pixels, 72 Green pixels and 72 Blue pixels; this gives us a total of 216 pixels for the processed image compared with 288 pixels for the sequentially filtered image. The sequentially filtered image therefore will have one-third more resolution.

Does the above matter? You might think so but in reality it doesn't matter very much. We have to return to the cost of producing CCD sequentially filtered sensors, which is high relative to CMOS Bayer filtered sensors. Thus it is not hard to perceive a situation whereby the camera manufacturers who wish to use CMOS Bayer sensors can, with only a relatively small increase in cost, simply add 33 percent more pixels to their sensor and get back to an even playing field with CCD censored cameras and, in the main, this is what they do.

You should keep in mind that another utterly crucial matter in the quality of the resultant image from a CMOS Bayer sensor is the quality and effectiveness of the algorithm applied to the RAW file when the excess of Green pixels is compensated for. If this is done well all will be well, but even the slightest compromise made here can easily end in disaster further down the production process.

14.9 Using Sequential Pattern Filtering

The disadvantage, as we have seen, of sequential pattern filtering is that there is a danger of getting interference patterns between the frequency of a pattern on the set and the frequency of the pixels on the sensor. The simple answer is to have a much higher pixel count on the sensor. As sequential patterned sensors are usually CCD devices and are therefore already expensive, substantially increasing the pixel count will put that already considerable cost up at what may be an alarming rate. If you can afford to do this then all will be well and you should have an excellent image from your camera that gives an RGB output with little or no after-processing being needed. This could be a considerable advantage when you get to post-production.

CHAPTER 15

Data Files – A Simplified Guide

15.1 RAW Data Files, etc.

RAW data files have only really become an issue since the use of single-chip complementary metal-oxide semiconductor (CMOS) sensors in moving picture cameras. With cameras utilizing three charge-coupled device (CCD) chips the use of RAW data files is rarely encountered, as by their very nature each of the three chips sends data already encoded as a single color, this having been done by the prisms optically splitting the colors, and therefore the chip block inherently outputs three distinct signals, Red, Green and Blue. With a Bayer patterned CMOS chip things are very different.

With a Bayer patterned CMOS chip the exit data stream is really only a monochrome signal, each pixel simply sending a value, and in addition to that there is metadata (data about data) that tells the file which color each pixel has been filtered by. As you can imagine, without some fairly strong interpolation this stream of data can hardly be looked at as a cogent image by most display devices. This may or may not be a problem; let us see.

If you are familiar with the use of RAW files in the world of still photography you must now accept that things are going to be a little different, for downstream from the master image the requirements are also different. In the stills world one often manipulates a RAW file and then finally outputs it in a universal format such as JPEG or TIFF or something similar. Here the RAW file will be considerably bigger than the JPEG or TIFF, as those file formats utilize some form of compression. In the motion picture world we try to avoid compression as much as possible and herein lies the difference.

In the motion picture world we would like RGB (Red, Green, Blue) files where the three primary colors have entirely independent signals, all of them uncompressed. If a RAW file is manipulated to give the finest possible uncompressed RGB file then, unlike the stills world, the complete three-color RGB file will be considerably bigger than the RAW file as what was simple metadata is now unscrambled and expanded to produce the pure RGB file.

All the above has lead some camera manufacturers to come to the conclusion that it may be sensible to keep to RAW files within the camera and to ask the downstream computer that lives in the cutting room, and runs off mains electricity, to do the interpolation from RAW to RGB. They may have a point.

Why? Well, look at what happens if your camera inherently starts with RAW files after the analog-to-digital processor and now has to convert these files, within the camera, to a full uncompressed RGB file. First, there is going to have to be another fairly heavy duty processor to add the monochrome data to the metadata and bring all this together as the required RGB file – and what will the result be? Considerably more power requirements for a start. The camera will already be having a hefty power draw down just to run the analog-to-digital (A-to-D) converter which, unlike a film camera, must run all the time in order to provide a signal for the viewfinder unless you are using an Arriflex D-21 or a Dalsa that have optical viewfinders. Now you must add possibly an even more power hungry RAW to RGB translating processor – even more power required all of the time. If you have added all this extra power consumption what will be the first problem with which you now have to deal? A great deal of extra heat. Almost certainly a lot more heat than can comfortably be dissipated by any external heat sink, so if you previously did not have a fan in your camera you now most certainly need one, and if you did have one you now need a bigger one or quite possibly more than one. I know of at least one High Definition (HD) camera that has three fans.

So you put your extra fans in and your two power hungry processors are kept sufficiently cool, but you now have to drag around a much bigger and considerably heavier battery. Job done? No! From considerable experience on set I can tell you that you now have one very unhappy sound department, for in the background of their lovely dialog there is this continual whooshing noise. Now, say you are on a three- or four-camera shoot and that whooshing noise is multiplied by the number of cameras. Do you really think that the Producer is going to be happy to pay for days and days of automatic dialog replacement (ADR) just because the camera designer thought it essential that their CMOS chip camera had to output an RGB signal? I think not.

Hence the move by many newer camera manufacturers who have chosen to have CMOS Bayer patterned sensors in their cameras to record RAW data and let something downstream, run on a mains power supply, convert that RAW data to RGB. A small whoosh from a single processor in the cutting room has to be preferable to many whooshes on set.

Fortunately, in order to obtain a signal from a camera that essentially records RAW data that can be interpreted by an electronic viewfinder, things are nothing like as serious as trying to provide a recordable RGB signal.

One more thing. Although I have talked about RAW files things are not quite as simple as that. Were they ever? There is no such thing as a universally accepted format for a RAW file. In the stills world, for instance, Nikon alone have used several RAW file formats for various models of their cameras. If you are using a camera that records to RAW files it is therefore absolutely necessary to check that the post-production workflow you are intending to use can cope really well with exactly the file format you will be sending them. I speak from a seriously bad experience here when a reputable post house swore it knew what it was doing and blamed the onset crew for horrible picture noise in the shadows. It took many days and several scarred reputations before they finally tried another way of converting the camera's RAW files to one their editing suite liked and, miraculously, the noise in the shadows disappeared. Strangely, no apology was forthcoming from the post house. No surprises there. Be warned and check all is well downstream before you start principal photography.

15.2 4:4:4, 4:2:2 and All That

I am going to be daring and say 4:4:4 and 4:2:2, and other combinations of numbers, are often figures bandied about by people in post-production just a little bit to frighten those of us at the sharp end where we actually take the pictures and, perhaps, in order to increase the size of their invoice.

The assumption is that using 4:2:2 may produce a less pure image. However, unless you are shooting a movie with heavy post-production involving a lot of CGI etc., this may not be relevant, provided you are using a decent camera of almost any make. I can hear howls of derision from many quarters, but not from those, like me, who have actually photographed any significant number of conventional movies on HD. I have been lucky enough when shooting digits that I have always had reasonably good cameras. I am happy to state I have never, repeat never, seen any artifacts on my movies relating to any kind of compression. So what's all the fuss about? I have trouble seeing the problem unless you are on one of those high CGI movies.

Back to 4:4:4. If you are recording in 4:4:4 then the fact is you are recording all the information from each of the Red, Green and Blue signals in its entirety. What is important here is that the three numbers are equal, denoting equal weight being given to Red, Green and Blue. The number 4 is a hangover from the early days of digital video, where the signal was sampled at a frequency four times that of the color subcarrier. 1:1:1, 2:2:2, etc. would be equally valid. That will be just fine and you will have a very pure image. It will also be unlikely that you will have a camera you would like to put on your shoulder! Indeed, as far as I know there is no tape recorder or video cassette recorder (VCR), that can record totally uncompressed 4:4:4 so you will have to be using hard drives or flash drives or something that at the present time will be expensive, have a short recording time and need that new figure – a Data Wrangler.

Alternatively if you see no problem in recording 4:2:2 with some well-thought-out compression you could put a camera on your shoulder about the size of, and weighing roughly the same as, a 16 mm Arriflex and it will still happily fill that criterion of mine, the screen at the Odeon Leicester Square.

Now reducing your recorded signal from 4:4:4 to 4:2:2 significantly reduces the amount of data you need to record. Let us see how.

First, it is important to realize that the three numbers no longer correspond to Red, Green and Blue as with 4:4:4. Rather, the first number refers to a signal called Luma. This corresponds to the black and white portion of an image and is produced by adding appropriate, fixed, proportions of Red, Green and Blue together. This signal carries not only the brightness portion of the image but also the vast majority of the detail, since our eyes are more sensitive to changes in brightness than color. The largest component of Luma, some 70 percent, is obtained from the Green value. Remembering that we are trying to reduce the amount of information used to describe our image, we now form two color-difference signals by subtracting both Red and Blue values from Luma. These are the signals describing the Chroma or color portion of our image and due to the aforementioned relative insensitivity of our eyes to changes in color we can afford to sample them at half the rate of the Luma signal, i.e. only analyze them with half of the same accuracy; hence 4:2:2. Note that here the use of 4 gives us the ability to use 2 rather than end up with unpleasant ratios like 1:1/2:1/2, etc.

I am simplifying here but please don't be offended as I am only trying to give enough information for those on set to make some sensible judgements.

But how do we get back to our full RGB output? In the post-production environment data handling circuits can simply input the 4:2:2 data and take the "4" part that is Luma and sum it with the "2" part that represents Luma minus Red to give a complete Red signal. The same goes for Luma minus Blue. It is then straightforward to recover the remaining Green signal. What you now have, if all those circuits were designed well enough, is exactly the same three signals of Red, Green and Blue that composed the original scene. Believe me, with good circuits, it works really well.

15.3 Look-up Tables (LUTs)

LUT stands for look-up table and I have to say I think it is a poor description of what happens. What one is doing when applying an LUT is changing the look of an image into something better, more appropriate or more appealing. This is done electronically, usually by adjusting gamma, contrast, brightness and saturation, sometimes all together. The LUT is a reference by which and by how much each of these parameters is altered for any given circumstance. You may, for instance, when starting with a master file use a different LUT if you are preparing that image to go to television and quite a different LUT if the same image were going to be printed out to film. You never actually refer to a table, it is all done quite automatically.

15.4 De-Bayering an Image

De-Bayering, on the other hand, requires bespoke algorithms we use to modify the RAW image from a Bayer patterned sensor to give a true representation of the original scene. The original image will often appear to have very little contrast and be somewhat green. There will be parameters for changing gamma, contrast, brightness and saturation that will give a correct and pleasing result. This is one solution where the results achieved will be directly related to the time and effort put in: the simplest de-mosaic looks less good but is fast in pseudo-real time; the best quality requires considerable computational power and time.

CHAPTER 16

The Video Tape Recorder (VTR)

16.1 The HDCAM Format

It is useful to investigate a specific format in order to understand how video tape and cassette recorders work, and as HDCAM is probably the most used format in the professional environment I have chosen to discuss it here. It should be borne in mind, however, that virtually all professional video tape recorders (VTRs) and video cassette recorders (VCRs) work on very similar principles. Some smaller recording formats lay down and/or encode the information in a different manner, but the mechanics of doing so are by and large the same.

The HDCAM format writes the information to the tape in exactly the same way whether it is recording a Progressive scan or an interlace scan image. Every frame is recorded as a totally separate and individual part of the recording. Each picture frame is recorded in 12 diagonal stripes across the tape. This, and the phenomenal head to tape speed required to record such a huge amount of information, is achieved by using a helical scanning drum (see below).

Four playback and record heads are used, with newly introduced signal processing and error correction and concealment circuits so powerful that perfect pictures can be recorded and replayed even if one of the four heads completely ceases to function. Each frame is laid down on to the tape as two separate segments; this must not be confused with the way an interlace picture has traditionally been recorded, it is a completely different process. When recording a 24 frames per second (fps) Progressive scan image, each segment will be laid down in one-forty-eighth of a second. This is known as the segmented frame format and is approved by the International Television Union (ITU) in its recommendation 709-3.

16.2 Helical Scan Recording

If the tape were to travel straight past a static recording head, as in a conventional sound-only tape recorder, the tape would have to travel at a terrific speed to be able to record the quantity of information being delivered by the recording head. The use of a helical scanning drum maintains the required record head to tape speed while dramatically reducing the linear tape speed. It does this by wrapping the tape, which is half an inch wide, around more than half the circumference of a drum, approximately 3 inches (75 cm) in diameter. As can be seen in

Figure 16.1, the tape is not wrapped around the center of the drum but makes first contact at one edge and leaves the drum adjacent to the opposite edge. The tape path has therefore described part of a helix, a shape just like a turn on a screw thread, and from this comes the term helical scan. This helical wrapping of the tape would not, in itself, increase the record head to tape speed but, as the drum is then made to rotate the relative head to tape contact speed is dramatically increased. There are four record heads, each halfway between the outside edges of the drum and spaced at 90-degree angles around the drum. As the tape is wrapped around more than 180 degrees of the drum, and as there are four heads on the drum, there will always be at least two heads in contact with the tape. Because the tape is wrapped in a helix around the drum, the recording head will, relative to the tape, travel not only along the tape but from one edge of the tape to the other. By switching the record heads on and off sequentially, strips of recording can be laid down at a shallow angle across the tape, as shown in Figure 16.2. In addition, there are a series of linear, static, recording heads to lay down several control tracks and the time code track.

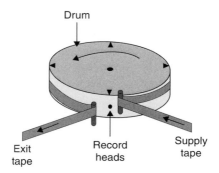

Figure 16.1: The Helical Scan Recording Drum

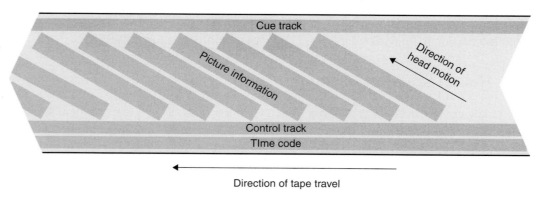

Figure 16.2: Layout of information on HDCAM tape

In practice the mechanism that performs the above operation is far from simple. Figure 16.3 shows the VTR side of a Sony 750P with the side panel removed. What always amazes me is how much electronics are carried on the drum and, given that it must remain very light weight, how extraordinarily reliable they always prove to be.

If you study Figure 16.4, where the cassette is loaded and the tape has been wrapped around the drum, you may notice two things. First, if you look at the top of the drum, on the left-hand side the tape is clearly further away from camera than it is at the top right-hand side, thus showing how, with the slight tilt of the drum, the tape is forming a helix around the drum. Secondly, you can see that the tape is wrapped more than three-quarters of the way around the diameter of the drum, thus ensuring that three of the four record heads on the drum will always be in contact with the tape.

16.3 Mechanical Considerations

If treated with respect, the VTR will give years of unfaltering service. It does, after all, come from a fine and very reliable lineage – the Digi Beta camera and before that the Beta SP camera. In both these cameras it proved to be very reliable indeed, so it has a fine lineage.

The drum is so light not just as a contribution to the portability of the camera as a whole, but to reduce the inertia associated with spinning the drum at a high speed. This reduction in the inertia

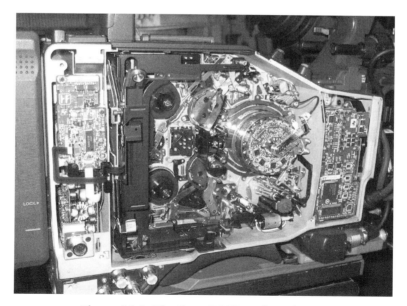

Figure 16.3: The Sony 750P on-board VTR

Figure 16.4: The Sony 750P on-board VTR with the tape loaded

of the drum brings two benefits: it can be brought up to operational speed very quickly and will consume very little power to keep it spinning. This second factor reduces the drain on the battery and therefore indirectly contributes to a reduction in the weight of the on-board battery.

16.4 The Drum Lacing Mechanism

In order to remove a loop of tape from the cassette and wrap it around nearly three-quarters of the drum, the mechanism has first to open the door of the cassette as it enters the door of the VTR. Two rollers then come behind the short, straight, length of tape that is free at the mouth of the cassette. These rollers then travel round the drum in a circle larger than the diameter of the drum but allowing the tape to wrap around the drum. Again, due to weight considerations, this mechanism is made of high-quality but very light materials.

16.5 Operational Considerations

There is little chance of the VTR failing to operate, though there are precautions that should be taken. While the cassette door opens by itself it must be closed manually; please do this gently but firmly. Experience with old and tired SP and Digi Beta cameras leads some operators to bang it shut; banging it shut will eventually lead to its having always to be banged shut and this is doing no good at all to the mechanisms contained within the VTR.

16.6 A Jammed Mechanism

Perhaps this is a good moment to mention an invasive operation that one very occasionally has to carry out on the camera. The following only applies to the Sony range of HDCAM cameras and I include these instructions as Sony cameras and their derivatives, such as the Panavision versions, are by far the most common.

On the opposite side of the camera to the operator, at the bottom of the camera casing, roughly halfway along the camera body, is a rubber plug about a centimeter, or roughly half an inch, in diameter. If you remove this plug it reveals a red plastic button with a Philips-type cross-head slot in it. Should you have an electrical breakdown such that the camera will not unlace the tape and let you remove the cassette you can, with the camera switched off, insert a cross-head screwdriver into this button and turn it; at this point make sure you are turning it in the direction of the very small arrow on the red plastic button. You can then very, very, gently hand crank the lace/unlace mechanism, thus allowing you to retrieve the cassette. A warning – if you turn this button the wrong way you will very likely seriously damage the lacing mechanism. The gear ratio is very low, so this will take some time. I have had to do this a couple of times and would counsel you to carry out this procedure only as a last resort. It is much safer for your tape and your camera if you can get the camera back to the supplier, where a more thorough and safer method can be deployed. You should only consider this mechanical unlacing of the camera if your rushes on the tape are very important and retrieving them is a matter of the greatest urgency.

Part 4
High Definition Cinematography

CHAPTER 17

Lighting and Exposing for HD

17.1 An HD Camera's Equivalent ASA Speed, or ISO Rating

I check the speed, or sensitivity, of any High Definition (HD) camera using the same technique I would use when testing a film stock's ASA (American Standards Association) or ISO (International Standards Organization) rating. Note that the numbers will be the same. When checking a film stock's ASA speed, I set the camera up facing an 18 percent reflectance gray card and make a range of exposures, noting the setting on my meter for each one. Then I ask the laboratory to make me a middle of the range one-light print. Whichever exposure most exactly matches the tonality of the original gray card I deem to be the correct rating for that particular film stock. If I use this method and send the test film to the laboratory that will be processing the rushes for my forthcoming production, I have refined the process to give me the ASA rating of that film stock when processed by that laboratory; they all differ slightly.

With any HD camera my approach is the same but the technique a little different. I set the 18 percent gray card up as before and, close by, set up a carefully lined up decent sized monitor, preferably a 24-inch monitor. Making sure that the card is evenly lit, I adjust the exposure until the gray on the monitor exactly matches the gray of the card; with a 24-inch monitor they will even be roughly the same size if they nearly fill the screen. Now I take a reading of the card with a digital spotmeter and set the reading in the viewfinder on its scale. I then adjust the ASA setting on the meter until the aperture shown is the same as that on the lens. The ASA setting on the meter is now showing the equivalent ASA speed of the camera. With the majority of HD cameras this works out at around 320 or 400 ASA, though as development continues I am finding cameras' sensitivity to be increasing – so never assume, always check.

17.2 Tonal Range

There is much discussion as to the length of the tonal range of HD cameras; I have a very simple test. Using a Kodak 18 percent Gray Card Plus, which has a black and a white patch both sides of the gray (Figure 17.1), I light it evenly to a brightness that gives a perfect exposure with the lens set at, say, T 4 – a stop I know works well for this test – and have the image up on a carefully set up large monitor. Without touching the lens setting I now

Figure 17.1: The Kodak Gray Card Plus

reduce the lighting level while watching the monitor and keep on reducing the level until the gray area on the card is only *fractionally* lighter than the black patch next to it. I now take a spotmeter reading on the gray area; this will be the lower end of the camera's tonal range. Again, without making any adjustments to the lens, I now increase the lighting level until the gray area of the card is again only fractionally darker than the white patch next to it and take another reading on the gray area of the card; this will be the upper end of the tonal range. The number of stops between the first reading and the second reading is the tonal range. It is important in the above test that you have just the very slightest difference in brightness on the monitor between both the black and the white patches and the gray area of the card, for if they are exactly matched you might be at the limit, or you might be far beyond the limit, and you won't be able to tell, as either situation would look the same on the monitor. Just before the limit the camera is still – just – recording detail and this point can be thought of as definitely within the tonal range.

Sometimes when I demonstrate this test to colleagues I have to repeat it a second time, as they simply cannot believe the result. The tonal range of Sony HDW cameras, for instance, by my test is at least 11 stops. Now, those 11 stops are from limit to limit and the characteristics of the camera, particularly as I set up the camera, are similar to a film emulsion in that there is a straight-line section of linear response over most of the range, but there is a certain amount of roll-off at both the extremes of black and white. I have spent some time trying to grasp where these roll-offs start and stop; this involved changing lighting levels minutely in the stop and a half from pure white to pale gray and at the other end of the scale from pure black to dark gray, taking readings with my spotmeter all the while. My conclusion is that you can safely work on the basis that there is a nine-stop linear section of tonality with around a stop

```
 1  stop difference in exposure = lighting ratio of 2

 2  stops difference in exposure = lighting ratio of 4

 3  stops difference in exposure = lighting ratio of 8

 4  stops difference in exposure = lighting ratio of 16

 5  stops difference in exposure = lighting ratio of 32

 6  stops difference in exposure = lighting ratio of 64

 7  stops difference in exposure = lighting ratio of 128

 8  stops difference in exposure = lighting ratio of 256

 9  stops difference in exposure = lighting ratio of 512

10 stops difference in exposure = lighting ratio of 1024

11 stops difference in exposure = lighting ratio of 2048

12 stops difference in exposure = lighting ratio of 4096

13 stops difference in exposure = lighting ratio of 8192
```

Figure 17.2: Lighting ratios relating to difference in exposure

of roll-off at each end – very like many modern film stocks, which must contribute, in part at least, to the pictures from the camera looking so very like film.

17.3 Lighting Ratios

Many cinematographers, especially those from a film background, are used to thinking through a lighting scheme by relating their ideas to the concept of a lighting ratio. A lighting ratio is a simple enough thing; it is a number given to the difference in brightness between one part of the scene and another. If you have taken readings of two parts of your set and the difference between them is one stop, what would be the lighting ratio between them? As it requires twice as much light to increase an exposure by one stop, the lighting ratio will be 2. If the difference had been two stops the lighting ratio would now be 4. This is because every stop increase in brightness doubles the amount of light required and therefore doubles the lighting ratio.

As we have seen, modern HD cameras can photograph a tonal range around 11 stops, so if you refer to Figure 17.2 you will see that the total lighting ratio of, say, a Sony HDW camera is 2048 from maximum white to minimum black. Figure 17.2 also shows how the progression from a single stop of brightness difference, giving the expected lighting ratio of 2, moves through the different stops of brightness differential. As we have seen, each change of one stop doubles the lighting ratio.

If you want your HD pictures to look as much like film as possible, then the lighting ratios you choose to use when lighting for HD should be exactly those you would use for film. If a film camera can photograph it, so can you with a decent professional HD camera. There is, to my mind, however, a more elegant way to light for HD – light to the monitor.

17.4 Lighting to a Monitor

If you are about to execute some fairly sophisticated lighting, then I would strongly recommend you work to a well set-up 14- or 24-inch monitor. An argument goes that if the camera works with 11 stops of tonal range, and even the very best cathode ray tube will be hard pressed to display six stops of tonal range, how can you trust the monitor? Well you can. Both the camera and the monitor have within them circuits to subtly squeeze all the camera's ability into a shorter range with sufficient cleverness that the human eye/brain combination, when looking at a high-grade monitor, will believe it is seeing the full 11 stops of tonal range in a perfectly natural way. Believe me, it works. I have lit several pictures using HD now and have always lit to the monitor using my exposure meter for nothing more than lining up the monitor's contrast level and, in whatever medium they were eventually displayed, the pictures were always exactly as I expected them to be. There is a great joy in working to a monitor; it is very like painting – instead of doing mathematics while staring down a spotmeter I am freed to, quite literally, paint with light. Every mark I make on the set will instantly appear on my canvas, the monitor's screen. It is hard to describe the freedom I felt when I first started working this way; it was very liberating. Instant gratification I suppose.

17.5 Highlights and Shadows

There is a misconception that blames "video" for the poorer handling of highlights than film in some circumstances and with some cameras. It is not the image being recorded on video that is the influencing factor, but the fact that you are working with a positive image rather than a negative one. Those of you who have shot reversal film or still transparency will be familiar with a similar image, one where the shadows seem to look after themselves more than when using a negative/positive process, but where more care must be taken with the highlights, and so it is with any video camera – they shoot a positive image. So whereas with film you would probably spend more time reading the shadows with your meter to establish that they will be recorded just as you wish, you must get into the habit with HD of walking back to the monitor and checking your highlights first.

17.6 Exposure

17.6.1 Using a Monitor

There is an absolutely sure-fire way of getting your exposure spot on. Light the set by eye and, when you have all your keys, cross lights and backlights to your liking, walk back to your monitor and with one hand on the lens aperture ring adjust it until you think your highlights are perfect – to my mind that will be when they have just a little information in them. Now complete your lighting by adding your fill light until you are equally happy with the shadow detail and then check those highlights once more, as some of that fill may well have added brightness to your highlights. How could it be simpler?

17.6.2 Using a Meter

On the other hand, I had one colleague, let us say he was of the old school, who was about to shoot a picture with a young director. I had spent some time with this Director of Photography (DP) explaining HD and he was very enthusiastic about the picture quality and how the cost savings might allow more young directors to get their films made. He may be old school but he is certainly not against progress. After much thought he confessed to me he hated monitors so much that even when shooting film he refused to look at the video assist. What was he going to do? I assured him that the camera was very stable in its equivalent ASA speed and he could safely assume that the camera he was going to use had an equivalent speed of 320 ASA to tungsten light, we had checked, and if he lit with his exposure meters in his usual fashion all would be well, and it was. The young director came back at the end of the picture and expressed the opinion that the DP must be a genius for the pictures were terrific, but he had done it without once looking at a monitor! How times change.

So here are two very different approaches to exposure control; both work perfectly so use whatever works for you. I will be sticking to my monitor, for me that is much more fun.

17.6.3 Auto Exposure

Most HD zoom lenses intended for broadcast use have a side handle much like traditional video lenses, on which there is usually both a button and a sliding switch associated with exposure. The sliding switch normally has two positions, auto and manual. If left on auto the camera will continuously adjust the exposure to its own liking. If set to manual you can simply grab the iris ring and set it to your preference, or if you press the button on the hand grip it will give you a one-time-only auto exposure, which might be a very good starting point for making your own assessment. To my mind most video cameras tend to overexpose when set to auto, which is curious as this will exacerbate the video, or positive image, highlights problem. There is a page in the menu on many cameras, certainly Sony HDW cameras, where you can give the auto exposure control a bias and I tend to set this to reduce the exposure by around one-third of a stop.

Panavision Digital Primos and Zeiss Digi Primes do not have a handle on the lens, and neither do many "film-style" lenses from other manufacturers, so with these lenses you will have to work to the monitor or use an exposure meter in the traditional way.

17.6.4 Exposing Using a Waveform Monitor

Before I describe how to use a waveform monitor I must confess I am not a fan of it. On the two occasions I was persuaded to have one on set I thought my lighting was not as brave as it normally is; the waveform monitor was making me more cautious. I understand what it does and respect those that like using it, but it is definitely not for me.

On the screen of a waveform monitor you will see a graph where the vertical component is the signal level and the horizontal component is the position across the width of the scene. It is not a single line graph, for it is filled in with the energy levels of the vertical components of the picture.

There are two horizontal lines on the screen, one near the top and one near the bottom, which represent the voltages of peak white and peak black. The general idea is to adjust your lighting and exposure to keep the highlights under the top line on the screen and the shadows above the bottom line on the screen. One tends to come to think that any part of the display that is outside these limits must be an error. This is not necessarily so.

When I am lighting for film I am conscious that some parts of the scene will be too bright, and some too dark, to have detail in them. Knowing which parts of the scene will exceed the ability of the film stock and handling them in an artistic way is part of my craft. If I am lighting in the same manner I know I can ignore the top and bottom lines on the screen of the waveform monitor, but for some reason that is psychologically very hard to do.

It is particularly distressing when you have a beautiful picture on the monitor and someone with too little knowledge spies your waveform monitor and expresses the opinion that you are overexposed because a few spikes go above the top line or even flatten out. So, for me at least, the waveform monitor stays back in the stores.

CHAPTER 18

Setting the Color Balance

18.1 White Balance

If you are using a Sony HDW camera there are three positions for the switch on the side of the camera that determine which form and setting of white balance you are using. Most professional High Definition (HD) cameras will have similar controls so I will describe those on the Sony here. The positions are labeled Preset, A and B. With the switch at Preset the camera will set the white balance to its own internal setting. You can create your own white balance on position A or B by switching to them and operating the white balance switch on the front of the camera.

18.2 What is White Balance?

Most digital video cameras are set up to show a color correct image when the scene is lit with tungsten light, but not all, so check the situation with the camera you are using. The RED One, for instance, has a native color balance of 5000 K but can be programmed for the two more conventional settings of 3200 and 5600 K.

With the Sony HDW cameras the nearer of the two filter wheels to the camera body, situated just above the lens mount and on the operator side of the camera, contains three filters and a clear glass. With the clear glass in place, the overall effect is to make the camera have the same color balance as tungsten balanced film. The other positions give various color corrections, the values of which are shown in Figure 18.1. This wheel places a colored filter between the lens and the image splitter block, much as one would put, say, a Wratten 85 filter in front of a film camera lens in order to have the correct color balance when shooting under daylight with tungsten balanced film. Curiously, Sony correct to a slightly warmer color more akin to using a Wratten 85B on a film camera. This often looks very pleasing but corrects to 6300 K, not a commonly used value. The cross filter has no effect on color. It is the equivalent of a light four-point star filter. I have no idea why Sony incorporated this filter as I have only ever used it twice and always have a couple of light star filters in my filter kit anyway. More recent Sony cameras are beginning to appear with the star filter replaced by one correcting the color balance to 5600 K, a very welcome change in my opinion.

Position A	Cross Filter
Position B	Balanced for 3200 °K
Position C	Balanced for 4300 °K
Position D	Balanced for 6300 °K

Figure 18.1: Internal Camera Filter Wheel settings for the wheel nearest to the camera body on a Sony HDW 750

Position 1	CLEAR
Position 2	¼ ND
Position 3	1/16 ND
Position 4	1/64 ND

Figure 18.2: Internal Camera Filter Wheel settings for the wheel farthest from the camera body on a Sony HDW 750

18.3 Neutral Density (ND) Filters

On the Sony HDW cameras the filter wheel farthest from the camera body deploys four filters that have no effect on color but only affect exposure. The value of these filters is shown in Figure 18.2.

18.4 A Warning!

On the Sony cameras, with the exception of zero ND and the star filter, each position on both the ND and the color correction wheels will have an independent white balance written to it. This means that if you have white balanced at zero ND and you swing the filter to an ND 0.6 you will now have the last white balance setting you made when you used an ND 0.6 filter. This function can be switched off in the internal menus.

18.5 Setting the White Balance Using a White Card

Having chosen the filter in the filter wheel that most accurately reflects the light you are working under, select either position A or B on the Preset selector if using a Sony camera or the similar control on the camera you are using, fill at least 70 percent of the screen area with a white card or paper that is illuminated by the primary source of light you are working under and press the white balance switch on the front of the camera. The following applies to virtually all digital cameras when carrying out a white balance. In just a couple of seconds you should see in the viewfinder "White Balance OK". The camera has now electronically given you the best possible color balance for the conditions you are working under. Until you make another white balance on the A or B setting you have chosen, the camera will always give you the same color set-up every time you switch to your chosen position.

It is important that you have a correct exposure when you carry out a white balance as the camera is set up to make the correction in this mode, otherwise you may get a message in the viewfinder telling you the brightness is too low or too high and the balance will not have been set.

Be careful what white card or paper you use to white balance. Office papers that are sometimes called "high white" or something similar are, in fact, tinted a little blue to give them a whiter appearance and this may affect your white balance. If you use one of these papers you may find your scene looking a little warmer than you expected. This can be attractive but you need to be aware it is happening. Keeping a piece of good white art card with you is a much safer option.

18.6 Setting the White Balance Using a Colored Card

One way to make any video camera show an image that does not have the same color cast as the original scene is to white balance to a card or paper that is not white. I don't use white balance very often but should you, perhaps, wish to warm up the overall look of a scene you might white balance to a pale blue card. The white balance process will remove the blue from the set-up and the overall result will be warmer by the same factor as the card was cool. The reverse is true if you use a pink card; the result will be cooler as the pink will have been removed.

Green and yellow, or indeed any color, can be used in this way and the result will be a color change diametrically opposed to the color of the card you are using. I find colors other than pink and blue of very little use unless I still have a green cast from fluorescent lights after doing a standard white balance, when balancing again to a very pale green card can sometimes help.

You can easily obtain pastel-colored thin card in almost any color from art shops; they usually come in large sheets but are not expensive and easily cut to standard office paper size. I always carry a folding clipboard with me in which I keep my colored cards, several white cards in case they get dirty, and my star chart for setting the back focus. As the clipboard has a folding cover, it keeps everything clean and dry, and can easily be folded backwards so that it can be propped up if I am white balancing or setting my back focus when on my own. If you choose to use a cover like this, make sure you use a black one. When the paper is clipped to it some of the folder will be in shot; the color of the folder may then affect the white balance. I say this from experience as my first folder was red and it took me some time to work out why my white balance always looked a little cool. We can all be fooled!

18.7 Setting the White Balance Under Fluorescent Lighting

With any digital camera I rarely use the white balance facility, for I prefer to stay on Preset and occasionally use filters as if I were filming. The exception to this rule is when I am filming under fluorescent light. Here I find the best way to white balance is, having checked all the fluorescent tubes are the same make and specification, to take the white card quite close to a tube and balance it there. This is to make sure that no spurious light that may have picked up some other color from reflection off another surface is being allowed to influence the setting.

18.8 The Outer Filter Wheel on a Sony HDW Camera

The filter wheel farthest from the camera body on a Sony HDW camera has no effect on color; again, it has a straight-through position with the other three positions having ND filters of varying strength in them. Many other cameras have the capability to employ ND filters. Most HD cameras have an ND switch somewhere reasonably obvious and to hand. This is to allow you to keep the lens working at a reasonably wide aperture when filming under bright light. At first glance you might think that using as small an aperture as possible, and thereby getting a great depth of field, would be a good idea. After all, in these circumstances keeping focus would hardly be difficult. This is not always a good thing for two reasons. First, some lenses do not perform at their best at very large apertures; the Panavision Primos, Zeiss Digi Primes and Cooke S4s and a few other lenses are an exception to this rule, as often they are at their best at the wide end of the aperture range. Secondly, one thing that most film people dislike about video is that everything seems sharp and it is impossible to separate the foreground from the background using discriminatory focus. Deploying these ND filters can overcome both these problems.

18.9 Black Balance

Black balance is primarily used to reset the voltage at which an image signal reaches the lowest point the camera or the recording format can cope with. This can change for a variety of reasons, a change in temperature of the circuitry, for example. It is therefore very important to maintain the system's ability to record the best possible black available; operating the black balance should do this.

With the Sony HDW cameras, pushing the same switch as is used for white balance in the opposite direction operates the black balance. It is worth familiarizing yourself with how black balance works on the camera you are using. With any HD camera you should black balance the camera first thing every morning and whenever you change the position of the gain switch on the camera. It is also a wise precaution to carry out a black balance if the camera has experienced a large change in temperature, though this is probably being hyper-cautious.

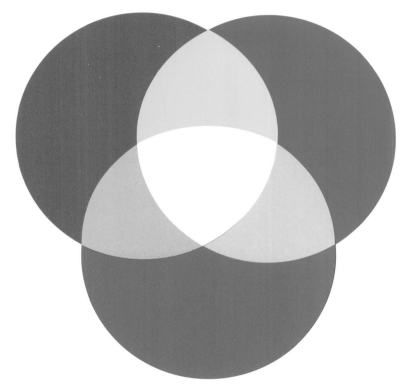

Color plate 1: Three color additive mixing

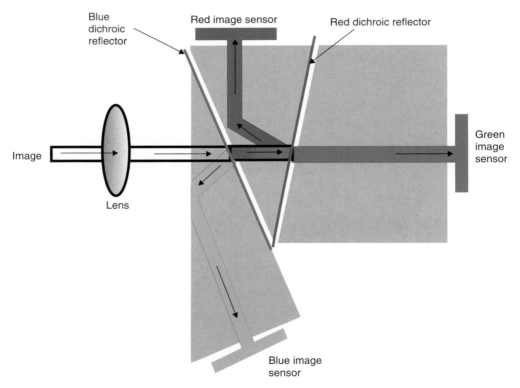

Blue dichroic reflector

Red image sensor

Red dichroic reflector

Green image sensor

Image

Lens

Blue image sensor

Color plate 2: The light path through a video camera beam splitter

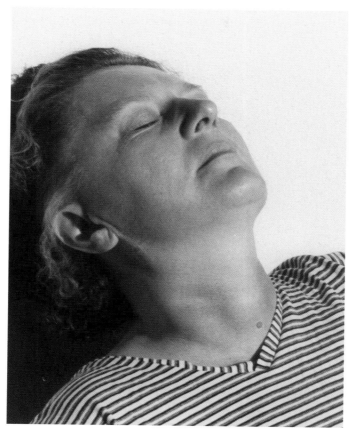

Color plate 3: The image in its original RGB full color format

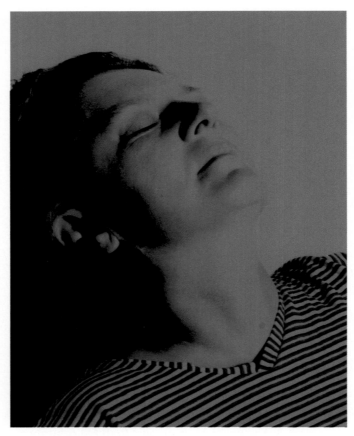

Color plate 4: The image as seen by the Red image sensor

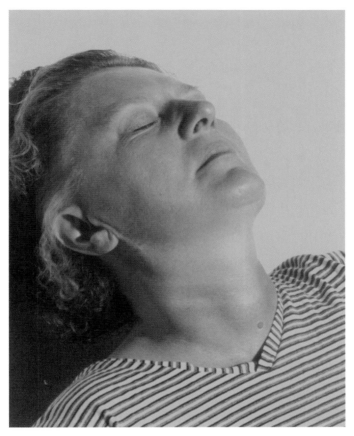

Color plate 5: The image as seen by the Green image sensor

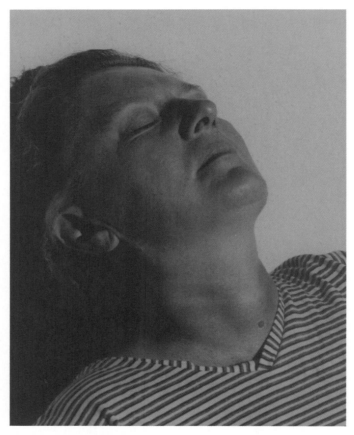

Color plate 6: The image as seen by the Blue image sensor

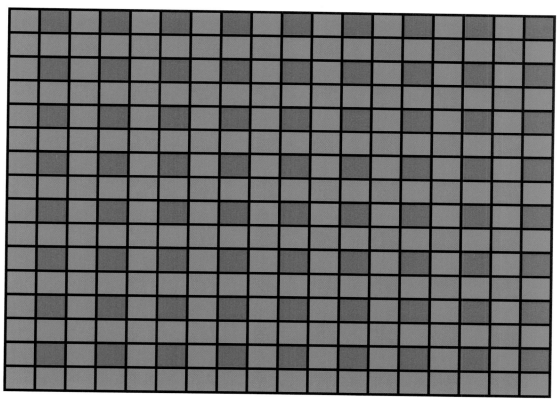

Color plate 7: The effect of Bayer filtering

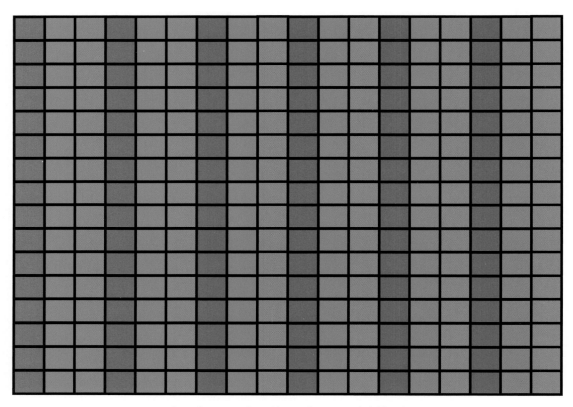

Color plate 8: The effect of sequential filtering

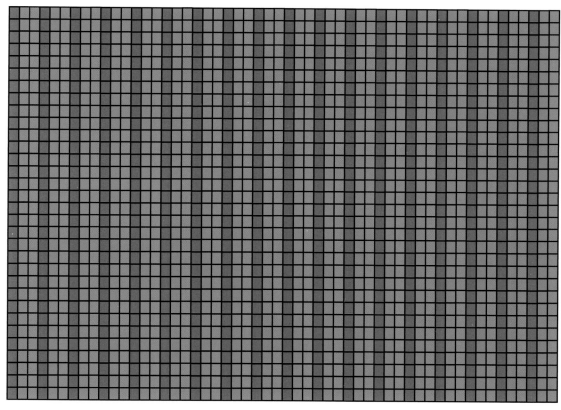

Color plate 9: Sequential filtering representing six sub pixels for each of the pixels as shown in Color plate 8

Color plate 10: EBU line up bars

Color plate 11: SMPTE color line up bars

Color plate 12: *King Lear*. The opening scene – Cordelia, played by Romola Garai, awaiting her father, King Lear, played by Sir Ian McKellen

Color plate 13: *King Lear*. Goneril, played by Frances Barber, standing in one of the shafts of light awaiting her father, the King

Color plate 14: *King Lear*. King Lear, played by Sir Ian McKellen, about to divide his empire among his daughters

Color plate 15: *King Lear*. The gouging of the eyes of Gloucester, played by William Gaunt, with Regan, played by Monica Dolan (left), and Regan's husband (right foreground)

Color plate 16: The set of *King Lear*

Color plate 17: *King Lear*. The lighting control desk

Color plate 18: *King Lear*. The Director's desk

Color plate 19: *The Optician*. Interior of the optician's practice, featuring
Chris Barrie and Carolyn Tomkinson

Color plate 20: Chris Barrie as *The Optician*

Color plate 21: Chris Barrie as *The Optician*

Color plate 22: The optician's proposal is accepted

Color plate 23: The optician knocked unconscious by a car – night exterior from a crane

CHAPTER 19

Camera Checks Before Shooting

Unlike starting a film shoot, where there are clearly defined checks on the camera equipment that have to be made, many of them required by the picture insurance company, for High Definition (HD) with less than 10 years of existence things are not so simple. So far I know of no formal checking procedure for a digital camera. For a film camera one might include the following:

1. Check every lens comes up to the focus scale engraved on it correctly.

2. Check that all long focus lenses go past infinity so that they can make infinity with several glass filters on.

3. Run film through the camera using every magazine and check for scratching.

4. Run a steady test on every camera body.

5. Make an accurate check that the camera runs precisely to speed at all the frame rates you expect to use.

6. Again, check for scratching on all magazines at the highest frame rate you expect to use.

A good camera crew in the days before photography starts on a film would consider the above only the beginning – they would run between 20 and 30 checks before even thinking of putting that camera kit on a movie.

But we can't run most of these checks on a digital camera so what are we to do? I am not sure but what follows is a list of checks I would like my crew to carry out. Most of them I put here as a result of problems I have had in the past – so be warned!

19.1 The Camera Body

19.1.1 Menus

You need to check the menus sequence properly and you understand that sequence. Sony are notorious for changing the order of the pages in the menus and they are not alone.

- Check the lens mount works and is clean and does not stick. I once managed to drop a £60,000 lens because the lens mount was stiff and suddenly gave way. I can't tell you how glad my assistant was that I dropped it and not he! The manufacturer modified the lens mount shortly afterwards, which is my feeble excuse.

- Check *all* the switches on the camera body work reliably.

- Check that Time Code and User Bits, if they apply to your camera, are running and can be set reliably.

- Check that all handles and accessories are firmly fixed to the camera body. I know this seems obvious but I have seen a camera nearly hit the floor because a simple screw was not tight enough.

19.2 Lenses

This may seem stupid but about once a year I find a lens that rattles. That means that at least one element in it is not firmly fixed where it should be. If this happens to you reject the lens immediately.

- Check that all the lenses will hit infinity and that the longer ones will go past infinity. You will need this because if you put several glass filters on a long lens they bring the focus forward and if you only had infinity with the basic lens you will not get it at all with filters attached.

- Check whether you are using film-style lenses or broadcast lenses. If using film-style lenses you will need to measure focus from the datum point on the camera that is the notional film plane. If you are using broadcast lenses there will probably be a green ring around the lens somewhere near the front. If there is, this is from where you measure focus.

- Check all front and back elements are scrupulously clean.

- Check that all the lens mounts go easily onto all your camera bodies and that they are clean and undamaged.

And that's only the beginning!

19.3 Electronic Checks

This is where it gets really tricky! You can't just check for scratching as with a film camera and it can be very hard indeed to see, even on a Grade 1 monitor, defects that may show up in post-production. But it is your duty to try.

19.3.1 Dead Pixels

A huge number of cameras out in the field have a few dead pixels. Most of these cameras handle this situation very well and if they have handled it well you can discount the problem from your shoot. *But*, if your camera has some dead pixels that have not been dealt with, you need to find them.

Finding out if your camera has pixels that are dead and may be recorded is, fortunately, not too difficult. Cap your lens or put the lens port blank into the camera so that no light whatsoever can enter the throat of the camera. Now wind the gain on your camera up to its maximum. With a high-grade monitor plugged in look for any bright spots on the screen – pixels most often die *on* so they will glow bright. If you have any bright spots reject the camera.

19.3.2 Ringing – Or Whatever the Manufacturer Calls It

This is a very curious effect that can rarely be seen on a location monitor but, if you have been unlucky enough to have a camera with this problem, it may only become apparent somewhere down the post-production route, often quite late in the process.

What is happening is that somewhere in the camera's circuitry there is an error occurring that is something like an electronic echo and this will, most often, show up as a very low intensity second image of the scene, more often than not displaced to the right of the original image. You need to do your best to check if you have this problem. If you are in the slightest bit suspicious for heaven's sake shoot some tests and send them to your post house where, in ideal conditions, they should be able to make a finite judgement. You are very unlikely to be sure if you have this problem on set, believe me.

The best empirical check you can do is to set up a relatively low-key scene of a very even tone with one clearly defined patch at a brightness roughly halfway between white and black, that is a mid to light gray, and set it right in the middle of the picture. Now look left and right and see if you can see a very low level secondary image of the brighter area. If you think you can, reject the camera body. I once had this problem and no one spotted it on set. It only came to light after the picture was cut and going into grading. Only a small percentage of the cut picture was affected but I am told it cost £30,000 in post to remove the echo! It is a rare but potentially costly problem.

19.4 Temperature

With an increasing trend to solid-state recording, or the use of hard drives, both of which are inherently quieter than a tape transport mechanism, some camera manufacturers are being tempted to try and build their cameras without any cooling fans at all, thus making them totally silent. If they provide a sufficiently large and efficient heat sink, as in the Arriflex D-21, then things should be fine. On the other hand, if heat dissipation is not handled really well it can lead to cameras tripping their protection switches or crashing the internal processors – not something you want to happen in the middle of a shoot.

I would therefore suggest that if you have the slightest suspicion that the model of camera you are using is prone to overheating or even has a reputation for doing so then there is a simple check you can carry out. On your first test day build the camera as soon as possible and add all the electrically driven accessories you are likely to be using during the shoot and then leave the camera running for the rest of the day, including over lunch. This should not be inconvenient as you can still carry out all the tests you need with the camera switched on. If it has no problems by the end of the day you are probably OK.

19.5 Matching Cameras

I have photographed a number of three- or four-camera shoots and it is rare that all the cameras match precisely. So long as the differences are minimal and you are aware of them this is hardly a problem. Solving the problem completely is next to impossible, which is one reason why in television studios and outside broadcasts there is a control room, often known as "racks", where an engineer sits with complete remote control over all the cameras, with a picture monitor and a waveform monitor together with a vector scope so that the output from each camera is tuned, such that before the signal enters the control room all the pictures look the same. Coming from a film background I would hate to work this way, so I have to devise strategies to overcome the tiny differences in the cameras' outputs.

The most often encountered difference between cameras is in exposure. This rarely amounts to more than a quarter of a stop, so my solution is simple. Rather than remember, or ask the crew on that camera to remember, the difference we simply put a small piece of tape over the datum point on that camera's lens next to the aperture ring, line all the cameras up so that they exactly match and then mark a new datum point where that lens matches the setting on the other cameras. Simple and effective.

If you find a noticeable difference in one camera's color balance or contrast then I suggest you change that camera immediately. If this is not possible then rather, as I prefer, running all the cameras on a preset white balance you may try simultaneously white balancing all the cameras. The word simultaneously is most important in the above. On the occasions I have resorted to this ploy we were very careful to light a perfect white card very evenly and pull all the cameras back from it so that they would all be on as near the same optical axis as was possible. I do exactly the same thing when on multicamera film shoots but then I shoot an 18 percent gray card so that the laboratory can grade all the camera's rushes (dailies) to the same card. If I am going down this road I insist on a white balance first thing every morning, immediately after all the cameras have had a black balance.

19.6 Matching Lenses

If you have all your lenses from the same manufacturer, and I strongly suggest you do, then this is hardly likely to be a problem. Sony and some other manufacturers do have pages in the camera's menus where you can set different parameters for each lens you will be using. I have only known one production where this facility was deployed and it took a considerable amount of time and at the end of all that work I confess I could see no discernible difference even on a Grade 1 24-inch monitor.

Trying to match lenses in this way is something I have never found to be a particular problem.

19.7 Lens Vignetting

Virtually every lens known to man vignettes, though it is very unlikely you will ever be conscious of this. I believe this is a good thing and let me tell you why. When my hobby was taking and printing exhibition-quality black and white prints, during the printing process I would arrange for the outside 5 or 10 percent of the image to be given an extra 10 percent exposure. Nobody ever saw this but it is well known – read Ansel Adams' books – that this effect helps draw the viewer's eye into the picture where the most important parts of the image usually reside. You can do this in post but you will spend quite a lot of time and money in your grading suite doing this for the whole picture, for it is not a global thing; light and dark scenes will need a different approach and scenes of distinctly different color values will need treating differently.

The vignetting inherent in a lens is far, far, less than 10 percent. It comes about because the distance from the back of the lens to the center of the image is smaller than the distance from the back of the lens to the outside edges of the image and therefore there is just a little more fall-off in brightness at the edges. You can hardly ever see it, but I strongly believe if it is well below the observable limit it makes the picture more pleasing and easier to read – just as it did on my black and white prints.

I have only ever known one production dial out this vignetting inside the camera's menu and that was because, they claimed, that they were going to be doing so many layers of CGI that it might interfere with the post-production process. That production spent two weeks with laptops plugged into the back of the cameras just getting a perfect match and I, for one, could never see the difference.

19.8 What Does It All Mean?

If you are looking at a first-class monitor, you can see no problems and you have checked out all your kit as well as you can, you should be just fine. Remember Wheeler's First Law, which states: if it looks right, it is right!

CHAPTER 20

Lenses

20.1 How to Choose a Lens

There are many parameters that define a good lens and separate a good lens from a bad one. For High Definition (HD) cinematography, where there is a mixture of both film and video backgrounds, the most important include resolution (i.e. what is the smallest dot in the scene that can accurately be recorded?), contrast (does the lens have a short, hard tonal range or a long, gentle one?), color rendition (this breaks down into two separate parameters: the overall color hue of the image and edge fringing) and, finally, breathing (which describes the effect of an image size change when the lens focus is racked).

20.1.1 Resolution

There are many ways to define the resolution of a lens but the simplest is to consider the same parameter that is used to compute depth of field charts, the circle of confusion. The circle of confusion does not exist until we choose it. Typically for 35 mm cinematography using spherical lenses a circle of confusion of 1/1000 of an inch, or 25 microns (25 μm) is used and this remains current when using a single-chip HD camera with a chip size approximating the area of the 35 mm film frame.

Before we go any further let us define a circle of confusion. The correct circle of confusion is the diameter of the largest dot on the recorded image that will still look sharp to the audience in the most taxing presentation venue in which that picture will ever be shown. The principle is that if you try to photograph an infinitely small dot, how large would you allow that dot to grow as it becomes less well focused on the image plane and at what size will it appear to the audience to be out of focus?

If you are going to show your images in a large cinema, say in a capital city, this will be a very taxing presentation on the parameter of resolution. As we have seen in Chapter 10, in Section 10.5, for regular 35 mm cinematography 1/1000 inch (25 μm) is considered adequate. Next we must consider the difference in recorded image size between the 35 mm frame and the area of a 2/3-inch HD image chip camera. The 35 mm frame is 2 1/2 times larger than the HD chip, so for a dot on the HD chip to seem to be as sharp on the same cinema screen as one projected from a 35 mm print it must be 2 1/2 times smaller, that is 1/2500 inch or 10 μm. There are only a few lenses that can achieve this.

20.1.2 Contrast

This is a difficult subject, for perceived resolution – that is, how our eye/brain combination assesses sharpness – can be materially affected by the contrast of the image. A very contrasty lens might give you a picture on even a 24-inch HD monitor that looks very sharp, but if that image is expanded to a large cinema screen the lack of resolution that has been masked by the excessive contrast will now be very apparent.

20.1.3 Perceived Sharpness with Regard to Contrast

The eye/brain combination perceives sharpness quite differently from the way we might measure resolution on a lens-testing bench. Perception is an impossible thing to measure yet we, as cinematographers, need to get a grasp of how our audience will see our work and need to know if they will consider our pictures to be sharp.

Increasing the contrast of a scene will, most likely, increase the perceived sharpness of the scene. That said, it might also reduce the artistic value of the scene or even take it away from the cinematographer's initial concept of the scene as represented in the script. A cinematographer might wish to show a scene with a reasonably high resolution but having a gentle, low-key, feel to it. To do this the cinematographer needs lenses that have a very long tone range and a gentle contrast but still appear sharp.

Let us look at some of the sharpness we perceive in a scene as against the actual resolution of the image. In Figure 20.1 we have two nearly identical images; don't study them too carefully, but at a glance which do you think is the sharper? I would guess you chose the bottom one. Wrong! All the images for this example were taken on my Nikon CoolPix camera; the top picture was downloaded at 300 dots per inch (DPI) and the lower picture at 75 DPI – the difference is the top picture has a much lower contrast than the bottom picture; contrast has fooled you into thinking the resolution is higher when the contrast is higher.

Now look at Figure 20.2. Which do you think is sharper here? I guess you will again choose the bottom picture. Both pictures were downloaded at 300 DPI. Again it is the contrast of the bottom picture that makes it look sharper.

Don't look at Figure 20.3 until you are holding the book at arm's length and then try and decide which picture is sharper. My guess is you will think they both look the same. Now bring the book to your normal reading distance, normally 10 inches or 25 centimeters; if you look at the top of the gate you should see a jagged line in the bottom picture but a true and straight one in the top picture. Both pictures have exactly the same contrast but the top picture

Figure 20.1: The effect of resolution

has a resolution of 300 DPI and the bottom a resolution of 75 DPI proving, I hope, that viewing distance is also a critical factor.

The conclusion from all this is that a lens that appears sharp may not be, so it is therefore important that you measure resolution and judge contrast – separately.

Figure 20.2: The effect of contrast

20.1.4 Color Rendition

20.1.4.1 Overall color bias

All makes of lenses tend to have an individual character: some are cold and clinical, some are warm and gentle and some are utterly neutral. Most of the time my own preference is for a neutral lens, for I can then add the character I require scene by scene with the aid of filtration.

Figure 20.3: The effect of resolution and contrast

Perhaps the simplest way to discover the difference in color bias between different manufacturers' lenses is to mount them on the camera and line them up at the standard 18 percent gray card we use in the film world. Fill most of the frame with the card and set the correct exposure. Having first lined up the monitor correctly, can you now see any color difference between the card and its corresponding image on the monitor? You should easily be able to tell the difference between warm, cold and neutral lenses using this simple test.

20.1.4.2 Color fringing

This is a phenomenon almost unheard of with any lens from the film world built in the last 30 years. Unfortunately it is all too commonly found on even some of the most recent video lenses. The reason is twofold: first, the film Director of Photography (DP) is used to paying considerably more for lenses than the equivalent video cameraperson, so there are the financial resources available to film lens manufacturers to design out the problem; secondly, until the advent of HD a video image was very rarely shown on a big screen and consequently the problem was not immediately evident on a normal size television screen, though it can nearly always be detected if you look closely.

20.1.4.3 What is fringing?

If you look closely at a hard edge on a picture on a television screen and find that it is not totally pure but there appear to be single or multiple colored lines around it, this is fringing. It is caused by the lens being unable to bring all the colors in the visible spectrum into focus at exactly the same place.

For HD cinematography a lens showing even the slightest hint of fringing must not be accepted.

20.1.5 Breathing

Breathing is when the image size changes when the lens focus is changed. It is very common indeed with most lenses used for television video camcorders and almost unheard of with film lenses. Again, the acceptable cost of the lenses is the main contributing factor. A DP working in film is very unlikely to accept a lens that shows even the slightest sign of breathing, but a news cameraman using a camcorder where the image is moving much of the time will hardly notice the effect.

Unfortunately there are a number of lenses purporting to have been designed specifically for HD, most of them coming from established video lens manufacturers, that show not just slight but considerable breathing. This to me is wholly unacceptable.

20.2 Setting the Back Focus

Setting the back focus is a requirement for all professional 2/3-inch three-chip cameras; it is not required in any way on single-chip cameras. Three-chip cameras require it for a number of reasons, the most likely being the difference in contraction and expansion rates between the three glass elements of the color splitter block and the metals of the lens mounts in the camera and on the lens itself.

The back focus should be checked first thing every morning, every time you change a lens and if there has been a significant change in temperature since you last carried out a check.

Conventional wisdom suggests that one uses a star chart very like the one I prefer, which is illustrated in Figure 20.4.

20.2.1 Zoom Lenses

1. Set the lighting to give a correct exposure with the lens wide open. It is quite acceptable to deploy the neutral density (ND) filter wheel to achieve this.

2. Put a star chart (Figure 20.4) at around 6 feet, or 2 meters, away from the camera.

3. Zoom right in and focus the lens in the normal way. If you can possibly do so, check all the focus adjustments on a monitor, with the chroma taken out, so you have a black and white picture.

4. Adjust the lens to wide angle and rotate the back focus ring until the star chart looks sharp.

5. Zoom in and adjust the lens focus.

6. Zoom out and adjust the back focus.

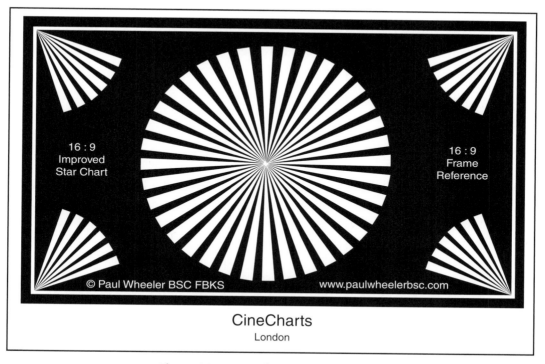

Figure 20.4: PW's improved Star Chart

7. Repeat steps 5 and 6 until no further improvements can be made.

8. Lock the back focus ring.

9. Run through steps 5 and 6 again to check the back focus ring did not move when you locked it.

Note: You may have to go through steps 5 and 6 several times before the focus is correct at both ends of the zoom without any refocusing being necessary.

20.2.2 Prime Lenses

Set up whichever chart you prefer at a convenient distance that is marked on the lens scale and measure this distance very carefully; now set the lens to this mark – this should be no closer than the minimum focus plus 6 inches. Remember that "film-style" lenses measure from the notional film plane – where the Green chip is with 2/3-inch cameras – and it is totally different if you are using a broadcast lens; there should be a green ring somewhere around the front focusing barrel of the lens. With a broadcast lens the green ring is where you run the tape from, not the notional focal plane. If you are taping focus this is also true of broadcast zoom lenses. Now adjust the back focus so as to produce the sharpest image possible. Now lock the back focus ring while very carefully trying not to move it. As a further precaution now focus the lens on the chart; if it comes up to scale all is well, if it does not something is wrong – almost certainly you inadvertently moved the back focus ring when locking it and I am afraid you need to start the whole procedure again.

All the lenses should have their back focus checked before you go out on a shoot. You owe yourself the confidence boost of knowing all was perfect when you started.

20.3 Focusing the Lens Using Back Focus Charts – Beware!

Before you can successfully focus any lens on a 2/3-inch three-chip HD camera you must have assured yourself that the back focus is correct. You may be tempted to use a star chart as shown in Figure 20.4 as a target when carrying out eye focuses at various distances – this is unwise. A star chart works perfectly for setting the back focus at 6 feet or 2 meters, but although it looks like a perfect image to focus on for, say, an actor's position, experience has proved this not to be the case. I once had a phone call from a crew complaining that one of the Panavision Primo Digital zooms they had with them was not focusing to scale. The lens was immediately swapped out and, following up the call, I put it on the lens test bench; it focused very accurately to scale and the definition was above specification, so what was going wrong? I telephoned the unit and found that, quite sensibly as things stood at that time, they were using the star chart as a focus aid when making eye focus checks through the lens. The next thing was to repeat that with the rejected lens so I set up the lens on a camera back at Panavision where I was helping introduce HD at the time, back focus checked it at around 6 feet and then very carefully set the star chart up at 12 feet and did an eye focus. The scale showed 11 feet 9 inches, exactly what the crew had been getting.

It was time for greater minds to be brought to bear on the problem. I asked Panavision's head of camera maintenance to focus the lens; it came up at exactly 12 feet. Puzzling. Asking a number of technicians in the building to focus the lens proved that less than one in five got it right and those that did all had considerable experience of using various lens test charts. Your average crew member, embarrassingly including myself, always came up with something near 11 feet 9 inches. Not one of us focused long and this I cannot explain.

I spent the next few days pondering this and driving everybody in the building mad by asking them to go through the same routine with all kinds of charts I wanted to try. Eventually I came to the conclusion that because the star chart was of such high contrast what we were seeing was a function of apparent sharpness being influenced by the contrast of the image. Incidentally we were all getting the same results whether we focused through the viewfinder with or without the peaking turned on and even on a 24-inch monitor.

After some days I came up with the chart similar to that shown in Figure 20.5. Originally the rings were round. I now prefer the oval rings as camera assistants prefer the fact that they work just as well on a standard office size paper where the circular rings worked best on paper twice the size – hard to put in a kit bag. During all my testing I had decided that because the pixel layout in the camera is made up of horizontal and vertical lines, straight lines might be confusing the result. I had also come to the conclusion that the target must be of a low-contrast nature whilst still being easy to judge focus on. Further, prior to all this, I had never used the peaking control on the viewfinder as I found it disturbing during normal photography, but was rapidly coming to the conclusion that with the right chart for eye focusing it could be an advantage.

20.4 Back Focusing Using the Oval Rings Chart

If you set a camera up on what I have called the "oval focus target" (Figure 20.5) and wind the peaking in the viewfinder up to maximum when you focus the lens, you will see the peaking move up and down to the top and bottom of the finest set of rings you can resolve at any given distance. When the peaking effect is at its closest top and bottom you are in perfect focus at any distance. The peaking effect is unlikely ever to form a perfect and complete circle. This chart can therefore safely be used for eye focus checks and, using the same technique, can be used as a back focus chart.

This in no way negates the use of the star chart for setting the back focus; it still works perfectly well, but if you want a chart that can be used for back focus and general eye focusing on the set then the oval rings are a better bet.

20.5 Comparative Focal Lengths

What follows refers to lenses designed for 2/3-inch three-chip cameras. Almost all single-chip cameras emulate 35 mm photography so closely that the performance of a lens designed

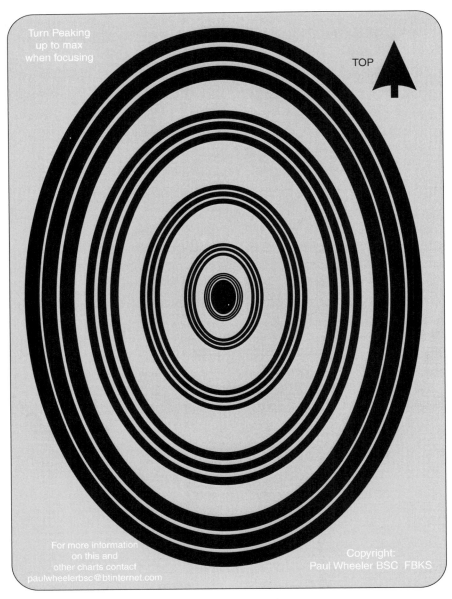

Figure 20.5: The oval rings focus target

for 35 mm photography, when it is mounted on a single-chip camera having a chip size close to the 35 mm frame, will allow production of pictures with virtually identical results.

Because the dimensions of the 2/3-inch chip in a three-chip video camera are considerably smaller than the frame size on 35 mm film, the focal length required to obtain an identical shot will be shorter for the HD camera. In fact, a ratio of 2 1/2 times is correct, meaning that a 25 mm lens on a 35 mm camera will have the same field of view as a 10 mm lens on the HD camera. The ratio of 2 1/2 times will become familiar to you as it applies to many of the comparisons between these two formats.

To compare HD to Super 16 mm the ratio is roughly 1 1/3. Figure 20.6 shows the lenses that will obtain the same horizontal angle of view on 35 mm anamorphic lenses, 35 mm spherical lenses, HD lenses and Super 16 lenses.

If you are using a single-chip camera with a chip size similar to the 35 mm film frame then the depth of field you will obtain will be virtually identical to that of a 35 mm camera. You are, after all, using the same lenses, this being the main point of hiring such a camera.

20.6 Depth of Field

One of the signatures of the video look, when shooting with a 2/3-inch three-chip camera, is, in comparison with 35 mm film, a considerably greater depth of field. Depth of field is a function of three things: the size of the image required, the focal length of the lens and the aperture being deployed. This part of the video look comes about because, to obtain the same field of view, the focal length of the lens on a video camera using a 2/3-inch chip will be 2 1/2

35 mm 2.4:1	35 mm 1.85:1	HD 16 x 9	Super 16 1.78:1
25	12.5	5	6.75
30	15	6	8
35	17.5	7	9.5
40	20	8	11
48.5	23.75	9.5	13
50	25	10	13.5
70	35	14	19
100	50	20	27
125	62.5	25	34
135	67.5	27	36.5
175	86.5	35	47.25
360	180	72	97
524	262	105	142
560	280	112	151

Figure 20.6: Equivalent focal lengths

35 mm 2.4:1	35 mm 1.85:1	HD 16 x 9	Super 16 1.78:1
2.8	2	0.8	0.9
4	2.8	1.1	1.3
5.6	4	1.6	1.8
8	5.6	2.2	2.8
11	8	3.2	3.5
16	11	4.4	4.8
22	16	6.4	7

Figure 20.7: Apertures to obtain same depth of field

times shorter than that on the lens required on a 35 mm camera or most single-chip cameras; this is because the image size is so much smaller. It is possible to get the same depth of field by using a wider aperture; in fact, you will need to set the lens 2 1/2 stops wider so T 4 on the 35 mm camera will have the same depth of field as T 1.6 on the 2/3-inch chipped video camera. Figure 20.7 shows the apertures required to obtain the same depth of field on 35 mm anamorphic lenses, 35 mm spherical lenses, HD lenses and Super 16 lenses.

20.7 Calculating Depth of Field

With single-chip cameras, use whatever way you have always used for 35 mm film. The simplest and probably the best way to calculate your depth of field when shooting with a 2/3-inch chip camera is to use a proprietary rotary slide rule designed for the job. In my opinion the HiDef Kelly Calculator designed and manufactured by the Guild of British Camera Technicians (GBCT) is one of the best available. It comes with comprehensive instructions, the cover of which is shown in Figure 20.8, and if you are familiar with earlier Kelly calculators you will not be surprised to discover that it works in exactly the same way. In the HD version one side of the calculator functions with imperial measurements (Figure 20.9) and the other side works in the metric system (Figure 20.10). To avoid confusion the solid part of the scale is gold on the imperial side and silver on the metric side.

Using the Kelly could not be simpler. You choose the appropriate focal length of the lens you are using and find it on one of the circles. Rotate the top disk until the arrow aligns with the distance set on the focus barrel of the lens (this is inscribed on the under disk), and either side of the original arrow the distances that can be considered to still be in focus will be adjacent to the aperture you are using.

There is a considerable amount of additional useful information in the instructions that come with the Kelly Calculator. I have been using the film versions since I was a focus puller and swear by it.

Figure 20.8: The cover of the GBCT High Def depth of field calculator

20.8 Neutral Density (ND) Filters

One of the two filter wheels at the front of the Sony HDW series, and many other similar cameras, contains a clear glass plus three ND filters as they are always referred to. A neutral density (ND) is one that will reduce the amount of light passing through it without changing the color at all.

On the Panavision 900F the nomenclature is: for filter 1 – Clear; for filter 2 – 0.6, 2 stops; for filter 3 – 1.2, 4 stops; and for filter 4 – 1.8, 6 stops. This is all very logical, for a density of 0.3 reduces the amount of light by exactly half. On the Sony version of the camera the filters are the same but, very confusingly for a person from a film background, they are labeled: 1 – Clear; 2 – 1/4 ND; 3 – 1/16 ND; 4 – 1/64 ND.

To keep the lens on the 2/3-inch three-chip HD camera's aperture 2 1/2 stops wider than the 35 mm equivalent often requires the use of ND filters; this is why the camera has three ND filters on a wheel within it. These filters are of a sufficiently high quality that you should have no hesitation in using them in appropriate circumstances. If even deploying the 6 stop filter leaves you with an unacceptably small stop, then there is absolutely no problem in using extra ND filters in front of the lens just as you would with a film camera.

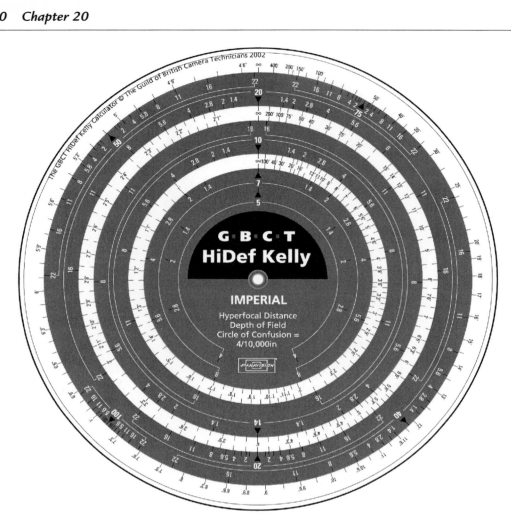

Figure 20.9: The Imperial side of the GBCT High Def depth of field calculator

20.9 Limiting Apertures

All optical devices have the equivalent to an aperture – that is, there is a limit to the amount of light they can pass. This is true of the splitter block in most 2/3-inch three-chip cameras. The beam splitter that is used behind the lens to break up the image into red, green and blue light is described in Chapter 13. The limiting aperture of this block is usually T 1.4 or T 1.6.

This means that if a lens with a wider aperture than the limiting aperture of the splitter block is used then the exposure will never be more than that aperture, for this is the maximum amount of light the block will pass.

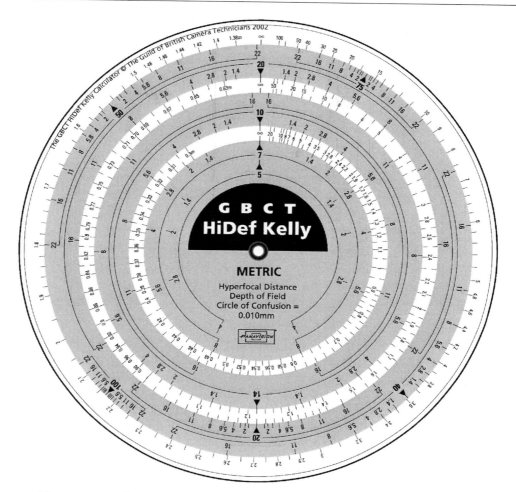

Figure 20.10: The Metric size of the GBCT High Def depth of field calculator

20.10 Filtration

20.10.1 Color Correction

All the filters you might use to correct or adjust the coloration of the image with a film camera will give you exactly the same results in the final image. I am not entirely happy with the color correction filters used by many manufacturers and, when shooting in daylight, frequently leave the clear glass in place on the color correction filter wheel, marked 3200 K, and put a Wratten 85 filter in front of the lens. This, it seems to me, makes the resultant image look even more like film, which is what I am used to.

20.10.2 Diffusion

Diffusion filters are another matter entirely. Again, this is influenced by the smaller area of the 2/3-inch HD chip as against the 35 mm frame. The strength of diffusion you must use to gain the effect you desire is relative to the area on the camera image, so just as you would use a lighter filter on Super 16 than you would on 35 mm you must be lighter still on 2/3-inch HD. My experience is that Super 16 requires roughly half the diffusion that you would use on 35 mm and 2/3-inch HD requires a little less than that which you might use on Super 16.

Curiously the diffusion filters I regularly use on Digi Beta, which has the same size chip but with far fewer pixels, does not have the same effect on 2/3-inch HD. My favorite filter when shooting Digi Beta is a 1/4 white Tiffen Promist. With this filter on a 2/3-inch HD camera it appears to be much stronger, so I drop to a 1/8 Promist when shooting for cinema. I gather various filter manufacturers are bringing out lighter strength diffusion filters than they have offered in the past to give cinematographers working with HD greater control over the image than traditional film filters would allow.

When shooting with a camera having a single chip roughly the same size as a 35 mm film frame, then the diffusion filters you are used to using on 35 mm film will nearly always produce the same effect. When shooting HD I avoid any diffusion filter that deploys tiny glass beads to create the diffusion; they can sometimes interfere with the pixel pattern and therefore become noticeable.

It should be noted that the effect of diffusion when judged even on a 24-inch monitor will not correspond to the same effect when shown on a large theatrical screen. If you are only shooting for television then it is perfectly correct to judge your filtration on a 24-inch monitor. This is not a safe practice if the pictures are going to be shown theatrically. If you are shooting your first HD picture and you are fond of diffusion then it is essential that you shoot some tests and have them post-produced in the same manner as the final delivery system.

CHAPTER 21

Monitors and Cabling

If, like me, you choose to light to your monitor then this chapter might just be one of the most important you ever read. Setting up monitors is not difficult or particularly time-consuming but for someone from a film background it can, at first, be a little daunting.

21.1 What Kinds of Monitor are Available?

21.1.1 Cathode Ray Tube (CRT) Monitors

Monitors using CRT technology have been the most common to be offered by high-end suppliers, though this is beginning to change as high-quality flat-screen monitors are now available. They nearly all come with a 16×9 screen, for which the most likely dimension of the diagonal of the picture will be 9, 14 or 24 inches. The early High Definition (HD) CRT monitors were interlace scan only and the picture therefore stuttered slightly when the camera was panned rapidly if that camera were set up to shoot in Progressive scan. This effect is never recorded, it being partly a function of having to display a progressively scanned picture on an interlace scan monitor and partly a function of the high modular transfer function (MTF) of HD in the middle tones of the image. More recently, true Progressive scan monitors have come into use and with these the stuttering picture never appears. Not surprisingly the Progressive scan monitors are more expensive.

21.1.2 Liquid Crystal Display (LCD) Monitors

Early HD LCD monitors had, most commonly, a screen diagonal measuring 6 or 7 inches. These sizes are now more often used as on-board screens either as the viewfinder if the camera operator prefers this or as a viewing guide for the focus puller. These screens are far too small for the focus puller to judge focus by, but do at least confirm what is actually being photographed. Recently, LCD screens have become available in much larger sizes, with a 14-inch becoming very popular as a Director's monitor. LCD monitors rarely exhibit the stutter shown on CRT monitors as the difference in their technology masks this effect, or at least masks a great deal of this effect. They are usually light weight and quite pleasant to look at, though I would hesitate to judge lighting or sharpness on a smaller one.

21.1.3 Plasma Screens

Plasma screen technology allows for large screens, often with a screen diagonal sometimes measuring between 42 and 61 inches; even larger screens are now coming onto the market. They can be very attractive to look at provided you are not too close. They are very slim but do not quite have the quality of picture of a large CRT screen. They are also expensive but do mask the stutter effect perhaps even better than an LCD monitor.

21.2 Lining up Your Monitor

One must take great care in lining up your monitor especially if you are going to judge your lighting via your monitor; fortunately this can be carried out both quickly and accurately.

Most cameras will generate either European Broadcasting Union (EBU) color bars (Color Plate 10) or Society of Motion Picture and Television Engineers (SMPTE) color bars (Color Plate 11); many will generate both, with the selection between them somewhere in the camera's menu. The object of the exercise, with either kind of color bars, is to get the bars correctly displayed by adjusting the brightness, chroma and contrast controls. EBU bars really require some sort of meter capable of reading the screen brightness, though in an emergency they can be lined up reasonably by eye. SMPTE bars, on the other hand, can reliably be lined up without a meter for they were designed so that an "eyeball" line-up would be reasonably, if not very, accurate. It is still possible to increase the reliability of your line-ups if you can measure screen brightness accurately in some way, even when using SMPTE bars.

Being British I used to favor EBU bars but since working more extensively with HD, where SMPTE bars are more often used, I have changed my mind and now feel much more comfortable lining up to SMPTE bars.

21.2.1 An SMPTE Line-up

The first parameters to set are brightness and contrast. Find the red bar and looking slightly below it find the three narrow vertical gray bars. Now switch the monitor to blue only. If at first you can't find them then increase the brightness until they appear. Your monitor should now look very much like Figure 21.1. You now need to reduce the brightness until the left and the middle bars just disappear, leaving only the right hand of the three little bars still just visible. These three small bars on your monitor should now look very like Figure 21.2.

Towards the lower left-hand segment of the screen you will find a white square. Using the contrast control adjust this square until it just bleeds into the adjoining areas; now back off the contrast control until this effect just disappears. This is often described as reducing it until it ceases to "glow". Or you can use some exposure meters to set contrast (see below).

Figure 21.1: SMPTE Color Bars with "Blue Only" switched ON – incorrectly set up

Figure 21.2: SMPTE Color Bars with "Blue Only" switched ON – correctly set up

With any television format the brightness and contrast controls are never wholly independent of each other, so you may well have to go through the loop of making adjustments to both controls until you find you are no longer making any more changes.

The third parameter to set is chroma. On the screen you should see four vertical white bars with three much darker bars between them. If chroma is incorrectly set this part of the screen may look something like Figure 21.1. Below each bar you may be looking at a much smaller and rectangular section to the bar. For the moment ignore all the other portions of the screen.

What you have to try to achieve is a situation where all seven long bars match, as near as possible, the smaller rectangular sections below them. The control we are going to adjust is chroma. Adjust the control until you have the best possible match between the large vertical bars and the smaller sections below them on all seven bars. When you have successfully done this the screen should look something like Figure 21.2; in other words the smaller rectangular sections have effectively disappeared.

When you are satisfied with your result switch off the "Blue Only" control – your line-up is now complete.

21.2.2 Lining up Using EBU Bars

First set the monitor to underscan, which sets the picture slightly smaller than the screen. Using the brightness control adjust the right-hand black bar to match the density of the surrounding unused screen area. Now switch the monitor to "Blue Only". Using the chroma control adjust the second bar from the left again until the density of the bar exactly matches the surrounding screen density. Using the contrast control adjust the extreme left-hand bar, which is white, brighter and brighter until it just appears to "glow", then back off just a little until it stops glowing. You can set the contrast with some exposure meters (see below). Switch off the "Blue Only" control. Switch the camera back to picture and your monitor should be perfectly lined up.

Monitors should be lined up a few minutes after being switched on and *every time* the lighting environment surrounding the monitor changes.

21.2.3 Using an Exposure Meter

If you have an exposure meter that can cope with a flickering image, such as a Cine Meter II or a Spectra Combi II, place it with its flat disk attached over the extreme left-hand white bar on EBU bars or the white box bottom-left on SMPTE bars and adjust the contrast till the meter reads 27 foot candles. The same trick works with a Seconic L508 Cine with the dome retracted but the correct reading with this meter is 54 foot candles. The difference in reading is caused by the way meters behave when faced with a scanned picture. To find out if your meter should read 27 or 54 foot candles simply do a careful eyeball line-up and place your meter on the appropriate part of the screen; it will now read very close to either 27 or 54 foot candles. From now on set your screen contrast to the appropriate value nearest to your test reading. Some meters will not give an accurate reading from a screen; these are easily discovered as the reading will be unstable and jump around – these meters should not be used for lining up a monitor.

21.3 Cabling your Monitor

How you cable your monitor may not seem important; in fact, it is vital to your success.

There are three commonly found ways of outputting an HD color picture from a camera to either a stand-alone video recorder or a television monitor. They are called RGB (Red, Green and Blue), HDSDI (High Definition Serial Digital Interface) and SDSDI (Standard Definition Serial Digital Interface). As the name suggests, three cables would be required for the RGB signal, one for each color. HDSDI provides a high-quality digital signal, which can be carried on a single coaxial cable. HDSDI or the lower quality SDSDI, which again is carried on a single coaxial cable, are the most common signals for monitoring camera outputs on a professional shoot.

There is another way of monitoring a camera's output, a Composite signal. The advantage of the Composite signal is that it can be carried on a single cable and this is the more common way of outputting a signal from the camera to a monitor screen in the amateur or domestic arena. It is simple, convenient and only requires standard quality coaxial cabling. However, it only delivers a standard definition picture and this picture will not be as good or as robust as an HDSDI or SDSDI signal.

21.3.1 Single Coaxial Cables

Most HD cameras either deliver an HDSDI output signal or can easily be fitted with an adapter to make this output available. The advantage of using an HDSDI feed is that you only need a single coaxial cable between your camera and your monitor. The disadvantage is that should you want to see menu information on your monitor, HDSDI will not deliver it; it only delivers picture.

When feeding HDSDI signals down a BNC (Bayonet N Connector) cable, the standard cable used in most broadcast applications is not of sufficient quality to reliably transmit a satisfactory HD signal, except where the cable is very short. It is unfortunate that the HD industry has, in the main, continued to use BNC connectors; they were never designed for the rigors of location work and therefore are rather unreliable. We hang a $100,000 camera on the end of a plug costing less than a buck – I, for one, find this ridiculous.

21.3.2 Triple Coaxial Cables

Alternatively, on many cameras, you can take a three-core coaxial cable out of the three BNC plugs on the side of the camera labeled Y, PR and PB. Down this cable you can send both the picture and all the menu information. The disadvantage of this triple cable is that it is some 20 mm or 3/4 inch in diameter and quite stiff. If you wish to see menu information but do not require a color image you can use a single coaxial cable between the sockets on both the camera and monitor labeled Y. This will give you an HD black and white image with the menu if you need it.

21.3.3 Termination

If you are simply feeding one monitor directly from the camera then termination should not be a problem. If you are looping from the camera to one monitor and then on again to another monitor, understanding termination is vital. The simple rule is that the last monitor in the line must be terminated. This may, on some monitors, be automatic, may be done with a simple switch or you may have to put a termination plug onto the Video Out socket of the last monitor on the line. If you don't the danger is you will see a different image on each monitor and it is quite likely that none of them will be correct.

21.3.4 Serial Monitors

Even if you get your termination right the number of monitors hung onto a single camera output can disastrously affect the quality of the image. Do not accept an image amplifier between any source and the monitor you, the Director of Photography (DP), are going to watch. They may claim to be transparent – that is, adding no changes to the image – but believe me I would never stake my reputation on it.

21.4 Best Practice

The monitor the DP is going to watch should come from a single output on the camera; no other monitors should be fed from this output and no monitors should be fed down line from the DP's monitor. This rule should never be broken.

Choose another output from the camera or HDSDI converter for any other monitors and do not be swayed from this opinion. I have let this happen in the past and it was a disaster – please learn from my experience.

CHAPTER 22

Shipping

22.1 It's Not ENG!

Although High Definition (HD) cameras tend to look a little like the earlier generation of Electronic News Gathering (ENG) cameras they are very different and have to be treated accordingly. For instance, the Sony HDW F900 is virtually the same size as, and has all the switches in the same place as, the generation of Digi Beta cameras that preceded it, namely the DVW 790. The HDW F900 has even been described, by my good friend Peter Swarbrick, as a Digi Beta on steroids – an excellent comparison, if a little unscientific!

More recent cameras such as the Sony 750P, 730 and 900R are, amazingly, slightly smaller and a little lighter than the original Digi Beta.

With any HD camera we are dealing with a camera capable of recording an image of massively greater resolution. Curiously the NTSC system delivers almost exactly the same data rate per second as the PAL system. This is a result of the limiting transmission bandwidth available to both systems at their inception. NTSC has to transmit 525 lines of information 30 times a second; 30 complete frames per second derives from their 60 cycles per second mains supply frequency. So $525 \times 30 = 15,750$ lines per second. PAL has to transmit 625 lines 25 times per second, the local mains here having a frequency of 50 cycles per second. So $625 \times 25 = 15,625$. These are remarkably similar figures given the gap of the Atlantic Ocean, caused by very similar limitations on the amount of data that could be economically transmitted.

Now let us compare a single frame and its resolution. For simplicity I am only going to use the PAL model; the figures for NTSC are very similar. A single PAL image (the image does not use all the lines transmitted in either the PAL or the NTSC systems) is actually made up, per color, of 576 pixels vertically by 720 pixels horizontally, giving a gross single frame a resolution of 414,720 pixels. Compare this with HD, where the true vertical resolution is comprised of 1080 pixels and the true horizontal resolution is made up of 1920 pixels, giving a gross resolution of 2,073,600 pixels. Gross picture resolution is therefore nearly five times the resolution of a domestic television. So an HD camera is having to work at least five times harder per frame than an ENG camera. To keep it in perfect working order it therefore deserves much more respect.

149

22.2 Shipping Lenses

ENG cinematographers are used to shipping their cameras with the lenses mounted on them, although the more careful do try and take them as hand baggage. As we have seen elsewhere in this book, to be able to fill a large cinema screen and cause the audience not to question how the image was recorded when they are used to watching 35 mm film, the HD lenses should be able to approach a resolution of 2 1/2 times that of the 35 mm camera lenses. As we have seen above, the camera itself must be able to record five times the gross resolution. Put these two factors together and no matter how strong the lens mount, the camera/lens combination is unlikely to perform to maximum specification if they have been shipped attached to each other.

As an extreme example the largest of the Panavision zooms weighs 8.5 kilograms or about 18.75 pounds; just think of the bending forces involved on that lens mount should the camera, with the lens attached, receive a blow. A sensible technician will ship the lenses separated from the camera body just as film technicians have always done.

22.3 Transit Cases

There is a curious divide between the case and padding philosophies either side of the Atlantic. In America a professional shipping case will, as often as not, be made from resin-coated plywood lined with soft foam. This is a great case with a lining that allows the equipment to float about to some extent, but as the foam is always quite thick between the equipment and the case wall the equipment can never receive a harsh blow. Europeans, particularly the British, take a different approach. Their cases are as often as not ribbed aluminium and filled with high-density foam that very snugly fits the equipment. The philosophy here is that you do not allow the equipment to move but any significant blow will almost totally be absorbed by the high-density foam.

I have worked extensively with cases following both patterns and am confident that both types protect the equipment equally well. As I come from the UK you will not be surprised that I slightly favor the European aluminium case with its high-density foam. It does not offer any greater protection than the US version but the foam lasts a lot longer and the case/foam combination does lead to slightly smaller, and therefore easier to handle, cases.

22.4 Camera Set-up When Shipping

I have shipped both Digi Beta and HD cameras all over the world for many years and have never found that the shipping procedure alters the camera menu set-up. That said, I always take the precaution of writing the set-up to a card or memory stick so that should I find the need to re-program the menu it is the work of moments.

I have been in the situation where I have programmed a card or memory stick on one continent and shipped just myself and the program to another continent and then loaded the program into a locally supplied camera. My experience is this is a safe and reliable procedure.

22.5 Size and Weight

If you compare a full feature film camera kit with a similar HD kit the individual boxes may be of different weights but the whole shipping manifest is unlikely to show much change. But note, I said camera kit. If your team want to have full HD monitoring facilities, and I would heartily recommend they do, then your monitor shipping weight will almost inevitably be more than a black and white video assist kit. My favorite 24-inch monitor, in its case, weighs around 87 pounds or about 40 kilograms! But worth every pound, or kilogram.

22.6 Batteries

You will need more batteries than if you were shooting with a 35 mm film camera. There are two reasons for this: first, any digital device tends to be power hungry and, more importantly, you are consuming power just to make the viewfinder work, whereas with a film camera it consumes virtually no power when in the equivalent of a standby mode.

On-board batteries are very convenient but even large and efficient ones will only last between 1 1/2 and 4 hours depending on how much recording you make in any given time. Often overlooked is the simple expedient of using a block battery, just as we often do with film cameras. Most video cameras are 12-volt devices, though the newer high-end cameras are moving over to 24-volt just as film cameras are. As a guide, a good 12-volt block battery will run a Sony HDW F900 all day in all but the most arduous circumstances, so if you are in a studio or even on location but will spend most of the day on a dolly the block battery may be your answer.

CHAPTER 23

Multicamera Shoots

In Europe, especially in the UK, big multicamera shoots are not common. There is a small market for performance films – that is, taking subjects originally presented on the stage and transferring them to the screen – but it is limited. There are a few rock concerts shot with up to 10 cameras but again this is a very small market.

In the USA matters are very different. Traditionally sitcoms have been shot on 35 mm, most recently with a camera having a three-perforation mechanism as against the traditional four, which saves 25 percent of the stock and processing costs. The market is so significant that Panavision has developed a camera exclusively for this market. It is three-perf, as one would expect, has 2000-feet magazines and usually carries a big, long-range zoom. Two thousand feet of 35 mm film is heavy so the issue of the weight transfer from the front of the magazine to the back during a take becomes important. To overcome this, between the camera base and the tripod head there are two wedged plates slotting together with a lead screw arrangement so that the camera operator can smoothly move the camera fore and aft to re-balance the camera during a take. Optical viewfinders are also removed and the camera operators use video assist monitors as on a television studio camera. These video assist outputs are also used to feed audience monitors – often to induce laughter from the audience to be incorporated onto the soundtrack.

This camera is often mounted on a studio-style pedestal with all the cabling brought together in a loom. A loom is simply a sheath, usually made of nylon, which encases all the necessary cables so there is only one tail coming from each camera.

It is this multicamera television market that is embracing the High Definition (HD) philosophy faster than any other. The reasons are simple. There is little difference between the rental cost of an HD camera and a specialist three-perf 35 mm camera. If you add the cost of 5000 feet of 35 mm raw stock to the negative processing cost and further add telecine time to transfer it to tape for editing and then compare that total to the purchase price of a 50-minute cassette of tape you find the film cost is around 50 times that of the tape, a powerful argument in this market. Add to this the fact that in going over to HD there is no discernible change in picture quality, given a good Director of Photography (DP).

Things on set get simpler too. Tape changes are only needed after 50 minutes of recording time as against a little over 20 minutes for even the specialist film cameras. Wiring looms can be made up in exactly the same way. Instead of having to look at a video assist monitor, the Director is now viewing finished product in full HD resolution and color depth. Recording stock weight transfer problems become a thing of the past as the weight of the tape is negligible and it travels from the top to the bottom of the cassette during recording, so there is no fore and aft weight transfer as in a film camera.

23.1 Synchronization

Synchronization of the time code between many pieces of equipment has to be very carefully thought out, especially if you are using Sony or Sony-derived cameras. The problem is very similar to that experienced with the earlier Digi Beta cameras. Put simply, the problem lies in the fact that for ease of writing to the tape the total image is recorded in two blocks; this is more convenient and produces a higher tape writing speed. Time code, on the other hand, is written as four groups of two numbers, the groups representing hours, minutes, seconds and frames. A complete frame is the smallest unit it can handle. When you stop recording, the tape may come to a halt on either block of the picture information being laid down on the tape. This is not a problem as the recorder will start recording seamlessly on either a first block or a second block so the picture will be continuous. The time code, on the other hand, can only progress in whole numbers of frames. It is therefore possible to restart recording where the time code has, in effect, made a jump forward in time equivalent to half a frame relative to the picture information. This is not a drawback if you are recording picture and sound on a single camera, but is a crucial matter if you are using two or more devices that need to be synchronized via their time code. Even two identical cameras cannot be relied upon to stop and start with greater accuracy than a time space interval of half a frame.

Therefore the only solution is somehow to lock the time code of every piece of equipment together with frame accuracy.

23.2 Time Code on Location

If you are reasonably static on location it is possible to link up all the various sound and camera devices by running cables from time code out of one device and daisy-chaining BNC cables to time code in of the next device, taking time code out of that device to the time code in on the next device and so on. If you do this you will need to make sure that all but the first device is set to use external time code. In these situations the sound master will more often than not be something like a Digital Audio Tape (DAT) recorder, in which case this is usually used as the master time code source.

23.2.1 Lock-it Boxes

Film crews traditionally hate cables, so though the above solution is very reliable, the necessary cables will be most unpopular. There is a very elegant and not very expensive solution. Each device on set should be given an external time code generator. The version I use nearly all the time is called a "lock-it box". Roughly the size of a packet of 20 cigarettes, these boxes are extraordinarily reliable and very easy to use. Most often the lock-it box will be attached to the camera using a pad of Velcro – very convenient.

Usually the sound department will look after the lock-its and synchronize them all together at the beginning of the shooting day, then hand them round the unit as required. They are more than reliable enough to need no attention until the day's wrap, when they are returned to the sound department to have a power check and be restarted the following morning. It is claimed they will hold sync for up to a week, but good practice suggests a fresh sync-up every day is prudent.

It must be noted that the lock-it boxes used for Digi Beta will not suffice for HD – you will need boxes capable of delivering Tri Level Sync and this should be stipulated when ordering your equipment package.

23.2.2 Script Boy

There is a further refinement to this system. A device known as a "script boy" can be given to the Scrip Supervisor, or Continuity as they used to be known. It consists of a clipboard with a time code generator just like the lock-it with the addition of a time code display on the top of it. A simpler solution I have seen used recently was a digital watch, in this case a G Shock, which the sound mixer was able to set by hand every morning with an accuracy of within a second, usually more than good enough for the notes sent to the picture editor.

23.3 Time Code in a Studio

Film crews must now abandon all hope. In a studio situation with more than one camera there are going to be so many cables that the sensible approach is to go down that route and get really well organized.

The number of cables can easily mount up and a list might look like this:

- Power
- BNC High Definition Serial Digital Interface (HDSDI) monitor cable
- BNC time code in
- BNC time code out

- Genlock in
- Genlock out
- Remote camera control cable
- Audio channel 1 in
- Audio channel 2 in
- Audio monitoring.

You can have more: the monitor could be from the three-core socket instead of or in addition to the HDSDI single socket.

The solution to all this is to make up a loom for each camera long before shooting commences. Many suppliers will already have this available, so it is worth asking.

On a long or multicamera shoot it is also quite the norm to have a mains-driven time code generator and run every single piece of equipment from it, including sound department.

Although a nylon-sheathed loom cable may be an inch in diameter (25 mm), it is at least now the equivalent of a single cable and much more crew friendly.

23.3.1 Genlock

One cable we have not discussed is that labeled Genlock. Strictly speaking you only need to run this cable if you are cutting in real time via a control suite. Genlock ensures that all the cameras will open and close their electronic shutters at exactly the same moment. This can be important, for if you cut in real time between one camera and another imagine what would happen if you left one camera just as its shutter was about to open and cut to the incoming camera just as its shutter was about to close. You would have a totally blank frame.

By daisy-chaining the Genlock out to the Genlock in of the next camera you have all the shutters working in perfect synchronism.

23.4 Menu Set-ups

23.4.1 The Sony RMB 150

Many lighting directors from a television studio background like to have remote control over the camera set-up. I do not, but that's a matter of taste and background. There is a remote control box for the Sony HDW F900 and it goes under the title of an RMB 150 (Figure 23.1). The problem with using an RMB 150, as I see it, is that you can only control the image from each camera by referring to the monitors, which seems a shame when you have all those nice

Figure 23.1: The Sony RMB 150 remote control unit

digital pages in the menus. Now engineers from a television studio background do this with amazing precision, but it frightens the hell out of me!

The RMB 150 is capable of controlling many of the picture parameters such as brightness, gamma, black levels, etc., and has a remote run/stop. It controls all but the run/stop with rotary knobs, with little guide as to the extent of their effect. It should also be noted that having made changes using the RMB 150, if you now unplug the unit it leaves the camera with all the settings you have made; the camera does not go back to any previous setting.

Television studio practice allows for small differences in exposure and color correction from camera to camera; this is not the case in film. A film DP, if shooting with several cameras, will either light the set for a perfect match, my preference, or give each camera a separate exposure setting. Neither route is "correct", but simply the result of different experience and training.

23.4.2 Using Memory Sticks

I am sure it will come as no surprise that I prefer to have all my cameras set up to exactly the same parameters so that I can match the monitors by adjusting my lighting. That is not to say that I may not use slightly different set-ups from scene to scene, but I try very hard never to make any changes during an individual scene. This is because I have a hang-up about lighting and picture continuity in general, which comes from my film background where shots within a scene might very well have their order on the screen rearranged in the cutting room, so I try very hard to ensure that they will all match no matter what the order. If you are more used to working in a studio where a live cut is made, then you are much more certain of the eventual cutting order and need not acquire my neurosis.

My technique is simple. I set up the main shot, usually something like a master wide and, using the camera's menu, set this camera to my preferred look. I will then record the settings to a memory stick and, using the stick, load these settings onto all the other cameras. As a precaution I will keep an eye on the leading actors' close-ups during rehearsals to make sure my settings and the make-up do not conflict in any way. In these circumstances the majority of my lighting will almost certainly have been done in advance of shooting and I will have considerable control over the lamps via a dimmer board. My aim is always to have set the lighting for the whole scene well before rehearsals are over and not touch anything at all during the scene.

23.5 Matching Lenses

The ideal is to have all your lenses from a single good-quality manufacturer so that no adjustment between cameras is ever called for. If you source your cameras and lenses from a high-quality supplier offering a complete range of lenses from a single manufacturer you can be absolutely sure of a perfect match between all zoom and prime lenses and no adjustments whatsoever will be needed. My apologies to all the other manufacturers, but experience has led me to favor the Panavision Digital Primo lenses; they suite my style and are utterly reliable. A second, and very good, choice would be Zeiss digital lenses, which are also of excellent quality. Lenses from other manufacturers make me nervous if I am shooting for cinema presentation. For broadcast-only shoots many other makes are quite acceptable. I suggest you test any lens kit you are offered and make up your own mind.

If you find your lens set does not match in image quality and look, there are things you can do about it but usually you will be bringing the look of your better lenses down to the quality of your worst lens. If you look carefully in the Sony HDW F900 menus and, indeed, most of the Sony HD cameras, in the section named Operations you will find a page labeled Lens File. Here it is possible to assign individual settings to several different lenses. Many other manufacturers offer a similar facility within their menu system – look hard, it's usually there somewhere.

The problem is that to make a sharp lens match a softer lens you either have to reduce the image enhancement of the better lens and/or bring up the electronic image enhancement of the poorer lens so much the image acquires all the bad characteristics of the look of poor-quality video, so why are you spending so much money on an HD kit?

Personally I would not accept a lens set that did not match perfectly without any adjustment within the camera.

CHAPTER 24

Hazardous Conditions

There are many myths about video cameras in general, and High Definition (HD) cameras in particular, regarding their vulnerability to the elements. Most of this is nonsense. If you think of the amount of electronics packed into a modern film camera, what makes an HD camera more susceptible to hazardous conditions? Very little.

There are a couple of cut-out switches in the camera to protect it from abuse. It will stop if the humidity surrounding the tape record drum becomes too high, and it has to be very high indeed for this to happen. A film camera would probably be equally in trouble. This safety trip is a wise precaution, for if the humidity surrounding the tape drum ever reaches a critical point the tape will, eventually, stick to the drum. You don't want this to happen as it is not a field serviceable condition. The camera is going to need a whole new tape drum and that is going to be very expensive. I have been associated with a long-term shoot where a Panavised Sony camera was up a Scottish mountain in a gale for some considerable time; sensible precautions were taken, exactly as you would with a film camera, and there was never the slightest suggestion that the camera was threatening to shut down. There was a real chance that the crew would have to though!

There is a heat overload cut-out switch as well; this is mainly to protect the computer processors from overloading. I have never experienced or heard of this tripping out. I have been associated with an HD shoot in the Moroccan desert where the temperature was 110°F in the shade; the cameras worked perfectly. A personal experience of the reliability of HD cameras in this respect came when shooting in a studio during a particularly hot summer. As we neared lunch my camera operator put his hand on top of the Sony 750 we were shooting with in order to reach over for something and quickly pulled his hand away – it was very hot indeed. The ribbing on the top of the camera and under the handle is not a feature there to make the camera look more appealing; it is to better dissipate the waste heat from the analog-to-digital processor and do the job very well. When we broke for lunch my Gaffer, who had a voltmeter that could also be used as a temperature probe, measured the ribbing just before we switched the camera off for lunch – it was 32°C! I believe we really could have fried an egg on it. The moral of this tale is that the camera was still working perfectly, just as it had been designed to.

24.1 Resetting the Trips

If you look under a Sony camera at the rear on the operator's side you will see a small hole; this is the reset button. If the camera has tripped out then press a small, blunt object such as the end of a paper clip into this hole. The camera will not restart immediately. You need to take it where it is drier or cooler, depending on why it has tripped, and wait for the conditions to change. Removing the cassette and leaving the door open can help matters. The camera will come back to life when you press the reset some 20 minutes later. If you look carefully you will find a similar reset somewhere on most HD cameras.

Treat an HD camera with the respect you would give a high-quality 35 mm camera and you are unlikely to have any problems. Nevertheless, let us look at the precautions you might like to take.

24.2 Water

Please ignore the old adage "Water and electricity don't mix." The adage should be "Water and electricity mix only too well." In fact, they attract each other. If there is the slightest sign of rain keep the rain cover handy. If you are going into a very humid environment take the camera and lenses in some hours before you need to use them and let them normalize. Keep a hair-drier handy in these circumstances to speed things up – but not set on heat please! Use it on cold or you may melt something significant. All just as you would do with a film camera.

24.3 Heat

Referring to the above, don't put the rain cover on unnecessarily – it can cause a heat build-up as the fans cooling the computer processors won't get their heat away as efficiently. If Sound have insisted, as they often do with the quietest of cameras, that you cover it with something to make it quieter, take that something off as soon as the take is finished. Remember the front-end processors are working full time just to give you a picture in the viewfinder and therefore they will be dumping waste energy, in the form of heat, even when the camera is on standby. This is one difference from a film camera.

If you are shooting on a very hot exterior location you would be very foolish not to put an umbrella up over a film camera to ensure that the film stock did not reach temperatures that would change its characteristics; please do just the same with an HD camera even if the reasons are different.

24.4 Cold

It is traditional to "winterize" a film camera if it is going to an extremely cold climate. HD cameras probably survive cold better than film cameras do. HD lenses will need just the same attention as film lenses. The biggest problem might be cables; they can become very brittle in the cold, especially BNC cables. Check out a few different makes of coaxial cable in a cold store to find the one that will survive.

Batteries in extreme cold are always a problem. Two remedies come immediately to mind: one is putting a DC supply cable into the camera and keeping the battery on the other end of it inside your clothing; alternatively, if you are shooting more formally, say on a tripod or a dolly, then before you leave home have some block batteries clad in 1- or 2-inch polystyrene and then have an outer case made for them in plywood. In really freezing conditions you could have a double-thickness polystyrene layer underneath the block battery and mount a suitable car headlamp bulb under it as a heater. Your battery will run down somewhat faster but while it has a charge it should be lively enough to keep the camera running.

24.5 Dust

All the usual precautions apply, such as protecting your lenses, setting up wind-breaks where possible, perhaps using the rain cover to protect the camera.

There is one both essential and simple protection an HD camera needs over a film camera. The most vulnerable parts of the HD camera, with regard to dust, are the tape transport mechanism and the record head drum. Very fortunately the gaps around the cassette loading door are not used in any way as cooling ports, so if you are in a dusty, gritty or dirty environment simply put some gaffer tape over the gaps between the camera body and the cassette loading door.

24.6 Gamma Rays

Now this is a bit sci-fi but bear with me, it could be important. One of the few things that can kill a pixel on the imaging chip is a gamma ray hitting it smack in the middle. At ground level there is very little chance of this happening; the Earth's atmosphere absorbs or reduces the chances by a very large factor. On the other hand, if you are flying the camera at an altitude anything above 30,000 feet gamma rays are much more prevalent. I have only known one occasion where a camera has suffered gamma ray damage after flying and only one pixel was affected.

In all my time with both Digi Beta cameras and HD cameras I have only known one moment when several pixels were destroyed at the same time. Curiously, over a 24-hour period a camera in London was fine before lunch and after lunch had several dead pixels. The following day I had a telephone call from a crew in Prague in the Czech Republic saying there were a couple of dead pixels – very strange. Was there a sun spot that day or something? Who knows?

A pixel normally dies switched on so you will see a bright spot on the screen; it will be of the color relating to the chip it is on. Fortunately there are several ways to get rid of this bright spot. If you have missed it during shooting, and because it will always be in exactly the same place in the picture area, it is easy to eradicate in post-production. If you spot it before turning over then there is a better than 90 percent chance you can quickly solve the problem. Hold the black balance switch down for at least 3 seconds. The camera will now perform an extended black balance and an auto pixel check. This might take up to a minute and you may have to perform this operation eight or ten times to completely eradicate the problem. The camera has a sophisticated memory circuit in it and if it finds a dead pixel it will, for the rest of the life of the picture head block, take an average of the eight pixels surrounding the dead pixel and assign this average to the dead pixels' output. The memory is sufficient to cover for up to 40 dead pixels. I have never known a camera reach anything like that number of dead pixels, but should it, the only solution then is to change the prism block and the three receptor chips.

If the auto pixel check fails to clear all the dead pixels – and you are only likely to be in this position if the pixel has only partially failed, which will give a dull colored glow on the screen – then the pixel memory correction can be initiated manually. I am not going to go into the whole procedure here, but if you need to do it in some distant part of the globe then ring your supplier and they will happily guide you through the process. If you are on your mobile phone make sure you have a fresh battery; it is not difficult but it is tedious. It's very like playing an old computer game; you have to line up a vertical line and a horizontal line exactly over the pixel in question. With two million plus pixels per chip this can take a while and there is no scoring system, so it can be a thankless task.

CHAPTER 25

Camera Supports

Tripods and tripod heads should be chosen in much the same way as you would for a film camera. This means that for a Genesis, Arriflex D-21 or Sony HDW F900 you should have the quality and strength you would use for a 35 mm camera, and for the Sony HDW 700P range and their 900R, or a Panasonic HDC 20A, you could go down to the slightly lighter equipment you might use for a fully equipped Arri SR3 or a well-loaded Super 16 camera. Unless we are going to be taking the kit into difficult locations my preference is to always go for the 35 mm type supports as they are usually much more robust and generally nicer to use.

25.1 Fluid Heads

Any fluid head that is robust enough to take easily the weight of your chosen camera in its heaviest configuration, say with the biggest zoom and the on-board battery attached, will suffice. That said, I have a personal preference for underslung fluid heads where the tilt bearing is level with the optical axis. These are usually of a dog-leg or "L" configuration. My favorite is the Ron Ford Baker Fluid 7; it has been going for many years and has been in continuous development, so the current model will comfortably support an F900 or similar camera in any configuration.

Cartoni have introduced a head of similar configuration to the Ron Ford Baker Fluid 7, which they have christened the Lambda. It is more easily adjustable than the F7 and pays for this by being slightly larger and heavier. I have used one and it was very impressive.

25.2 Geared Heads

There is much discussion about the value of a geared head. Certain Directors of Photography (DPs) I know dislike the use of geared heads; they express the view that such a mechanical device produces a camera movement that is not hand made or personal enough – I disagree. The whole principle of the "boat" on a geared head is that you can both rotate and tilt the camera where the center of both movements is the nodal point, or optical center, of the lens. The human eye is a ball rotating in a spherical socket where the center of the ball remains in the same place, thus never moving up or down, left or right of the optical center of the eye, just like the camera on a well-set-up geared head.

If those DPs that dislike the use of geared heads could be persuaded to watch a monitor when the camera was operated by a truly skilled operator using a geared head, I think some of them might change their view. That said, the skill of the operator and their talent for the task will be much more in evidence when using a geared head than when on a fluid head. Talent will out, never more so than with he or she who cranks the handles.

Underslung or dog-leg fluid heads are capable of the same centering of the lens nodal point but nearly always the need to balance the head puts the nodal point ahead of the pan center.

All geared heads have a certain feel to them, which makes different operators prefer different makes of head. I am happy to use an Arri geared head, preferring a Mark 1 to a Mark 2; I have used a Panahead extensively and like it a lot. On a job some years ago I had been using an Arri head for some weeks when it needed to go back to the hire company for some minor adjustment that was unwise to carry out in the field; the company rang me to apologize for not having a spare Arri in stock and asked me if I would take a Mitchell Lightweight just for a couple of days until they could get the Arri back to me. I said yes, of course. I didn't return the Mitchell until the end of the job. Four weeks later I had bought my own Mitchell Lightweight. When I operate myself the sheer joy of driving a head you love and are familiar with is a very special pleasure.

25.3 Remote Heads

You should treat remote heads just as you would with a film camera, with one proviso. Not all the suppliers of cranes and remote heads are fully up to speed with the requirements of HD cameras. Sometimes they forget that whereas most 35 mm film cameras run on 24 volts many HD cameras run on 12 volts. The cabling is also very different; the BNC lead that is usually used for the film camera's video assist is unlikely to be of sufficient quality to be able to handle the data stream associated with an HD signal. You will probably get a picture, but not a very good one, especially if it is a long crane and therefore needs a long cable run.

Even the stop/start plugs and cables are different; zoom and focus may or may not be compatible. All these things must be checked long before you arrive on the set.

Remote heads are usually controlled by either a joystick or a pair of wheels emulating the controls on a geared head. The operator's viewfinder is now a television monitor. From what I have said about my affection for a geared head you will not be surprised that I prefer the wheels. Indeed, if an operator chooses the joystick I think the camera movements often look a bit "clunky".

If my operator is under pressure when the crane comes out, I sometimes offer to do the crane shot for them "just to take the pressure off a little", which is, of course, just an excuse. I love little more than flying a camera through three dimensions while "'ackling the 'andles". And it does massage my pride to show the younger members of the crew that some of the older members of the crew can still enjoy themselves.

25.4 Under Water

Underwater cinematography has much the same problems whether you are using a film camera or an HD camera. I have done it myself and would now always give the advice – bring in a specialist. In the end a skilled underwater cameraperson will save the production time and money and make a difficult shot look easy.

Housings need to be looked at carefully. Most HD cameras are a very different shape to film cameras; for a start they tend to be longer, so this should be looked at well in advance of the shoot. A number of manufacturers now have dedicated HD housings that work very well.

25.5 In the Air

I have seen a Sony HDW F900 very successfully mounted on several fixed-wing and helicopter mounts, including the Wescam. In the end there were very few problems. Again, the power supply voltage must be looked at in advance. It is a very good idea to make sure you can balance the camera correctly well before the shooting day. HD cameras can have their center of gravity in a very different place from many film cameras. This can apply to the left and right dimension as well as the fore and aft. On the test day it is wise to take along a selection of sliding base plates, especially an extra long one, just to make sure you get a good and balanced fixing.

25.6 Motion Control Rigs

With most motion control rigs you will have no problems other than the balance and voltage ones discussed above. There is, however, one fascinating piece of equipment available which, unfortunately, I have not as yet had the chance to try out. Panavision have a device they have named the Panahub that apparently fits on the non-operator side of their version of the Sony HDW F900. It will combine a large number of data streams; it can not only lay down all the lens data including zoom setting, focus and aperture, but can record many of the data streams from the axis controls of a motion control rig. Two of the four soundtracks available on the record tape are used so instead of recording sound on them it records metadata (metadata = data about data).

In theory, at least, this would mean that you could record a take, go away for several weeks and, provided you have the nodal point of the lens in exactly the same place on the rig, replay the tape and teach the motion control rig to carry out exactly the same shot as you took all that time ago. What an exciting prospect that might be.

CHAPTER 26

How HD Affects Other Crafts

In general, if most of the other crafts on set treat High Definition (HD) as a 35 mm shoot all will be well. There are a few instances, however, where certain specific matters are different, so let us look at them craft by craft.

26.1 Art and Design

In the main, sets and set dressing will need to be every bit as good as for 35 mm; the resolution of HD is as good so, if a join is going to show on 35 mm, it will show on HD. Colors are much the same but you may have to watch deep or dark reds as they tend to come through in the equivalent density but colored orange. This depends very much on the camera you are using. The later the camera, the less likely there will be a problem, but it is still wise to shoot a test before going into production.

There is a very slight tendency to moiré patterning, just as there will be with any pixel-driven imaging system, which includes virtually every video camera. Textures having very fine regular detail should therefore be camera tested at an early stage. As time goes by cameras are acquiring more pixels, and better imaging devices and strategies to overcome these problems.

Very pure whites can be a slight problem especially when put next to, or in, a very dark color. But this is something to keep a watch on even with film.

So, in general, few problems for Art and Design.

26.2 Costume

I have experienced a few problems with our friend moiré patterning on some costumes. Some loosely woven cloths can, at certain distances and size of shot, start to shimmer in the classic moiré patterning manner. Any materials you think might be even a slight problem should have a camera test before you make up the garments. Some check patterns will also have the same problem. Costume designers who are experienced in working in television will have little problem overcoming these effects as they will be familiar with them, but designers who have only ever worked in film would be well advised to have some camera tests shot.

It should be noted that these problems are likely to be less than if you were shooting on Digi Beta due to the closer density of the pixels on the camera chip and, as I say, cameras are getting better all the time at handling these problems.

Dark or deep reds can be a problem for the Costume department just as they are for all Art and Design.

26.3 Make-up and Hair

The problems here are different from the previous crafts as there are few color or moiré issues but there is a problem with using lens diffusion. It is quite common, say with a hairpiece mounted on a net, for the Hair Designer and the Director of Photography (DP) to work closely together to ensure the net does not show. With a 2/3-inch HD camera there is less the DP can do to help, for a diffusion filter that works on a 35 mm camera will be far too strong for the rest of the image on an HD camera. Any form of diffusion on HD has to be very light as it has a greater effect and this makes it very difficult for the DP to find that subtle level of diffusion where the lace will disappear but the rest of the scene will not look false.

HD cameras using a single chip roughly the size of a 35 mm film frame have fewer problems as exactly the same filters and tricks can be applied as have been used for many years on 35 mm film, for you will, most probably, be shooting with the very same lenses.

The above applies to the treatment of wrinkles on an actor's face.

The only solution the DP has when using a 2/3-inch HD camera in these circumstances is to pay greater attention to the lighting, so allowances must be made to give them a little more time in this area if the make-up problems are to be adequately addressed.

26.4 Sound

Sound have roughly the same problems on HD as with most film shoots, although you might say the camera crew are going to perceive a problem with the Sound department. It is more than likely that the cutting room, and the Producer, will insist that the floor-mixed sound be fed back to the camera, assuming you are using a camera with an on-board sound recording facility, the camera's soundtracks. This is for two reasons: the cutting room will most likely prefer to take their first soundtrack into the off-line edit suite directly from the video tape, as this is much quicker and they will almost certainly be conforming the digital audio tapes (DATs) later. Secondly, the Producer will see the soundtracks on the video tapes as a worthwhile backup of the DAT should there be a problem at a later date.

As most camera crews look upon extra cables coming out of the camera as a curse worse than a bad cold, much patience and forbearance must be brought to bear.

26.5 Script Supervision and Continuity

The most obvious difference here is that whoever logs the shots will be working to time code numbers rather than footage numbers. On many of the shoots on which I have worked, at the end of every printed take the focus puller calls out the focal length of the lens, the focus settings, the aperture and possibly the number on the footage counter. Surely the simplest thing is for them to simply replace the footage reading with the time code? It is not always as simple as that, for on most shoots the time code display will be showing the time of day plus the frame number and will be running continuously. There is a pause button on the time code readout but it requires some deft fingerwork to hit that button as well as shutting the camera down after a take. It cannot usually be arranged to happen automatically.

As I have suggested elsewhere in this book, the solution might well be a simple digital watch set as near as possible to the same time of day as the camera, which the person logging the shots can glance at on cut. A better solution might be to get them a script boy, which is a clipboard incorporating a time code generator that is locked to the camera every morning and has a screen to display the numbers. This can also be fitted with a pause and restart button so that immediately the button is pressed from a stopped condition the time code automatically catches up, jumping, as it were, the lapsed time during its off period. This device replaces the traditional stopwatch very elegantly.

26.6 The Second Assistant Cameraperson or Ex-Clapper Boy

Although not strictly another craft, as they are very much an integral part of the camera crew, I think special mention should be made here of a few of the changes to their responsibilities that have come about with the introduction of HD. The biggest problem they sometimes have is, as they are now in charge of the setting up, lining up and cabling of the essential monitors, they can easily be run ragged by other crafts persuading them to run extra monitors. It should be understood that it is an onerous and responsible task to make sure that both the Director and the DP have the monitors that they want when and where they need them, so the second assistant will be quite busy enough getting monitors ready for these two senior heads of department, especially if there has been a big camera move, without other crafts prevailing upon them to supply extra monitors for their convenience.

The practice I like is for the second assistant cameraperson to cable, from a single primary source on the camera, a feed for the monitor the Director and DP will be using. When this is done a second feed, totally independent of the one already fed, is supplied for anyone else to tap into. If the DP allows it then the second assistant cameraperson can rig a single monitor on this secondary feed for Continuity, Make-up, Wardrobe, etc. to share. It must be understood that anything beyond the first monitor on the second feed is nothing to do with the second assistant cameraperson – they will simply be too busy. If any other craft wants their own monitor they must find the labor to daisy-chain it from the first monitor on the secondary feed.

All this might sound a bit complicated but bear with me for, as I describe in detail elsewhere in this book, if a monitor is plugged into the DP's monitor and that monitor is faulty or unterminated then this can lead to the DP lighting quite incorrectly; hence monitor cabling discipline is essential.

CHAPTER 27

Troubleshooting

27.1 Stating the Obvious

Forgive me if some of the solutions listed below seem obvious, but I can readily recall times when a camera, mechanical or digital, has seemed to fail at an extraordinarily embarrassing moment and panic has set in. In a state of panic it has, on one occasion, taken me a full 5 minutes to realize that the lead leaving the camera was not actually plugged into the battery! Hence if you have need to grab this book in order to obtain help with a problem, the obvious is also here – hopefully you will then realize the lead needs plugging in a little quicker than I did.

Professional High Definition (HD) cameras are proving to be very reliable; therefore if you seem to have a fault do try and troubleshoot it yourself as a touch of finger trouble may well prove to be the answer. If you have been through all the troubleshooting checks and things are still amiss, then more often than not there is little you can achieve on location. Your best repair kit is your mobile phone; ring your supplier, they may have good advice and if things can't be made to work will almost certainly ship you a new camera immediately.

I was at a London camera rental house recently when there seemed to be a problem with one of their HD cameras out in the field that could not be solved on location. Within 2 hours a new camera body was on its way, traveling as hand luggage with one of their young engineers who, despite having to fly the length of Europe followed by a long jeep ride the other end, had a new camera, perfectly set up to the Director of Photography (DP)'s requirements, in the hands of the crew an hour before the on-set call time the following day. That's service! The irony was the problem turned out to be a little lack of experience on behalf of the crew – no matter, these things are to be expected.

27.2 Problems and Solutions

Please note that these solutions were initially written for Sony cameras, but they give a good starting point for most shoots.

Problem: No image on the monitor.

Solution:

1. If there is one, have you switched the High Definition Serial Digital Interface (HDSDI) adapter on?

2. Is the monitor powered correctly – does the standby light glow?

3. Is the monitor set to the correct channel?

4. Check all cable connections.

5. Is the BNC cable of sufficient quality?

6. Try another BNC cable.

7. Try using the output from the Y, Ph or Pr sockets on the side of the camera. If the image is good you may need to change the HDSDI adapter or the down-converter.

Problem: The monitor is showing coloration in the corners of the image.

Solution: Degauss the monitor – there should be a small button somewhere on the monitor to do this.

Problem: No image in the viewfinder but there is an image on the monitor.

Solution:

1. Is the eyepiece cable correctly inserted into the camera?

2. Is the camera powered correctly?

Problem: No image through the down-converter – if using an external one.

Solution:

1. Is the power light-emitting diode (LED) alight? If not, check power cable connections.

2. Check video cable connections.

3. Check power and DIP switches on the down-converter.

4. Check the monitor (see above).

5. If the cable connection is OK it is just possible that the internal camera fuse is blown – if you suspect this call your supplier; it may not be user replaceable.

Problem: Camera will not power up.

Solution:

1. Check power cables and connections.

2. Check battery voltage – try another battery.

3. If using the mains converter, check the power supply is on.

4. Did the camera overheat and shut off? If it did, let it cool down – this may take 20 minutes or so – and then press the reset button under the rear of the camera. Make sure the fan extracts are unblocked.

Problem: Camera will not record.

Solution:

1. Is the camera powered correctly (see above)?

2. Is the tape cassette or storage media write protected? Check that the red tab, or whatever, is flush with the cassette case and not pushed in.

3. Is the Humidity warning display on? If so, dry out the camera and press the reset button.

4. Go into the diagnosis menu and see if anything looks amiss – DO NOTHING. Consult your supplier with your findings.

5. There may be another internal problem – consult your supplier.

Problem: Monitor is too bright when using the component Y, Pb and Pr inputs.

Solution: The monitor is probably not terminated – if it has a switch, deploy it; if not, fit termination plugs to the video out socket.

Problem: Monitor is green when using the component Y, Pb and Pr outputs.

Solution: The monitor is probably configured for an RGB signal rather than a component Y, Pb and Pr signal – reconfigure the monitor.

Problem: Monitor shows a single pixel as a bright and constant color.

Solution: Perform a black balance repeatedly, holding the black balance switch down for at least 3 seconds, until the pixel disappears. It might help to turn the monitor brightness up to be absolutely sure the problem has gone away. It may still glow at higher monitor brightness – keep operating the black balance until it disappears. Try this eight or ten times before giving up. If it won't disappear, consult your supplier.

Problem: Image is vignetting on one side and/or blue flickering band at the top of the screen.

Solution: One of the internal filter wheels is almost certainly not perfectly in its indent position – check both internal filter wheels.

Problem: Image has excessive blur when panning.

Solution: The shutter is almost certainly switched off – make sure it is switched on and at the right shutter speed. Probably the shutter switch on the camera control panel has been moved.

Problem: Image looks soft – this might only be noticeable on a 24-inch monitor.

Solution: Check the back focus on the lens. This will most likely show up if you have zoomed in, eye focused and zoomed out; the image will go soft as you zoom out.

Problem: Footage marks on lens are no longer accurate.

Solution:

1. Check lens back focus.

2. Are you using a broadcast lens or a film-style lens? Film-style lenses should be measured from the notional focal plane, whereas broadcast lenses should be measured from the green line around the front of the lens.

Problem: The camera will not accept external time code.

Solution: Is the time code set to F-Run? If not, set if to F-Run.

Problem: No audio signal level on camera VU meter.

Solution:

1. Check cable connections.

2. Is the input switch situated above the XLR input socket on the back of the camera at the proper setting – mic/line?

3. Check the audio in switch – it should be set to rear not front.

Problem: Lens Ret – i.e. record preview – function on the assignable switch is not working. (N.B. Not all cameras have assignable switches.)

Solution:

1. Is the tape cassette write protected? – check that the red tab is flush with the cassette case and not pushed in.

2. Was the last take at least 3 seconds long? – it has to be for Lens Ret to function.

Problem: White balance is not functioning correctly – AWB: NG will appear in the viewfinder.

Solution:

1. If LEVEL HIGH appears in the viewfinder the exposure level is too high. On a Sony camera with a conventional lens with a hand grip, switch the lens to Auto Exposure and try again. With a Panavision camera set the level of the white card to approximately 70

percent – you can do this using the zebra function or, better still, take an incident reading immediately in front of the card and use this reading as the stop on the lens.

2. If COLOR TEMP LOW or COLOR TEMP HIGH appears in the viewfinder then you are not using the appropriate color correction filter in the filter wheel. Try different filters until white balance operates successfully.

3. If LEVEL LOW appears in the viewfinder there is simply not enough light reaching the camera head. Either open the iris or add more light to the subject. Do not solve this problem by adding gain.

4. If AWB: WHITE PRESET appears in the viewfinder then the white balance switch on the side of the camera is set to PRESET – move it to the A or B position where an auto white balance can be performed.

Problem: The audio in not in sync with a down-converted image.

Solution: The down-converter takes a few milliseconds to carry out its job so you need to insert an audio delay box into the audio line. This problem usually only presents itself when using a down-converted image for playback.

Part 5
Examples of Shoots

CHAPTER 28

Birthdays

Birthdays, an early HD production, is an 8-minute short intended for the UK cinemas and to be shown at film festivals in order to progress the young team's careers. There was simply not enough in the budget to shoot on 35 mm and as it was intended for cinema presentation it would not have been made if High Definition (HD) had not just arrived. On this occasion I agreed to be the Director of Photography (DP) as I liked the Director, Chris Atkins, and his company Stage 2 Screen. He had also written the script, and it gave me the opportunity to shoot without making any concessions to trying to make HD look like film. I would light the picture like film but would use no diffusion and would not vary the camera settings from the Panavision recommended settings for a write-out to film. This way I would discover what HD, when shown both as digital projection and as 35 mm film, would look like.

28.1 The Studio Shoot

The picture was scheduled to be shot in 3 days, with one day to film the "interlocutor" in a coved studio where the floor would be blue but the walls black so there would be a color for the artist to stand on but the background would be a complete void – not an easy concept no matter what you are going to record it on. Further, the Director's vision of this scene was that it would be very severely top lit with the minimal amount of fill light.

The day in the studio was not scheduled to have much of a lighting budget and the "dolly" consisted of a tripod on a rolling spider that could run on plastic piping as rails, not my normal scene, and I had offered to operate it myself to help with the budget. I love such operating when I can and that may have influenced my decision to take the job. The "dolly" rarely went in exactly the same place twice. As most of the time I only had to keep a mid shot on the actor that was not too difficult, but when we went for close-ups my focus puller was in for something of a challenge.

The lighting scheme could not have been simpler: two Par cans were rigged next to each other in the roof of the studio centered on the artist and very slightly in front of him. The only other lighting was an 800-watt redhead bounced off a polystyrene board. Simple, effective and when Chris saw the result on our 24-inch monitor he declared it exactly what he had envisaged. A good start to the shoot. Realizing that with a totally black background the sometimes excessive depth of field on HD was not an issue, for there was nothing there to be sharp, I could work without any neutral density (ND) filters and at least give my focus puller a decent chance; nevertheless with only two Par cans as a key light he still only got T 3.2, which with that shifting track kept him on his toes. The "panda effect" look of an actor very top lit with dark eye sockets is far from my normal style, but I have to give it to Chris it was powerfully effective in this context. The 4-foot square polystyrene reflector put a nice dot in the eyes as well as brightening the eye sockets to a point where I could accept them. I may be old school but it seems to me that the script, the writer, the Director and particularly the actor might all be wasting their time if it is impossible for the audience to read the meaning on the actor's face. It does not matter how dark the face is so long as you can read what is going on behind it. To my mind, most of that communication comes from the eyes, and hence I hate it if I can't see an actor's eyes.

28.2 The Location Shoot

The two location days would be all over central London including the Houses of Parliament, Millbank, the new Greater London Council Offices, Tower Bridge, some back streets in west London, Panavision Europe's office and a north-east London flat. With a lot of locations in difficult parking circumstances with a large camera, it was a good job my young camera team liked a challenge! It would have been much easier in some respects if the Sony HDW 900R had been available at the time.

We were very lucky with the weather, particularly as we only had 2 days to shoot our exteriors. It was very bright with big majestic clouds with enough breaks in them to give us sun for the shots without waiting around too much. It also gave me a chance to show off what the camera was capable of. One of the silly rumors doing the rounds about HD was that it wouldn't handle a bright sky; I had bright skies in abundance so this was my opportunity to show that they were not a problem. If you refer to Figure 28.1 you will see a still pulled directly from the HD tape. The scene concerns a chap who works for the police and whose job it is to stop people committing suicide, and the chap on the left is trying to throw himself off the top of a building site. Even in black and white and reproduced here you can see the big sky holding up very well indeed. I assure you it looks even better on the big screen.

Because we were going to so many locations and, to ease the parking problems, we were traveling in private cars, I decided to work solely from a 9-inch monitor run off batteries. For really difficult shots I would dive under a cloth to check my exposure on the color monitor but found I rarely changed it from the setting I had made using the black and white viewfinder. When traveling a lot during the shooting day you must be aware that control knobs on both the viewfinder and monitor can easily get knocked, so the first thing to do on arrival at a new location is to switch the camera on, leave it and the monitor for a few minutes (this can easily

Figure 28.1: A still taken directly from the master HD tape of *Birthdays*

be the time it takes you to set the shot up), then switch the camera to bars output and line up both the monitor and the viewfinder. You can get a detailed description of how to line up your monitor quickly and efficiently in Chapter 21. The line-up procedure is exactly the same when lining up a black and white viewfinder as for a color monitor, except you simply ignore the fact that there is no chroma control.

There were several important scenes in *Birthdays* where, because of the time pressure, we had shot a take before someone turned up with the monitor. With a carefully lined up viewfinder I was very pleased with my exposure even when the scene contained one of our big skies. In retrospect I think having finished product to look at, even be it only in black and white, made me braver with my exposure than I might have been if shooting film – it seemed I was not making that little cautious allowance I might when using a spotmeter and this was very much to the benefit of the pictures.

28.3 Exterior Tracking Shots

There were two major tracking sequences in *Birthdays*, one where the camera is static on a doorway through which our hero bursts and runs, in profile, down a street and a second where he literally chases after the camera. This being a very low budget production, the only vehicle available that was not full of equipment was the Director's Peugeot 306 hatchback. We did the burst through the door and into a profile run first. I simply got in the back seat, wound the window right down and rested the camera complete with the 6–27 mm zoom on the open window ledge.

There are some advantages to a heavy camera. I could have opted to take the High Definition Serial Digital Interface (HDSDI) adapter and battery off one end of the camera and used a prime lens on the other end; it would have been just as nicely balanced, but I chose not to. A heavy camera clearly has a greater mass and therefore a greater inertia so the camera simply does not want to change direction if it can help it. The result was that under the initial acceleration the camera wanted to tilt to the right; we were traveling right to left, but experience had taught me to expect this, so I had my right hand on the top handle to correct this yaw to the right. Once we were under way the inertia of the camera smoothed out virtually all the bumps in the road and we had as smooth a tracking shot as I could have wished for with a much more sophisticated tracking vehicle.

The second tracking shot with the hero running after the camera I approached in a different way. Still a great believer in tracking with as heavy a camera as is practicable, I got the Director to fold down the back seat of his Peugeot 306 and took a long hard stare at the available space. To everyone's amazement, including my own, we got the camera, again rigged with the 6–27 mm zoom lens, HDSDI adapter and battery, into the back of the car mounted on our baby legs and metal spreader. Again, I was banking on the mass of the camera smoothing things out and it did, quite wonderfully. Having got the camera in, the biggest problem was getting me and my focus puller in as well; it was a good job we had become friends by then as it was a very tight fit.

28.4 Interior Lighting

There is one scene in *Birthdays* where our hero and his best friend have a drink in a bar. It is, supposedly, lit by tungsten light and has a soft, intimate atmosphere. Normally in these circumstances I would reach for my filter box and add a little diffusion, but you might remember I had forsworn such tricks on this shoot. I also wanted to warm up the scene a little. Basically the two friends end up having an argument so I wanted this to happen in a very attractive environment, thus heightening the conflict between place and dialog.

The warmth I achieved with two crossed key lights from each end of the room; they were 2 K blonds and I bounced them both off folding Lastolite reflectors. I am a great fan of Lastolites, particularly on a heavy schedule; they are quick to rig if you use their proprietary universal support brackets, are not expensive and give a wonderful light. They come in a variety of colors but on this occasion I stuck to gold.

The cross keys worked to give an effect I use often; the key for one of the protagonists provided the backlight for the other, in both directions. The only fill I used was a Mizar bounced off 2-foot square of polystyrene board immediately in front of the two shot. The lighting plot can be seen in Figure 28.2 and a still from the master HD tape of this scene is shown in Figure 28.3.

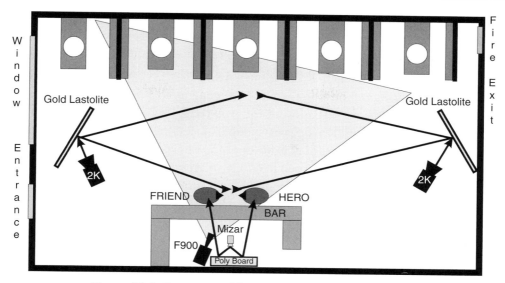

Figure 28.2: Banquets with practical hanging lamps over

Figure 28.3: The bar scene from *Birthdays*

28.5 Adding Gain

Appropriate though this looked, I still missed some diffusion in front of the lens. I had been experimenting to try to grasp what effect on the image quality adding gain to the image might have, expecting it to be detrimental; I confess I was quite surprised. On a low-key scene, particularly a warm low-key scene, it did not appear to reduce the apparent picture quality by any discernible amount but added a certain texture. I know video engineers will tell me that what I have really added is picture noise – I accept this, but it does not look like any video noise I have ever experienced before. It looks remarkably similar to moving from a modern high-quality film stock of around 200 ASA to an equally high-quality one of around 500 ASA. These days you will not really notice added grain but there will be a change in texture.

Had I been shooting *Birthdays* on film I would have gone up to a higher film speed for the bar scene; I did not need the added exposure and would have added ND filters to counter this just as I did with the HD camera. I would have done it solely to get a texture to the image more appropriate to the scene. In adding 6 dB (one stop of exposure) to the bar scene I put the effective ASA rating of the HD camera up to 640 ASA, very close to the 500 ASA film stock I would have chosen if shooting on 35 mm, and I got a surprisingly similar, apparent, effect. I have now seen this scene written out to 35 mm film and shown on a large screen and am still very impressed with the result, and will most certainly be using this trick again.

28.6 Hand Holding

In the flat where the two main characters live they have a fairly violent argument. Chris, my Director, wanted this to be a hand-held scene because the camera could then get involved, and involve the audience, in the physicality of the scene. I liked this approach but the downside for me was that I was operating the camera! Chris felt that several zoom adjustments were essential during the scene and the Panavised Sony 900f with a Panavision Digital Primo 4 1/2:1 zoom on board is a heavy camera. I asked my crew to put the big Anton Bauer battery on the back of the camera as I knew that this would make it much better balanced, but that put the weight up to the same as a British Army Infantryman's back pack, around 60 pounds, and the army does not, of course, have to carry that load on one shoulder and hold it steady! But I did have some tricks up my sleeve, as you can see in Figure 28.4. The "bull's horns", which

Figure 28.4: PW hand holding the Panavised Sony 900f

allow you to take control of the camera with handles down in a convenient and comfortable position, are an absolute boon in these circumstances. Having made the decision to use them I had, of course, no hands left to control the lens or camera, so as you can see in the illustration my First Assistant Cameraman (AC1), Alexander Golding, has control of the zoom. At this point I think it is right to point out that when hand holding a heavy camera it is absolutely essential that you have an assistant or grip to put the camera on your shoulder when the First Assistant Director says "Stand by" and take it off again the moment "Cut" is called. You get far more tired lifting the camera and putting it down than operating the shots. Hence it is simply good crew discipline and much to the Director's advantage to have a less tired operator.

One thing you have to get used to when hand holding a heavy camera is the sheer mass of the thing. It is not difficult to start a pan but when you want to come to rest on a shot you have to start decelerating surprisingly early or you will overshoot the desired composition.

28.7 Editing *Birthdays*

Chris's company, Stage 2 Screen, had recently purchased a Targa 3000 off-line editing suite, which was capable of handling images in full HD format, so at the end of shooting Panavision supplied him with a Sony HDW F500 VTR for an afternoon and he played all the material directly into the editing server. Initially there were some issues with producing Edit Decision Lists (EDLs) as we had shot at 24P and the Targa was working at 25 frames per second (fps), but these were quickly overcome. As this was Chris's first film on HD he was determined to go down the 24P route and make no compromises; it was a brave decision as it was still quite early days for HD, but we both learnt so much on *Birthdays* that it has stood us in good stead on later projects.

28.8 Viewings

I have now seen *Birthdays* on a 24-inch monitor, projected digitally and projected from a 35 mm print. I have to say I am very happy with the look of the pictures in all three presentation media. It seems that the pictures adapt themselves in some subtle way to each type of screen. What we have learnt is that for a top-of-the-range digital projector a tape graded on a well-set-up 24-inch monitor looks perfect. If, on the other hand, the digital projector is less than top of the range and will therefore not have as full a tonal range, making a tape copy with deeper blacks will improve the screen image immeasurably. Peter Swarbrick was the first to demonstrate this to me when we went to show another HD movie at the National Film Theater in London. We were disappointed in the blacks even after carefully setting up the projector when Peter made the blacks deeper simply with a control in the VTR. I therefore recommend you make two copies of your product if it is to be shown digitally, each to give the best picture depending on the grade of the projector. Do label them very carefully though, for if you get the wrong one on the wrong projector you will be very disappointed with the result.

CHAPTER 29

King Lear

29.1 The Project

When I was asked if I would like to come on board as Director of Photography (DP) for *King Lear*, the answer was, of course, "yes". I had worked on two previous productions with the same Producers, Richard Price and Chris Hunt of The Performance Company, and with the same directors Trevor Nunn and, again, Chris Hunt. The earlier productions were *Oklahoma!* and *The Merchant of Venice*, and I had enjoyed them both tremendously. We had shot *Oklahoma!* on 35 mm film and *The Merchant of Venice* on Digi Beta, but right from its initial conception *King Lear* was destined for High Definition (HD), which was very much to my taste.

The idea was to take the stage production, which had toured the world, and add a considerable amount of extra set onto the stage set. In the theater there was never a heath or battlefield, sets on which some 40 percent of the action takes place, and these would be created, albeit in a theatrical way, at one end of the stage at Pinewood Studios in Buckinghamshire in the UK.

In the theater the play lasted 3 hours and we were assured that at least half an hour would be cut, something all of us who had worked on this kind of performance program doubted would actually happen; we were not being the least bit cynical – when you think about it the actors had performed the piece 130 times already and the chances of them remembering the cuts after only 4 days of rehearsal for the filming were, quite understandably, slim. While on the subject of actors, one of the main reasons for loving this kind of project is the sheer joy of photographing such talent and experience, and as this cast was headed up by Sir Ian McKellen that joy was clearly going to be immense. The rest of the cast were equally good and I got particular pleasure from photographing Lear's three daughters.

29.2 The Schedule

At the outset the schedule looked very tight; it was, but we made it! We had roughly 12 days of serious preparation. This broke down into a week of thinking and designing basic lighting rigs, then 3 days of lighting rigging, after which the studio floor would be given over to the Design department to build the set while we concentrated on cabling the lights we had rigged and programming the dimmer board so that we had complete control over all the lamps once filming started. My initial order was for 144 lamps, so we had our work cut out.

The shooting schedule was for two 6-day weeks, each day consisting of 10 hours on camera. Tight, as I say, but with four cameras all manned by experienced crews and actors who never forgot a line, or a move, it seemed possible and so it proved. Our record was 27 minutes of screen time in one day, twice what I had ever achieved before! That was only made attainable by everybody's superb work and planning, and because that day's script contained two soliloquies that enabled word-perfect actors to give us 16 of those screen minutes in only two takes each. The two takes were not needed by the actors but enabled the directors to get more than 16 shots from those two takes.

29.3 Preparation

On shoots of this kind I always try to walk on set the first morning of the lighting rig with accurately drawn plots of where I want the majority of the lights, and *King Lear* was no exception. The first thing I need is a copy of the designer's floor plan and our Production Designer, Eric Walmeley, kindly supplied me with a full size plan and an A3 reduction. I scanned the A3 version into my laptop using my flat-bed scanner in two halves, for it only handles A4, and then stitched the two halves together in my favorite drawing program, Corel Draw (see Figure 29.1).

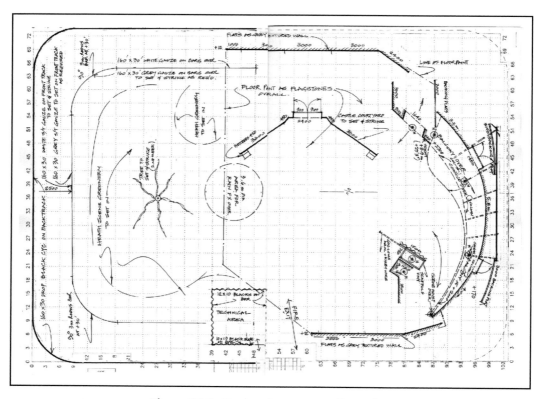

Figure 29.1: Design department floor plan

Because of the way my Gaffer, Garry Willis, had planned to rig the set I then drew my lighting rigs on top of the set plan, one drawing for each kind of lamp I intended to use. Before you look at the lighting plots, please remember that rarely were more that 25 percent of the lights going to be burning; I had to have enough lamps, in roughly the right places, for over 20 scenes.

The basic lighting scheme was to key almost everything from three-quarter back lights and have soft fill available from the sides and the front of the sets. I also needed a high degree of control over the color of the lighting as the script, after an initial procession, starts in the King's library where all is well until his youngest daughter, Cordelia, gives the King an answer he misunderstands and seriously does not like – the plot goes downhill from there. I therefore felt that it was important that just the very beginning of the play should have rich, well-saturated colors and as things, and the King's mind, deteriorate, the character of the lighting and its color would become less attractive and even at times threatening, thus hopefully echoing the course of the action and the dialog.

The lighting scheme of keying from behind and soft lighting most other places not only suited the script but enabled me to call for a Super Techno 50 camera crane plus a Jimmy jib and these, together with two static cameras on tripods fitted with rolling spiders, provided the four camera platforms. It was therefore essential to provide lighting that would not give shadows from the two camera cranes as well as being able to light the set dramatically. There was an added bonus in this idea for when our sound recordist, a little hopefully, asked if there was any chance of being able to use a couple of Fisher booms I was able to assure him that that would be no problem, for if I could keep my camera cranes from casting shadows in shot then his booms should not be a problem.

The first lighting plot I drew was for the 5-kW lamps; this can be seen in Figure 29.2. Please note that in none of the plots are the lamps to scale; they are merely drawn for easy reference by the rigging sparks. As you can see, there are some good strong backlights in position, especially down the left of the drawing, which is where our heath was to be built. In the center of the plot I hung two 12-foot (4-meter) square Lastolight reflectors on frames. I had had these made for *Oklahoma!* and found them very effective. The Lastolite facing the castle set was gold side to the set and the reflector for the heath had its white side to the set. Into each of these I pointed nine 5-kW lamps. The trick here was that we had steel blue filter on three of the lamps, straw plus Quarter magenta on another three and three lamps were naked. By using this configuration we were able to mix the three colors to give a nearly infinite number of tones. Furthermore, the lamps on the right of the reflector were bouncing off it and the light headed off in the opposite direction. By bringing up different lamps we were then able to push soft and attractive light of an appropriate color into quite discrete sections of the set. It by no means gave an overall soft fill when used in this way and never flattened the image.

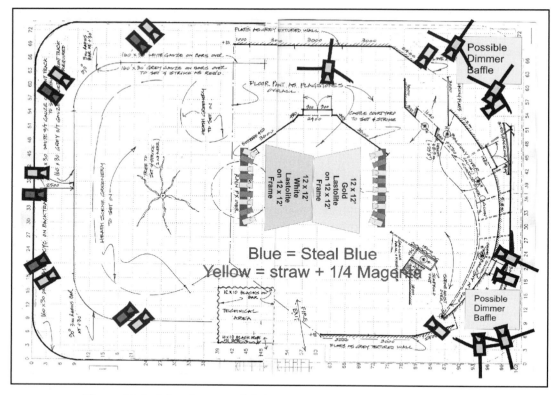

Figure 29.2: 5 kW lamps – lighting rig. *King Lear* **– Pinewood Studios**

If you look at Figure 29.3 you can see the rig for my 2-kW lamps. Eight of these were rigged with Chimeras so I had the option of bringing in a discrete soft light from almost anywhere around the set. It may look like they would flatten everything but remember that we rarely had more than two on at any time so this provided quite discrete lighting, which I often used as local key lights for the more low-key scenes. As these lamps were not too high and on hoists it took hardly any time to clip colored gels onto the front of the diffusers when needed. When we moved on to the heath scenes we moved this rig to face in the opposite direction. This was easily accomplished as we had arranged for the supports on each pair of lamps to be on independent rollers from the roof, so we knew that we could roll them from one end of the studio to the other in just a few minutes.

Figure 29.4 shows the rig for most of the 88 Par cans I had ordered. Par cans are often thought of as a crude lamp but, handled carefully, they need not produce crude light and they are very cheap. Again, we put various colored gels on them and as they were closely grouped we could, be simply adjusting the dimmers, provide a wide variety of mixed colors. As we had so many and they give a fairly narrow beam with suitable lamps in them, they were often used to give a discrete key light on a single actor. The narrow beams of light had the added advantage

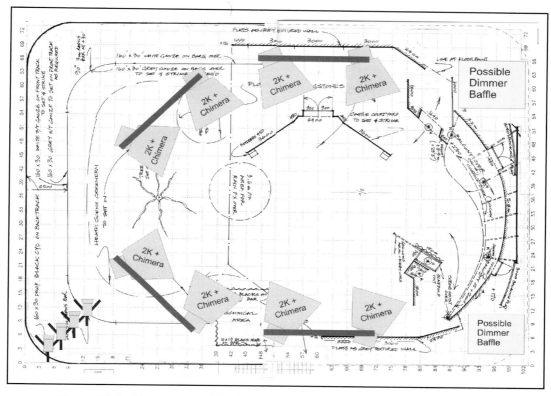

Figure 29.3: 2 kW lamps – lighting rig – castle. *King Lear* – **Pinewood Studios**

that they rarely produced shadows from camera or sound booms. Five Par cans were also hidden on the floor of the balcony of the castle set to give up-lighting between the columns.

The last rig to go in used the nine Source 4 projector lamps I had ordered, as shown in Figure 29.5. Five of these, the ones pointing to the left, were used to throw clouds onto the gauze background that surrounded the heath. By varying the position of the cloud projected by each lamp and altering the focus it was possible to ensure that no two scenes in 4 days of shooting ever had the same sky, a great advantage and quick to achieve. The four to the right were intended to light the corpses in the last scene but we later abandoned this idea.

29.4 Rigging and Equipment

Although we were given 3 days to rig the lamps, the Design department were under such pressure to get so much into the studio in so short a time we agreed that if there was any way, we would try and finish early. In the planning week I was sceptical that we could complete on time let alone early, but during this week we had a bit of luck. The original plan was to use chain hoists to hang trussing from the studio roof. The stage we were using at Pinewood is a multipurpose stage and is intended for use as both a film studio and a television studio;

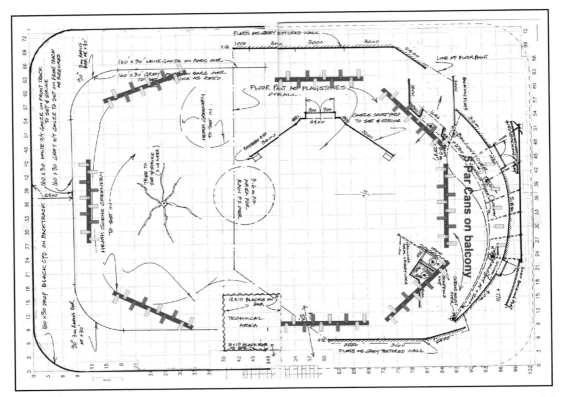

Figure 29.4: 1 kW Par can rig – all on 20 lightweight trusses – Yellow add straw gel – Blue add Steel blue. *King Lear* – Pinewood Studios

it had been assumed by us all that using the monopost lamp suspension system that had been installed tor television lighting would prove too expensive. When the lighting supply company saw the size of the lighting order they suggested that we move to using the monopoles and proved that it would not only save the cost of the trusses, but would save many man days of riggers. Thus we swapped to the monopoles, which made our rigging much easier, cost considerably less, meant the lights went in more quickly and allowed us to make changes to lamp positions in so little time we rarely held up the production for more than a few minutes. This all gave me a huge advantage as I had assumed that with trussing I would not be able to move lights other than overnight, but now I had a flexibility I had not previously expected. It also meant we finished our primary rig half a day early and were able to hand over the studio to a very grateful Design department.

Andy Picheta, our Line Producer, and I have worked together on quite a few projects and I have come to trust his judgement on more artistic matters than one would normally expect from a Line Producer. The opening of Lear was, in all our minds, some sort of procession where Lear's family and court come to venerate him and we the audience are introduced,

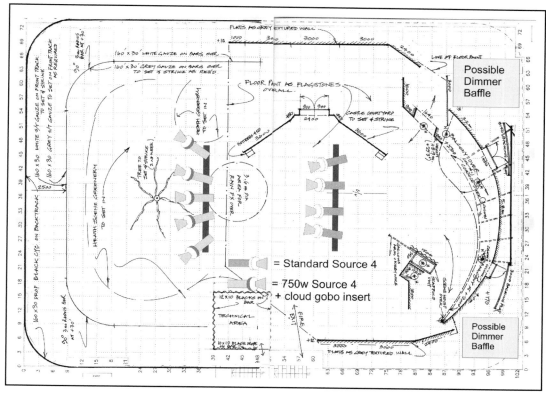

Figure 29.5: Source 4s – lighting rig. *King Lear* **– Pinewood Studios**

visually, to the main cast. This scene was also going to have all the main titles superimposed over it, so it was crucial that it looked stunning so that we did not lose the audience. Andy and I were banging our heads together over this scene when I think it was he who said "Can't you just put some shafts of light in, a bit like early morning sunlight from high windows in, say, Westminster Abbey?" "Yes, Andy, I can!" So we temporarily borrowed three of the Par 4 s from the other end of the set and rigged them as an experiment, dodging between set rigger and dressers all the while. The effect looked very good but not quite dramatic enough, so Andy allowed me to hire three big projection spotlights. These luminars come from a more theatrical background so have a variety of masks and shutters in them, and we were able to shape each beam with three straight sides and a curved top, giving very much the shape you might get from an old stone window frame. In Figure 29.6 you can see Andy and me checking the effect; we were very pleased with it. I gave Andy a copy of this picture and his reaction was "I paid for those lights and you are standing in them!" – fair enough!

In Figure 29.7 you can see my Gaffer, Garry Willis, sitting in for the King so that I can look at the effect of the three-quarter 5-kW backlight coming from the right of the set. The Best Boy, Ricky Jones, is on the right with one of the lighting adjustment poles ready to trim the

Figure 29.6: PW, left, and Andy Picheta, Line Producer, checking the lighting for Scene 1

effect. By this time in the rigging process most of the set was up and final decoration was in progress. When they saw this picture the crew immediately entitled it "Lear has the decorators in". You can clearly see at the top of the picture the poles with the Par cans on them, as well as one of the few floor-standing lamps coming through the door on the right of the set.

Due to availability of equipment one camera was going to arrive at the last minute, so towards the end of the 2-week rigging period I set up the other three cameras in a variety of shot sizes so that we could finesse the lighting for as many scenes as possible before we had the actors.

Figure 29.7: "Lear has the decorators in!" Gaffer Garry Willis sitting in for the King

Figure 29.8 shows the cameras on set as we do our best to set the Par cans for over 20 scenes. I have always found that by this time in the rigging process it is much more productive to light to the monitors, once the cameras are up, as with HD, a good monitor is, after all, the finished product.

29.5 Camera Equipment

You may have noticed my slight partiality for Panavision equipment but on this shoot there were few alternatives; anyway, I was being asked to produce the highest quality image the budget would allow and to do that I wanted the finest lenses I could lay my hands on and, if at all possible, they should be better than normal broadcast lenses. Zeiss lenses were certainly an option quality-wise but they do not produce the range of zoom that we were certainly going to need on a schedule this tight. Therefore it had to be Panavision Digital Primo Zooms. Going to film-style lenses, and some long ones at that, also meant we had to budget for first-class focus pullers in order to pull off the film look with the associated soft background for which we were looking.

My basic equipment list looked something like this:

- 4 × Sony 750 cameras with associated matte boxes and follow focus controls;
- 2 × 6–27 mm Panavision Digital Primo Zooms;

Figure 29.8: Finalizing the lighting on the morning of day 3 of the rig

- 2 × 25–112 mm Panavision Digital Primo Zooms;
- 1 × 9:1 Panavision Digital Primo Zoom;
- 1 × Super Techno crane;
- 1 × Jimmy jib;
- 1 × 24-inch cathode ray tube (CRT) Grade 1 monitor;
- 4 × 9-inch CRT monitors;
- 4 × 14-inch TFT monitors.

And that's just the basic bits!

29.6 The Shoot

As I have already said, it was agreed by all that the opening was crucial, so we went to some effort to ensure this. In Figure 29.9 you can see the effect of my three projection spotlights, which are lighting some of the courtiers awaiting the arrival of the King and his family. There was no other lighting for this scene, for with the help of a little smoke to diffuse the light and the light bouncing back from the floor, I had all the lighting I needed and this produced a most dramatic effect. I had also decided that if small areas of the actors burnt out as they passed directly through the spots this was fine, it added to the drama and I would happily allow this on film, so why not on HD?

Figure 29.9: Courtiers awaiting the entrance of the King

I did not add any more light throughout this scene and it worked, to my mind, very well. In Color plate 12 you can see the first entry of King Lear with his daughter, Cordelia, in the foreground. My decision to shoot most of the scenes at T 2.8 was a good one and you can see that the King is nicely soft; he will, of course, get sharper as he approaches his daughter. Remember part of the plot is about his misunderstanding of this daughter so she is, in effect and at this point, seeing her future before her.

By careful placement of the actors in the light available, something they were more than willing to cooperate with, some wonderful moments were photographed, as you can see in Color plate 13, where Goneril is awaiting the arrival of her father.

After this very dramatic opening all the royal family and their courtiers move to the King's library, where he intends to divide his kingdom among his three daughters. I wanted this to be a rich and slightly saturated scene in the hope that those in the audience not wholly familiar with Shakespeare's plot might just be fooled into thinking that all was well and therefore be more intrigued and surprised by how quickly the fate of all the characters goes downhill. I therefore gave Lear the traditional rich lighting with a three-quarter backlight, as you can see in Color plate 14.

Things are going severely awry by the time the plot gets to Color plate 15, where Lear's daughter, Regan, on the left of shot, and her husband on the right contrive to remove the eyes from one of Lear's most loyal courtiers, Gloucester, who is seen seated. This scene, as you can see, is severely backlit for effect and to keep a little off the light off the goriness of the prosthetics of the eye being gouged. In the movie it is a little more contrasty and quite blue as it happens at night.

As we near the end of the play renegade soldiers hang Lear's Fool, played by Sylvester McCoy. I understand that the fool has never actually been hanged in any other production up to this one, but the Director, Sir Trevor Nunn, decided that as very near the end of the play Lear has the line "And my Fool is hanged!" there was good reason to graphically show the act – hence you can see in Figure 29.10 Assistant Director Gemma Fairlie supervising the rehearsal of the hanging. Again, in the movie this is a heavily backlit and rather chilly scene.

29.7 Practical Matters

Although we had a reasonably big stage it always seemed very full. Every space was used. In Color plate 16 you can see a shot from above the set in action, in this instance a courtyard scene built to one side of the original castle set. On the extreme left you can see one of the static cameras and on the right its complementary static so that the directors can get matching close-ups. Yes, close-ups! This meant that the focus pullers really had to have their wits about them for, as you can imagine, they were right out at the longest focal length their zooms were capable of. Although I wanted to shoot most of the film at an aperture of T 2.8 I had, for various reasons, achieved this stop with a neutral density (ND) 0.3 filter on all the cameras. One reason for this was that I wanted good coverage from my lamps and lamps with too small a lens don't give you this so, by getting the coverage with bigger lamps, I was actually getting better lighting and was saving the production money, as two smaller lamps usually cost more than one larger lamp. This situation allowed me to pull the ND 0.3 on the static cameras when the focus pullers' job became nearly impossible and allow them a stop of T 4.

Figure 29.10: Sylvester McCoy as the Fool preparing to be hanged, with Gemma Fairlie, Assistant Director, supervising

You can also see in Color plate 16 how cluttered the set can get for even a relatively simple scene: two static cameras on each side, a Super Techno crane in the middle, a Jimmy jib over on the left of the picture and two Fisher sound booms tucked in between them all. Quite a party!

29.8 Monitoring, etc

To one side of the stage, the side that was never going to have a set built in front of it, we set up the technical control desk, as you can see in Color plate 17. On the very far right, almost out of shot, is a smaller desk with the lighting control board and its computer display. Central to the picture is my 24-inch Grade 1 monitor, which can be switched to any of the four cameras' outputs that are monitored by the four 9-inch screens, two to each side of the Grade 1. Just to the left of the desk you can see my laptop, on which I kept the relevant lighting plot for the scene we were shooting. Just to the right of that there is a small box that allows us to choose which camera will be fed by the router to the 24-inch monitor. We positioned an 8 feet × 4 feet sheet of black painted polystyrene above the desk to keep stray light off the screens and were able to set it at such a height that just by standing up we could see the set quite clearly.

Right in the middle of the studio and facing the set was the Director's desk, as you can see in Color plate 18. For the first 8 days of shooting it faced the castle set, but on the eighth night all the camera trainees had to stay late to turn it through 180 degrees so that the Directors could now face the heath. They accomplished this with amazing good humor.

Working from left to right across Color plate 18, in the bottom left-hand corner you can see a small monitor that is fed by a four-way splitter so that it sees all four cameras' outputs. This was to provide image playback to the Directors and the Script Supervisor when required. The playback operator can be seen bottom right and, very important, just to the right of the four-way split screen are the playback notes, which have to be very accurate so that the Directors can call up any scene no matter how long ago it was shot.

Central in the picture is the Script Supervisor, Tricia Canavan, whose job it is to make sure we are shooting the script as written and rehearsed, where we are in the script and where we have come from. Not an easy task with a 3-hour play when anyone, including myself, may suddenly get lost or forget the time of day of a certain scene and we only have the Script Supervisor to go to. In front of her and the Director to her right are four 14-inch TFT flat screens, each with an individual output from one of the cameras. On the right just in front of Trevor Nunn is a 36-inch monitor for director's playback from the DVCAM playback tapes.

CHAPTER 30

The Optician

30.1 How It Came About

I first met the Director of *The Optician*, Jane McGee, when we were both teaching at the New York Film Academy in London, she teaching Direction and myself Advanced Cinematography. Our first outing together was on a practical exercise and we immediately hit it off. I liked her and her work so much I offered to shoot a short for her if she ever had a script. It took a couple of years but eventually she sent me *The Optician*, which she had written – I loved it immediately!

Fortunately it was scheduled for a winter shoot, always a good thing if one is trying to shoot something on a limited budget as technicians are usually available and equipment can be hired at good discounts. I was able to pull together an ideal young crew and Panavision London supplied me with a Sony 750P and a couple of their superb zoom lenses.

We had recced (scouted) all the locations, including an optician's shop in north London, and Jane had got two terrific actors on board, Chris Barrie and Carolyn Tomkinson, when 3 days before the first day of shooting disaster struck – we lost the main location. I decided to see what I could do before she pulled the shoot so, on the off chance, asked the opticians I had been using for over 15 years, Tolley and Partners; they were truly magnificent and immediately agreed to let us have the shop for the weekend. Not only that, when Jane and her Producer, Christopher Billows, went to give J.R., my contact there, the fee his reaction was "I think you need that more than me, just invite me to the premiere." Thank you, J.R.

30.2 The Shoot

We had both day and night scenes inside and immediately outside the optician's shop, exteriors outside together with night shoots in a street elsewhere in London and a short scene in a cinema, both in the foyer and the theater itself. We accomplished this in two long days and an afternoon and half the following night. Not bad for a movie that lasted 14 3/4 minutes.

I was at the time very familiar with the Sony 750P and knew how wonderfully it would eat into the shadows at night, especially with the Panavision lens on the front. Also, I knew we had a good focus puller, Romain Choay, and therefore I could safely use a maximum aperture of T 2.8 on all the interiors and night shots. In fact, I often shot a little wider open and for the night exteriors outside the shop, was at T 2. Depth of field, i.e. keeping the backgrounds soft, was an issue in pre-production and I was not sure I had convinced Jane and the team all would be well. Once we started shooting I was able to prove on the monitor that I and Romain could pull off more than they expected.

If you look at Color plate 19 you can see a deep two shot where both actors are perfectly sharp; this is as it should be, for it is an early scene in the movie and we are still introducing the actors to the audience and want them to be able to recognize them clearly in later scenes. If you now look at Color plate 20, where we are introducing the optician as a character, his image in the mirror, center screen, is perfectly sharp but the back of his head on the left and the display of spectacles on the right are delightfully soft – just as we would hope for if I had shot in 35 mm.

Later in the plot the optician discovers he has acquired a pair of magical glasses that allow him to see 10 seconds into the future when he wears them. If you look at Color plate 21 you will see Chris Barrie in medium close-up beautifully isolated against a soft background. If you are thinking we were able to use particularly long lenses to achieve this you could not be more wrong; the shop simply was not big enough to do this. It is worth noting at this point that all the pictures used to illustrate *The Optician* are actual screen grabs from the master HDCAM tape. Again, when the optician's proposal for a night out with his assistant is finally accepted, but only due to the intervention of the magic glasses, we go back to another shot of him against the shop's window, in daylight (see Color plate 22), and again we see a soft background and a fine demonstration of how well good High Definition (HD) cameras can hold a bright exterior, so long as you get the exposure right. I was only shooting at around T 4 as I simply did not have a big enough lighting budget to achieve a smaller stop, so I had to rely on the camera's 11-stop tonal range.

The last illustration (Color plate 23) shows a night exterior of the optician having been knocked down in the street. The car headlight playing from the bottom of the frame is, in fact, a couple of Arri 650 W lamps.

The lighting kit was limited so I opted for a Dedo kit, some small Arri tungsten lamps and a couple of Kinoflow™ lamps. Night exteriors outside the opticians was just a 200-W HMI with a half CTO on it to lift the actors' faces and the night street in the last scene was the street lighting augmented by four Arri 650s, all as backlights, plus two 2-foot Kinoflow™ lamps hidden near the entrance to the heroine's flat as a soft cross key.

I believe the secret of pulling off a movie with such a short schedule, and with such a small budget, is to keep the lighting really simple and put what little time you have into placing a few lamps in exactly the right place. I was fortunate that I knew the location well and therefore needed little preparation time. The shop was predominantly lit by miniature halogen lights buried in the ceiling and the display fitments; the shop designer had done a good job so the shop looks really attractive. To obtain the look we had all decided was desirable it was necessary to work most of the time at an aperture of no greater than T 2.8, so we spent more time taking practical bulbs out of their sockets where they overexposed than adding light from our photographic lamps. This was quite a revelation to my young Gaffer. In the UK the Gaffer and the sparks do all the lighting and the grips are only concerned with anything that supports the camera, unlike in the USA, where the grips do most of the lighting with the sparks only being concerned with electricity and its supply. Well, that's the simplistic view!

30.3 How Did It Come Out?

When I saw the fine cut I was delighted; none of the compromises that are inevitable on a shoot with so little time available showed at all and the picture quality was very pleasing. Once the picture was finished Jane and Christopher hired the Princess Anne Theater at BAFTA (see my description of that theater in Chapter 5) for an invited audience. It was great that on the huge screen at BAFTA it looked like a real movie and I don't think anyone came out of that cinema thinking about what format we had shot it on. It truly looked the business in every department.

30.4 Conclusions

If you have the right team shooting on an HD camera, having three 2/3-inch chips does not compromise the images – it can still look like a real movie. *But* you have to have the right people who understand the equipment.

If you have a terrific script, the right personalities on board and you shoot in the winter months when people and equipment are plentiful you can pull together a great team at not too high a cost.

If you think your compromises will show they probably will, but if you aim high there is no reason why you can't produce a movie that will stand up as a real film. But you have to be well prepared and be quick on the shoot, otherwise you won't finish the movie before the money runs out.

All the above is only true if you have a really good script – it all starts there.

Part 6
Cameras

CHAPTER 31

Cameras in General

Since Sony introduced their HDW F900 camera and its HDCAM recording format in the year 2000 much has changed, but much has stayed the same. The HDCAM recording format is still very much favored as an international exchange format, particularly in the television arena, and Sony have introduced HDCAM-SR as a format capable of supporting an even higher image quality and, at the top end, this has become the preferred exchange format. So, in a sense, what we record our pictures on, particularly when those pictures enter post-production, has become nearly as important as the camera we use.

The High Definition (HD) ground was broken with cameras, in the main, using three 2/3-inch chips with each chip dedicated to a single color, Red, Green or Blue, and each chip was sent only the part of the image that contained that color. This was achieved by using three bits of glass, two in the form roughly of a prism, to separate the colors, for this was, and is in this configuration, essential because the pixels on each chip are only sensitive to brightness, not color. To date no one has devised a pixel that, independently, can discern color. I have to wonder at the fact that the human eye can do this using the cones in the retina, but even in this wondrous device, the human eye, brightness is independently assessed by the rods.

In the beginning most of these three-chip cameras actually had, and many still have, pixels on each chip that conformed to the 1920 pixel requirement horizontally by the 1080 requirement vertically. This was no accident for, as you can see in other parts of this book, this horizontal and vertical resolution, if handled carefully, can more than fulfill the current resolution expected by an audience in even the largest of cinemas.

For a few years the above more than sufficed but expectations and ambitions moved on. The 1920 × 1080 pixel array, even utilizing three 2/3-inch chips, can still hold its own but human nature isn't like that. A favorite author of mine, Bruce Chatwin, suggested that the natural state of man (ladies forgive the word, it is generic, and his) is movement. I think he may have been right. A picture generated by a camera with 1920 × 1080 pixels on each of three 2/3-inch chips is good, very good. But human kind, I suggest, as did Mr Chatwin, does not like standing still and therefore, in recent years, cameras capable of even greater image quality have arrived on the scene.

Those cameras that are capable of much greater image quality than above have, at the time of writing, October 2008, come in a number of configurations. Most of those looking for greater resolution have abandoned the beam splitter and gone for a single chip with each pixel filtered, in some way, individually. Some of these cameras try to cram even more pixels on the chip, which with current technology tends to require a rather larger chip. Others, often using similar but larger chips, utilize subpixels so that each of the resultant 1920 × 1080 pixels recorded are formed from even smaller pixels that, hopefully, leads to an apparent increase in resolution and, perhaps, a better encoding of color information. Some cameras hold onto their greater pixel count and, using advanced recording techniques, not usually tape, then offer the prospect of post-production in the higher resolution and, only when the film is completely finished, reduce this to the international standard of 1920 × 1080. If one is to try to post-produce in the higher bit-rate format, then this requires considerable data storage capabilities that, again at the time of writing, are rapidly becoming much easier to obtain at a reasonable cost.

One of the main advantages of single-chip technology is that, more often than not, it allows the camera to photograph through conventional and existing lenses that were originally designed for 35 mm motion picture film cameras, thus further enhancing HD's ability to emulate the picture expected by the audience in a conventional cinema.

31.1 The Choice of Cameras

When I wrote the first edition of this book there were very few cameras capable of 1080P and, perhaps, one serious contender that used the 720P configuration. There are now a plethora of cameras to choose from and also a considerable number of recording formats, far too many to include here, so I have had to make some difficult decisions. As you will have noted from my comments in Chapter 12, as a Director of Photography (DP) my own decision as to what cameras to shoot with comes down fairly heavily on the side of a 1920 × 1080 progressive shooting format, or better. I have therefore decided just to include, with one exception, only cameras that meet this specification, the exception being the Panasonic Varicam because of its variable frame rate capabilities, which it offers at a reasonable cost. This decision is with some regret, for there are some very interesting cameras that use, to my mind, a lesser format. However, unless there were very compelling reasons I would have to advise my Director or Producer as to my preference. I would be the first to admit that this decision is very much driven by the kind of work I do, which I guess makes me a lucky man.

31.2 In This Edition

This camera section has been considerably revised, with seven new cameras being added, one dropped and several updated to new models. HD cinematography has moved on apace since I last reviewed the more popular cameras, and that was only 2 years ago!

31.3 My Disclaimer!

What follows is my personal opinion of each camera. You may feel I have missed out a camera you would wish to learn about and consider noteworthy; my apologies but, in the main, I have only included cameras that I either know well from personal experience or, at the very least, have handled and put through their paces for some hours.

I have tried to have all the facts checked by either the manufacturer or a major supplier. There may be some errors – I do hope not. The opinions are, of course, entirely my own.

So here goes, opinions and all . . .

CHAPTER 32

The Arriflex D-21

32.1 The Camera

The Arriflex D-21 is the new version of the well-established D-20 and remains a delightful camera that will appeal, more than most, to someone from a film background. This is especially true of the look-through, which is still based on the front end of a typical Arri film camera complete with the traditional spinning mirror reflex shutter with an electronically variable opening ranging from 11.2 to 180 degrees. The image from the lens is presented to the operator via a viewing screen, again exactly as in the Arricam 435, and utilizes the same viewfinder optics and options; of course, the image is in full color, is available even without powering the camera and shows an area larger than that being recorded.

Figure 32.1 shows the Arriflex D-21 in full shooting mode. Though the D-21 is superficially the same as the D-20 there are many significant internal changes; indeed, I gather all but one of the circuit boards have been updated and some very significant improvements to image handling and manipulation have been incorporated, as we shall see.

The second most appealing aspect of the D-21 is its build quality – it feels like an Arriflex! The D-21 completed its takeover from the older model just as I was coming to the end of writing this edition, and I spent some time with Bill Lovell at Arri Media who kindly showed me over the camera and spent considerable time updating me on the new model. As always with Arriflex, the camera was impressive and the new improvements add to the appeal and usefulness of this camera.

The basic camera weighs in at around 11 kilograms (some 23 pounds) – weight that can be reduced for use on, say, a Steadicam rig by around 8 pounds by removing the viewfinder module, which is quite unnecessary for that application. The camera runs on 24 volts and consumes some 50 watts and therefore draws about 2 amps.

Arriflex have continued with their policy of not incorporating a fan into the camera and this makes it particularly quiet. The Arriflex shutter mechanism is virtually silent and the D-21, of course, has no intermittent mechanism. The camera has a ribbed "brow" on the top of the camera housing to dissipate heat. This is solidly connected to the sensor board and analog-to-digital processors that, as in most digital cameras, disperse a great deal of waste energy in the

Figure 32.1: The Arri D-21 in full shooting mode

form of heat. As it is of generous proportions no fan is required and the camera emits a noise level below 20 dB.

The D-20 had the most simple and intuitive menu system of any High Definition (HD) camera I have so far encountered and Arriflex have made the D-21 even clearer, despite having added a few extra controls. As before it appears on the on-board camera monitor and has two presentations, standard and advanced. Standard mode contains just about everything a Director of Photography (DP) would need on a day-to-day basis. The deeper functions, of which, again, there are refreshingly few, are hidden behind a four-digit pin number settable at the customer's choice by the supplier. Thus, no one but the DP can meddle with the "dangerous" functions in the menu, a very safe procedure. After around 20 minutes playing with the single control knob on the back of the camera, which is the sole manipulator of the menu system, I believe any competent cameraperson would know all that one needs to know in order to control this camera. This is quite an achievement that I feel is the result of a historic film motion picture manufacturer approaching the problem from the same starting point that they have always used.

The D-21 has several equivalent ISO sensitivity settings selectable between 100 and 800 ASA when outputting in the "Linear" mode. It can also output in the Logarithmic mode, preferred by some for it does achieve better shadow detail or, at least, shadow detail more recognizable as a film-like image. In this Log mode the camera can output images as "C" as in Cineon or "F" as in the Film stream (much like the Thomson Viper camera, but without the green cast). In Log mode the output is usually a 4:4:4 RGB full bandwidth image with an equivalent nominal ISO sensitivity of 200.

The D-21 can also output via two BNC cables a RAW "Data Mode" signal, which is now very usable as data recording has progressed so far this is now a viable workflow on set. It can be recorded to an S.2 digital field recorder (DFR) hard-disk recorder, or to other suitable recording systems. In Data Mode the full output of the sensor with its 2880 × 2160 4 × 3 aspect ratio image is recorded, thus not wasting a single pixel on the chip. This might be very significant as, unlike most HD cameras, the Arriflex D-21 has exactly the same size sensor as the film image used for anamorphic cinematography. This means that all anamorphic lenses originally designed for 35 mm film productions can be used on this camera. There is no discernible pixel fall-off at the extremes of the image so there should be no vignetting of the image.

In Data Mode the output of each pixel is recorded as a 12-bit value, with each pixel assigned an R, G or B signature. Only a white balance is applied to this output, which has the advantage that it removes the green cast associated with Bayer patterning without creating problems in the post-production arena.

32.2 Significant Improvements Over the D-20

Arriflex have made improvements to the way the D-21 reduces picture noise. Complementary metal-oxide semiconductor (CMOS) chips, as used in the D-21, have a tendency to be noisier in the shadows than charge-coupled device (CCD) chips and this has been a bugbear of many cameras that use them. Arriflex have come up with a very elegant solution to this, known as correlated double sampling (CDS). During the blanking period – that is, when either the mechanical shutter is closed or the equivalent electronic blanking is utilized between frames – the D-21 looks at the noise in the blank, black, frame. This will be exactly the same noise as will be generated on the chip during the exposure, so by subtracting the signal in the blanked period from that in the picture, or shutter open, period that noise is removed from the recorded image.

They have also developed something they call Automatic Defect Pixel Correction. This, in effect, checks for errors in each and every pixel in the image every time the picture is blanked.

This is the same as carrying out an extended black balance on, say, a Sony camera, but instead of the crew having to do this if they suspect a defective pixel it is automatically checked for every frame exposed.

The D-21 will run at 1–60 frames per second (fps) in HD 16 × 9 mode, 1–30 fps in RAW Data 16 × 9 mode and 1–25 fps in RAW Data 4 × 3 mode. All speeds can be crystal controlled with 0.001 fps precision.

32.3 The Camera Sensor

The Arriflex D-21 still utilizes the same CMOS sensor as the D-20, having 2880 pixels horizontally by 2160 pixels vertically. These pixels are set out on a chip with an active area approximately the size of a Super 35 mm frame. Times change not at all, it seems.

In order to allow the sensor to output a Red, Green and Blue image, the CMOS chip utilizes a Bayer pattern filter. The RAW output from the chip will look a little green and, perhaps, a little lacking in contrast. Within the camera are simply accessed electronic enhancements that will both record, and display, a picture extraordinarily close to the finished product that can therefore be relied upon to judge the finished product and so enables the DP to light to that image with confidence.

When shooting in Data Mode it is possible to send the image from the camera to the recorder via a fiber-optic cable and have the recorder interpret the image and then send it back to the camera and other monitors in a way that they can interpret and that the DP can rely on to light. In effect the recorder uses look-up tables (LUTs) to convert the image into something very near the final product.

The sensor has, as the above format would suggest, a 4 × 3 aspect ratio so it has to be approached with a certain amount of understanding as to how to use it in the wisest way. If using exactly the same lenses you would use when shooting Super 35 mm you will get the same look and feel as if you had shot Super 35 mm film, depth of field and all. Equally, of course, when utilizing the Data Mode (which outputs from the complete 4 × 3 area sensor), existing PL mount anamorphic lenses will allow an optical squeeze to be applied to the image while using the full resolution of the chip for finishing in a 2.35:1, or 2.4:1, aspect ratio.

If you wish the camera to output a 16 × 9 HD compatible image then the camera will read a central slice out of the chip utilizing 2880 pixels horizontally, the full potential of the chip, by 1620 pixels vertically, thus giving a true 16 × 9 picture. Clearly this is not compatible with the HD 16 × 9 standard of 1920 pixels × 1080 pixels. No matter, for internally the camera can convert the original pixel array to the HD pixel requirements. It does this so successfully that a certain increase in apparent quality is obtained, particularly in respect of aliasing (as in the lack of it!).

I believe Arriflex are about to announce a new approach to HD anamorphic shooting that they have named the "M Scope" format after Milan Krsljanin, who developed the idea. Using two BNC cables this will deliver the whole picture but, by doubling the output to two 4:2:2 streams to an SRW-1 recorder (a system originally intended for 3D recording), will maintain a full-resolution anamorphic picture.

The way the sensor, and its electronic processing, behaves allow excellent keys to be obtained from both blue- and green-screen shooting.

32.4 Interface

At the rear of the D-21 there are a number of connectors. It is possible to have up to three output boards fitted to the camera but it is normally supplied with only two, as this has proved to be more than sufficient for most shoots. The output sockets can be seen in Figure 32.2.

Figure 32.2: The Arri D-21 showing the outputs and inputs available

With two output boards it is easy to get outputs as High Definition Serial Digital Interface (HDSDI) (4:2:2 and/or 4:4:4) or Data together with analog PAL or NTSC. If you are working with 4:4:4 HD then you will need to utilize two of the four output sockets as 4:4:4 needs two BNC cables to transfer the required amount of data in that form.

32.5 Lenses

Any lens with an Arri PL mount that will cover the image size you wish to shoot on, right up to a full Super 35 mm format, will be suitable for this camera, thus giving one the same feel to the picture as you would achieve on 35 mm film. This, of course, includes standard 35 mm anamorphic lenses; there are no other HD cameras that can do this at present.

32.6 Recorders

All HD cameras' output can be recorded on something. Most can even be recorded on something convenient. In recent times data recording has come a long way and it is now possible to record a 4:4:4 HD output onto an on-board flash drive, or FlashMag as Arri call it, as can be seen in Figure 32.3, where the camera is rigged for hand-held use. The FlashMag is a solid-state Flash RAM device capable of recording 10 minutes of screen time in 4:4:4 mode

Figure 32.3: The Arri D-21 in hand-held mode with a FlashMag attached

or 15 minutes in 4:2:2 mode. If shooting requirements demand it, the FlashMag can be a very useful device.

It is still possible to output the data as RAW or as an image to an SRW-1 recorder, as shown in Figure 32.4. The SRW-1 video tape recorder (VTR) can record the 10-bit HD signal in a 4:2:2 or a 4:4:4 format with approximately 2:1 compression, known as HQ (High Quality), when shooting at 24 fps and in this mode the tape will last for 25 minutes. It can also record in the 4:2:2 format, known as SQ (Standard Quality), with approximately 4:1 compression and then a tape lasts for 50 minutes at 24 fps.

The SRW-1 is powered by 12 volts DC and consumes around 10 amps, which means that it will run for between 2 and 2 1/2 hours on a standard 12-volt block battery. There is, of course, a mains unit available that is tolerant of fluctuating voltages so it can safely be run from the production's location generator.

If your picture needs a lot of compact camera work where a separate recorder may be a hindrance and you decide to go for FlashMags, then this simply needs a slight reorganization of the camera crew's responsibilities. The crew member who used to be known as the loader on a film shoot now becomes a downloader. FlashMags are expensive, it has to be admitted, but with a little organization the person who used to have their hands in a changing bag now needs to be transferring the FlashMag data to, probably, a Sony SRW-1 tape recorder or alternatively an uncompressed disk recorder – as onerous and important a task as being responsible for opening a film magazine with raw rushes in it. Long live the loader!

Figure 32.4: The Sony SRW-1 HDCAM-SR Recorder

CHAPTER 33

The Dalsa Origin and Evolution

33.1 The Dalsa Origin

By any standards the Dalsa Origin is an extraordinary camera. Dalsa have produced a camera with an absolutely "no compromise" approach to picture quality. It is widely accepted that a 35 mm camera negative has an inherent resolution that, in the electronic world, is regarded as 4 K resolution, which means the picture can deliver 4000 samples horizontally. This means that if you sample an image 4000 times across its width this will provide the same resolution as with a photographic image on a single frame of 35 mm film camera negative. The Origin can undoubtedly do this – but, possibly, at some inconvenience downstream in the production process. For an argument as to whether one needs this sampling rate, and when one does, see elsewhere in this book. Nevertheless, if your post-production workflow requires, or needs, a full 4 K master and that master needs to be digital and have a 4 K horizontal resolution, then the Dalsa Origin will look very attractive.

There is another point. Let us say you are working on a high-budget production and your Director or Producer thinks they are making a film that will become a classic; there may then be a strong argument to store, for prosperity, an original master copy equivalent to a 35 mm negative and in those circumstances, the Origin has a good argument in its favor – provided you can store all that data, which will become easier in time.

In essence the Origin outputs what is described as an uncompressed RAW 4 K signal equivalent to a film negative, if you like. It, like film, needs "printing" in post to realize its full potential. To try to put this in a more technical context, a 4 K RAW file from Origin is roughly 16 MB per frame, whereas the full RGB files are 48 MB per frame – clearly a huge saving in storage needs.

The sensor is slightly wider than the distance between the outside of the perforations on standard 35 mm film. This is considerably wider than the image size of a Super 35 frame and here lies the first of the Origin's quirks. While the camera is doing more than most to replicate the image quality of 35 mm camera original negative, and will have a very similar depth of field to the image, if not a fraction less, not all the available 35 mm lenses will cover a frame this big, but with careful selection many popular lens sets will.

While the Origin can give a fantastic resolution and, having seen pictures from it I can only say they are superb, to a film person's eye the camera itself is not an appealing sight. If you look at Figure 33.1 I can't help wondering if you would agree with me that it does resemble a black, shiny, desktop computer tower with a lens stuck on one corner. A three-quarter view of the camera as seen in Figure 33.2 shows it in a more flattering light, but you have to admit it's a bit of a lump.

33.1.1 *The Look-through*

The Origin, in that corner of the box with the lens, has a mechanical front strongly resembling an Arriflex film camera body. Therefore, very like the Arriflex D-21, you get an image in the viewfinder that will be very familiar if you are used to shooting with film. It is a good look-through but, as with all cameras choosing this route, operators may love it but it tells the Director of Photography (DP) nothing about the recorded image. This is not usually a problem, for most DPs working in High Definition (HD) have long ago learnt to look at a high-grade, well set-up, monitor in order to judge their work. The markings on the viewfinder viewing screen are, again, those you would expect in a 35 mm film camera – all very reassuring.

Figure 33.1: The Dalsa Origin

33.1.2 The Sensor

The scanned area is an array of 4096 × 2048 – that is, a 2:1 aspect ratio of which 4046 × 2048 are optically active, giving a picture aspect ratio of 1.98:1. This differential is because the sensor utilizes 50 optically dark columns to provide a dark reference for signal processing purposes.

The sensor also utilizes a Bayer mosaic color filter and with the Origin's dedication to the purest image possible the interpolation of the Bayer pattern is left as a post-production matter. Alternatively it can output RAW data using 16 linear bits per pixel, which can be

Figure 33.2: The Dalsa Origin

reconstructed externally. Unreconstructed Bayer pattern images are often referred to as a "digital negative", for they need processing to arrive at the desired viewable image. Again, see elsewhere in this book for an explanation of Bayer filtering.

33.1.3 Interfaces

The Origin outputs each frame as a DPX file with 16-bit linear data. If one multiplies the active pixels, 4046 × 2048, this means there are 8,286,208 pixels per frame. Given the camera works in a 16-bit environment, then the camera needs to record 132,579,328 bits of information per frame or 3,181,903,872 bits of information per second if you are shooting at 24 frames per second (fps). The data rate for the RAW 4K 16bpp at 24 fps is 420 MB/second – still pretty formidable but becoming much more manageable.

At this bit rate conventional monitors and data recorders may not be able to cope. In order to overcome this Dalsa have given the Origin a conventional computer-type TV interface on the back of the camera, which enables just about any laptop computer to become a monitor. I viewed some pictures this way when I saw the Origin in London and was very impressed with the quality. This interface is the third socket from the top in Figure 33.3.

For recording purposes an interface capable of far greater data transfer rates is needed and the Origin provides this with an elegant solution. Using a military quality four-core optical cable all the necessary data can easily be outputted. Another access point on the back of the Origin allows for this very slim optical pipe. The diameter of the "cable" is around 1/4 inch (6 mm) and is immensely strong and flexible. Interpolator boxes for this kind of data transfer are not that difficult to come by provided they feed a recorder that can cope with this data stream.

33.1.4 Conclusions on the Dalsa Origin

The Dalsa Origin is without doubt a formidable camera. Large file data storage is becoming easier and more practical almost by the month, which will make the recording and storage problems of the Origin seem almost trivial in the relatively near future.

33.2 Currently Available Recorders

As discussed above, while the Origin gives a very impressive and high-resolution picture its output, in terms of the quantity of data, does leave it with some problems finding a currently available recorder capable of doing it justice. Flash RAM drives and disk arrays will do the job but rarely have a reasonable recording time compared with a film camera and can be mighty expensive. But, as I say, data storage problems are easing in short order.

Figure 33.3: A rear view of the Dalsa Origin showing the interface options

33.3 The Codex Digital Media Recorder

When I "met" the Dalsa Origin camera in London it was linked to a laptop via the interface described above, as well as to a most extraordinary piece of equipment with which I was most impressed, the Codex Digital Media Recorder. Given that most recorders capable of dealing with very high bit rates are, at the time of writing, both expensive as an item and use very expensive data storage that rarely has a recording time much longer than a single roll of film, and costs a great deal more, the Codex, while not being that cheap, does seem to address these matters in a way I have rarely seen bettered. It is also exquisitely made and, particularly if you admire Kudelski Nagra, very elegant and appealing to the eye.

The Codex, as you can see in Figure 33.4, where it is shown in its transit housing, is a relatively compact unit given the data it can store and those data are quite astounding for an on-site recorder. At the bottom half of the Codex you can see a couple of handles. Each of

Figure 33.4: The Codex Media Recorder

these is the front of a removable disk pack and each disk pack can store 720 gigabytes (GB) of information; 360 GB packs are available. If one utilizes two disk packs, both of which are 720 GB capable, then 54 minutes of 24 fps 4 K images, uncompressed and in full 4:4:4, can be recorded. If you are working with an output conforming to the 1920 × 1080sF format but still wanting a 10-bit 4:4:4 RGB at 24 fps, then one disk pack alone will record 50 minutes of screen time.

It should be noted that the disk packs have RAID-3 protection against drive failure and can be "hot swapped", thus reducing reload time to virtually nothing.

33.3.1 The Touch Screen

I took the photograph for Figure 33.4 indoors with a reasonably powerful flash and, as you can see, the screen is still very bright and clear. I questioned Codex about this and their answer was simple and very much to the point: "You have to be able to see it clearly in daylight." Quite! But how many times have you had to shield a display screen and struggle to see it even when you are not in full sunlight? Another pointer to how well the Codex has been thought out and designed.

33.3.2 *Monitoring via the Codex*

Again, the Codex comes with an elegant and simple solution for monitoring an input from a camera like the Origin. While shooting you can get a High Definition Serial Digital Interface (HDSDI), a Standard Definition Serial Digital Interface (SDSDI) or several other signals out of the Codex, for it contains its own down-converters. Sound and time code are equally provided for.

33.3.3 *Conclusions on the Codex*

At the time of writing I have not come across another recorder with the capability to accept the huge data streams that the Codex copes with easily. More important, perhaps, to my eye expecting a quality associated with film equipment, I have not seen a recorder as beautifully designed and built and as intuitive to use.

33.4 The Dalsa Evolution

Right at the time of writing Dalsa announced their new camera, the Evolution. As it has not made the UK yet I can only look at their website and report. Very much as one would expect, its specification closely follows that of the Origin but they have made the camera considerably smaller and managed to reduce the weight by some 20 percent without taking away any of the original features. The new shape makes the prospect of hand holding the camera much more attractive and the new configuration also reduces the acoustic noise.

Although the chip and processor remain the same high quality, work has been done to greatly improve dust protection in the sensor cavity, a problem that needs addressing with most single-chip cameras.

All in all, the Evolution looks as if it is what it says, an evolution of a very interesting camera.

CHAPTER 34

The Panasonic VariCam: AJ-HDC27H

34.1 The Camera

The VariCam is unusual compared with all the other cameras I review here, for not only can it shoot at any constant frame rate between 4 and 60 frames per second (fps), but it is capable of changing the frame rate during a shot, known in the film world as ramping. It is also the only camera here that has a native 720P, 60 fps (or 59.94 fps) image configuration. You will have gathered that I favor a 1080P shooting format, but if you need the facility of variable frame rate offered by this camera then the compromise simply has to be worth it. It should be remembered that subjectively 720P and 1080i look almost as good to the eye and 1080 usually only looks significantly better when shot in the progressive format. This means that in a television arena the VariCam should be capable of excellent pictures.

The camera always shoots at 60 fps but an extra code is added to the time code that records the frame rate you have chosen. The camera cannot replay the pictures at anything but normal speed but when the pictures are played back through a frame rate converter or on a video tape recorder (VTR) that includes a frame rate converter then the pictures will be displayed, and can be re-recorded, at the speed you intended at the time of acquisition.

Panasonic have put considerable work into generating internal Gamma curves, i.e. CineGamma™, and although I try not to use them I have to say that many of my colleagues like them very much indeed. I would suggest, though, that if you are going to use them you don't just check you like the look created on a monitor but record some pictures and check them on playback, preferably in the post suite you are going to use, and make sure the people handling your material are happy with this approach.

As you can see from Figure 34.1 the camera is of a pleasingly compact design with the switchgear in roughly the same place as most other professional camcorders. This, at least, makes it much easier for a Director of Photography (DP), or the crew, to swap between products as the needs of a shoot dictate.

The camera has a native sensitivity equivalent to 640 ASA (ISO) when shooting at 24 fps in its normal 720P mode.

Figure 34.1: The Panasonic VariCam (AJ-HDC27H)

34.2 Frame Rates

As the camera always records at 60 fps to obtain a frame rate of 24 fps the frame rate converter will utilize the classic 3:2 pull-down frame sequence so familiar in the American television environment. With some of the other frame rates life gets a little more complicated. At 25 fps, the European television standard, the frame selection from the full 60 frames will go as follows:

Frame 1, frame 4, frame 6, frame 9, frame 11, frame 13, frame 16, frame 18, frame 21, frame 23, frame 25, frame 28, frame 30, frame 33, frame 35, frame 37, frame 40, frame 42, frame 45, frame 47, frame 49, frame 52, frame 54, frame 57 and finally frame 59.

In other words, the frame rate converter is working on a selection pattern of:

$3 > 2 > 3 > 2 > 2$ and then starting that sequence again.

Somewhat complicated, but it appears to work. If you are replaying at 30 fps the frame rate converter simply takes every alternate frame – much simpler.

34.3 Exposure Times

The VariCam has two ways of setting the exposure, either by nominating a shutter opening in degrees, just like a film camera, or setting an actual fraction of a second for each frame. Clearly, as the camera always works at 60 fps, the maximum exposure time that can be adopted is one-sixtieth of a second, which is, in effect, shutter off. Shutter speeds of 1/100, 1/120, 1/125, 1/500, 1/1000 and 1/2000 are also available.

The advantage of being able to choose between a shutter speed and the equivalent of a shutter opening is that with a shutter speed you get the same exposure on each frame, whereas with the equivalent opening the exposure per frame changes in relation to frame rate. Both have advantages in different applications. If you are going to ramp the frame rate, being able to have a constant exposure on every frame could be a very considerable advantage and make life very easy compared to shooting the same shot on film.

34.4 The Chips and the Processor

The VariCam utilizes 2/3-inch chips, as do all the three-chip cameras described in this book, with 1280 pixels horizontally and, as you would expect, 720 pixels vertically, and although multiplying those numbers gives 921,600 Panasonic assure me that each of the three chips actually has 1,019,280 pixels, certainly enough for the 720P High Definition (HD) standard but roughly half the number used on a chip that can fully support the 1080P standard. I can only express my personal opinion here – it works on television but I would want those extra pixels for cinema release.

The camera head utilizes a 12-bit processor that is impressive though, of course, there has to be some compression in order to get all those data down onto tape. Here the lower pixel count becomes a positive advantage, for it substantially reduces the total data that need to be recorded.

34.5 The VTR

Panasonic favor the HVCPRO HD recording format with which they have considerable experience in its earlier guises. The format is also referred to as DVCPRO HD. The VTR records in an 8-bit format, so there is some compression involved to bring the camera head's 12-bit format down to the capabilities of the VTR.

This format is well established and there are a multitude of VTRs etc. to support it, though not all will replay at anything but 60 fps.

34.6 Time Code

The camera generates 30-frame time code so problems can arise when shooting at frame rates other than 30 fps, when locking several cameras together or when ramping the frame rate. The solution is to use external time code generators such as lock-it boxes. When using external time code the time code so generated should be recorded on Audio Channel 2, for time code works in audio frequencies. Clearly it will be necessary to inform whoever is handling the post-production that you have made this decision.

34.7 An Overview

This is a very clever system; I say system for its cleverest trick cannot be viewed without additional equipment, frame rate converters of one kind or another. That said, at the time of writing no other HD camera can change its frame rate with such alacrity. As a result of it really being a system one has to be aware that the camera images may not be what you get in post-production and it is therefore very important that you shoot tests to confirm the correct shooting procedure required to give you the pictures you want. Having done this, shooting requirements should be quite simple. Time code also has to be addressed if shooting at any speed other than 30 fps. If you are going to use the camera's in-built Gamma curves these too should be passed by the post house before shooting commences.

All this said, if a 720P image format is not a problem for you and you would find a large range of variable frame rates an advantage, then this could be the camera for you. Both its purchase price and rental price are surprisingly competitive.

CHAPTER 35

The Panavision Genesis

35.1 The Camera

The Genesis reminds me of the old joke that goes "If it looks like a duck, talks like a duck and walks like a duck – then it's a duck!" I am fairly confident that if you walked onto a set without knowing it was a High Definition (HD) shoot and glanced at the camera you would assume it was a Panavision Millennium. Just take a quick look at Figure 35.1. If you gave it a second cursory glance you might think it had an unusual viewfinder and the futuristic 65 mm 400-foot magazine was new to you. Further enhancing the feeling that this was just a slightly unusual film camera would be the intelligence that the camera crew were behaving exactly as you would expect from a normal film crew. Personally I have never worked with a completely normal film crew, but that's entirely another matter. Believe me, it looks like a Panavision Millennium, is as quiet as a Millennium and the crew runs it like a Millennium – therefore,

Figure 35.1: The Panavision Genesis

233

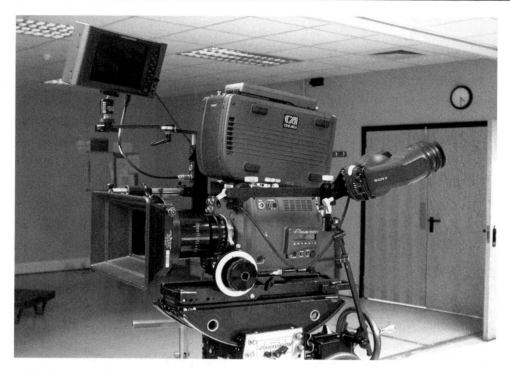

Figure 35.2: Panavision Genesis with a prime lens, the Sony viewfinder and an eyepiece leveler

it's a Millennium; well, more or less. Except, in some ways, it's better, it is a Genesis and if you like film and you also like HD then this camera could be for you. If you look at Figure 35.2 you will see the camera with the alternative Sony viewfinder, fitted with a Primo prime lens and a focus puller's HD liquid crystal display (LCD) monitor.

You can mount the "magazine", which is in fact the video tape recorder (VTR), either on the top of the camera or at the back, just as you have been able to do with any Panavision camera for several decades (Figure 35.3). As the camera utilizes a single charge-coupled device (CCD) chip similar in size to a Super 35 mm frame, virtually all the lenses Panavision normally supply for 35 mm photography will fit this camera, the lens mount is identical, and they will produce, again exactly, the same feel to the image and the same depth of field.

Being a camera derived, at least philosophically, from Panavision's more than 50 years in the motion picture business, this camera will accept just about all the accessories you could attach to a Panavision film camera and they will function and feel just the same.

It may seem strange that Panavision, with all their access to film camera bodies, have not gone down the route of utilizing a spinning mirror shutter. Apparently their thinking when designing this camera isolated a number of issues attached to optical viewing, two of which

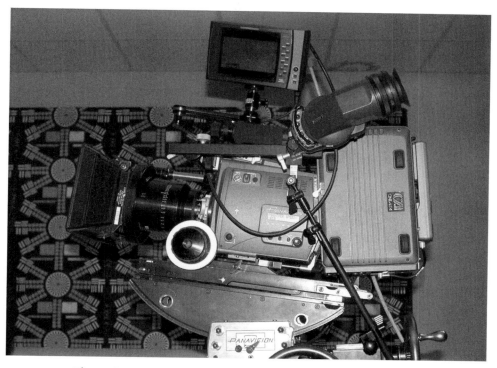

Figure 35.3: Panavision Genesis with the VTR back mounted

seemed to them to militate strongly against such a path. First, cameras designed for theatrical release tend to be heavy and opting for electronic rather than mechanical viewing reduced the body weight by some 3–4 pounds. Secondly, there is an inherent problem with single-chip cameras – dirt and dust on the sensor. If it gets there it stays there, unlike film, where dirt within the frame, as against a hair in the gate, moves away with every frame. Panavision have utilized the space freed up by not deploying a spinning mirror to seal a cavity between the actual sensor and the surface on which dust may arrive. The distance between the sensor and this surface is sufficient to ensure that any dust particle will be so completely out of focus within the image arriving at the sensor that it is impossible to discern its presence.

A further advantage of not deploying a mechanical shutter is that the camera can be set to have an equivalent shutter opening of between 3.8 and 360 degrees – as in "Shutter Off" – allowing some interesting effects to be obtained. The shutter angle affects exposure in exactly the same way as with a traditional film camera, so if you choose to shoot at a 360-degree setting then you will get one stop more exposure than at the more regular setting of 180 degrees, which is fine so long as you are happy with the additional motion blur you will be photographing.

If you wish to reduce the camera to its minimum proportions and weight, it is possible to introduce a cable between the camera and the VTR. This in no way reduces the quality of the image nor takes away from the number of available controls. The control unit, as shown in Figure 35.4, can be connected via an extension cable and does not have to be permanently mounted to the VTR itself.

Figure 35.4: The Genesis VTR control unit

Unlike most cameras that utilize the Sony SRW-1 recorder, the Genesis does not need the additional interface unit, which is as big as the VTR itself, since all the necessary connections are made directly when docking the recorder to the Genesis body. In addition to this, the camera and VTR have a bidirectional control link that ensures the two are always correctly configured for recording format, frames per second (fps) and so forth; this also allows the camera to include a VTR run switch and to receive feedback from the VTR.

The camera and the VTR are capable of running at any speed between 1 and 50 fps, in addition to which are several commonly used preset frame rates. These are 23.98P, 24P, 25P, 29.97P and 30P. In addition, you can select 50i, 59.94i and 60i. The camera will not ramp between speeds.

35.2 Menus

The camera menus are very similar to the Sony 900 menus, with a few additional pages such as the variable speed option etc., though Panavision take a different philosophical approach to how one should treat them. Panavision's view is that they would prefer to set the camera up for what they consider to be optimum performance and then suggest to the client they leave well alone. Personally I like this approach. All the original menus are still readily available should you wish to personalize the camera, with the exception of one.

35.3 White Balance

You cannot white balance a Genesis for neither can you white balance a film camera; instead, you use filters and the menu set-up Panavision prefer is tailored to the use of standard motion picture filters for all your color correction.

35.4 The Camera Sensor

The Genesis uses a CCD chip having 12.4 megapixels. To obtain an HD image utilizing the standard 1920 × 1080 pixel array, each HD pixel is formed by six subpixels. No Bayer pattern filtration is used; instead the subpixels are color filtered in the traditional Red, Green and Blue manner and then arranged so that three horizontal and two vertical subpixels come together to form one complete RGB macropixel in the 1920 × 1080 arrangement. By having six subpixels form each macro HD pixel, the picture quality is substantially increased and the problems of aliasing are just about completely eliminated.

The use of pure, singly filtered, CCD pixels brings a further benefit: all three colors are output at precisely the same resolution and relative sensitivity, so there is no green bias in the image as is the case with a camera using Bayer pattern filtration.

Arguably, say Panavision, the combination of the sensor size, the number of subpixels and the use of a CCD sensor brings the optimum combination of both resolution and tonal range. The films I have seen that were shot on a Genesis suggest they may be right. The downside is that with 14-bit-per-color processing that is then encoded into a 10-bit quasi-logarithmic signal using a CCD sensor, the camera does need a substantial battery as this combination is power hungry.

The Genesis sensor is the width of a Super 35 mm frame and the height that would be associated with shooting a 1.78:1 aspect ratio, and it is this configuration that enables the camera to utilize virtually all the lenses you would expect to be able to use on a regular 35 mm film camera.

The size of the sensor and the decisions Panavision have made make the front of the camera, without a lens mounted, look extraordinarily like a 35 mm film camera, as can be seen in Figure 35.5. The lens mount's the same, the frame size is the same and the accessories are the same – a bit like that duck, really!

35.5 Formats, Outputs and Interface

The Genesis primarily produces a 12.4-megapixel picture that is binned into a 6.2-megapixel, 14-bit-per-color linear signal, which the camera then converts to a 10-bit quasi-logarithmic signal having 1920 × 1080 pixels. The output from the camera is available as an RGB (4:4:4) or Y, Pb, Pr (4:2:2) configuration. If the SRW-1 VTR is being used, which records in the HDCAM-SR format, then each frame will be recorded, independently, with 10 bits of information for every single pixel. It is worth noting that most productions that have shot with the Genesis to date have recorded in the RGB format.

The Sony SRW-1 will record a 4:4:4 signal up to 30 fps, but if you wish to record at between 30 and 50 fps then you need to feed the SRW-1 with a 4:2:2 signal as this is the highest data rate it can cope with.

If you prefer to record a slightly purer image than can be handled by the SRW-1, then it is perfectly possible, and easy, to record a Genesis 4:4:4 output at any speed and without any compression, via Dual Link High Definition Serial Digital Interface (HDSDI) outputs, and send these signals to, say, a separate hard drive, flash memory or other external custom device that can cope with the increase in the data stream.

Monitoring the picture is achieved via a single HDSDI output socket on the side of the camera.

35.6 Solid-state Recording

Panavision recently added a solid-state recorder to their equipment line-up, the SSR-1. This handy unit can record 21 minutes of 4:4:4 data (SP mode) or 43 minutes of 4:2:2 data (LP

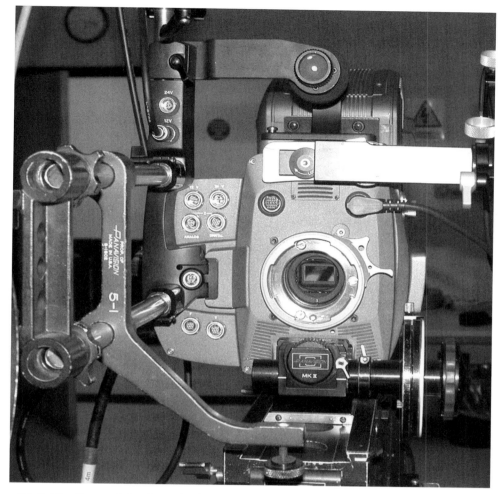

Figure 35.5: The front of the Genesis showing the lens mount, the throat of the camera and the sensor chip

mode). This solid-state recorder behaves just like the SRW-1 VTR, so it is very easy for the crew to swap between the two recorders.

The SSR-1 is about half the size and less than half the weight of the VTR and consumes considerably less power.

35.7 Viewing Logarithmic Images

Images encoded in a logarithmic way, though perhaps technically better and probably more appealing after post-production, tend not to look too good on a conventional monitor. Whilst this can be mainly overcome by the Director of Photography (DP) adjusting the monitor to compensate, Panavision offer a more elegant solution, a device they term the Genesis Display Processor (GDP). The problem is that whilst the logarithmic output from the Genesis, produced by what Panavision call the Panalog 4™ transfer curve, allows capture of the maximum tonal range for the image, it doesn't match the response of most display devices. The GDP enables viewing of the image in a very close approximation to the final result to be delivered when the film is completed. Whilst this device can bring great confidence on set as it utilizes look-up tables (LUTs), it would be prudent to consult with your post-production house before choosing the exact LUT you intend to use.

CHAPTER 36

The RED One

36.1 A Little Background

The RED One is the latest in a long line of cameras produced by people aiming to revolutionize the way we make movies.

My father knew August Arnold and Robert Richter, the founders of Arnold & Richter who, in 1937, announced the world's first motion picture camera with a through-the-lens viewfinder utilizing a spinning mirror in place of the conventional black shutter. This they called the Arriflex, a truly revolutionary camera, which was a cornerstone of the very successful Arriflex company of today (see Chapter 32).

Several of my friends knew Robert Gottschalk, the founder of Panavision, who in the 1950s revolutionized the way anamorphic lenses were designed and constructed, and went on to build Panavision into a world-class motion picture manufacturer and supplier (see Chapter 35).

I have met, and spent a wonderful lunchtime with, one of my heroes, Jean-Pierre Beauviala, who in 1973 introduced the Aaton 7 Super 16 mm camera. He was encouraged by the BBC and, as luck would have it, and as a new cameraman at the BBC Film Department, I was given the seventh Aaton camera they acquired as my personal issue camera. I went on to shoot with two later versions of the Aaton and I enjoyed shooting with them all. Believe me, when I put that first Aaton on my shoulder it was love at first touch – a truly revolutionary moment.

Now I sit down to write a chapter on the RED One. Will this be a revolution? I think it may. Why? It too is the creation of a person with a vision who wants to do something innovative and ahead of their time, one Jim Jannard. Whereas Messrs Arnold, Richter, Gottschalk and Beauviala were, in their time, fundamentally engineers as well as innovators, Mr Jannard comes from a slightly different background, but he is still certainly an innovator.

Jim Jannard started his career in 1975 working from his garage and calling his company Oakley. He soon launched a revolutionary handlebar grip for motorcycles. Mr Jannard has been quoted as "having a raging distaste for mediocrity and a fierce devotion to innovation". But if you trawl all the information you can find on him he has, to me, a Cinematographer, one outstanding and seemingly unique qualification over all the camera innovators I talk about above – he takes extremely fine photographs! Having sold Oakley, which he had transformed into one of the most successful sunglass companies, he added digital motion pictures to the things he wanted to do better than anyone else and so started the RED Digital Cinema Camera Company.

36.2 First Impressions

When the RED One was first announced with its very high specification and its equally low price I was mightily sceptical. How could the RED completely ignore conventional wisdom as to the usual premises for a camera and be acceptable to the motion picture crews around the world? How could RED claim to know what the market wanted better than the established manufacturers? Even if all this were attainable, how could they possibly do this at such a staggeringly low price? *How could I have been so wrong?*

I have now spent time with the RED One over five sessions and seen finished material both printed to 35 mm film and projected on a Barco DP100 projector, and I can confidently say the camera works, and works really well.

I first saw the RED One at a demonstration given by the camera supply company Decode in London and was immediately impressed by the physical build quality; I had not expected it to have the feel of a serious piece of motion picture equipment, but it has. It immediately felt right despite being a shape I had never encountered before. Decode were kind enough to let me have access to the camera twice more and I became increasingly convinced that I was looking at a seriously interesting camera. But could it live up to the hype?

Some weeks before writing this I was lucky enough to be invited to a viewing staged by the data/image handling company 4K London of some material shot on a RED One and printed out to 35 mm film, a viewing that claimed to be the first material so shown in the UK. I saw a compilation of what they had, clips from a feature film shoot shot at 4K but posted in 2K, some material, again from a feature, that was from a boxing picture where the camera had been in 3K mode in order to take advantage of its higher frame rate capabilities at this resolution, and an available light shoot shot and posted at 4K. All were very impressive and all were shot with a camera in build 14 mode. Although all the pictures from the 35 mm prints were of very good quality, the boxing film having been heavily graded, it was, as it always is, somewhat difficult to judge the camera as it is impossible to know the Director of Photography (DP)'s original intentions and what they had been asked for by the Director. Nevertheless, one could hardly fault the finished product. Please remember we were being asked to judge the pictures as full-blown feature films, a high standard.

The last viewing was of an intimate dinner between two young people, the table candlelit but in a reasonably bright sitting room. This had been shot in 4K and posted in 2K and we saw it projected on the Barco DP100 projector. I thought it looked even better than the material that had already impressed us on a film print.

The only criticism I could possibly raise was that, for me, there was not enough detail in the shadows, though I have to admit that those shadows were very clean and contained no noticeable noise as one might expect from a camera using a complementary metal-oxide semiconductor (CMOS) sensor with Bayer patterning. My conclusion has to be – it works and it works well.

36.3 The Camera

In Figure 36.1 you can see the camera more or less as it comes out of the box, with top and bottom 19 mm bars and the RED 18–50 mm T 3 zoom attached. This is probably the minimum kit with which a typical RED purchaser would start. With just a battery to power the camera you could take pictures with this rig, but I don't think a professional would consider it viable. The reverse side of the camera, where all the connectors live, is shown in Figure 36.2.

My next visit was to a London camera supply company, VMI, where DP James Friend and his First Assistant Cameraman (AC1) Romain Choay were prepping a RED One prior to starting principal photography on the feature film *Transient*, produced by Daniel Pickering

Figure 36.1: The RED One camera with just the top and bottom bars attached and the RED 18–50 mm T 3 Zoom

Figure 36.2: The non-operator side of the RED One showing all the output options

and Richard Kerigan for Annix. You can see them at the VMI prep room in Figure 36.3. The camera is now beginning to take shape as it now has the top handle, front "bull's horns", the 18–50 mm zoom and a battery pack attached.

By the time James and Romain had the camera fully built with their preferred Arriflex focus unit and matte box and all the other RED bits needed to turn this camera into something fully capable of shooting a motion picture at full theatrical release quality (see Figure 36.4), we had found that, despite this crew having worked with the RED One three or four times before, it had taken them almost 2 hours to rig the camera using several sizes of Allen keys. Their conclusion was that for the shoot proper they were going to have a transit case made for the RED that allowed it to be put away each night with all the solid physical bits left permanently attached. Lenses, matte boxes, follow focus and hard drive would be removed but everything else would stay on board. This, they reckoned, would enable the camera to be rigged each morning on the shoot in less than half an hour, much like any 35 mm film camera. Incidentally, the fully built camera now weighed as much as a similarly equipped 35 mm camera, a fact we cannot really complain about, for it is attempting to do exactly the same job.

One thing that was entirely new to me on this meeting with the camera was the on-board viewfinder, which had only recently been announced; you can see me checking it out in Figure 36.5. The image down the RED viewfinder is very good, being clear and crisp with

Figure 36.3: 1st AC Romain Choay and DP James Friend starting to build up the RED for their shoot

Figure 36.4: The RED One fully built and ready to shoot

Figure 36.5: PW checking the RED viewfinder with Romain Choay on focus

seemingly good color reproduction, but like most High Definition (HD) finders currently available there is a noticeable stutter to the image on panning the camera. You can choose to have just the image or a variety of extra information, just as you can on the assistant's monitor (Figure 36.6). The look-through viewfinder has another very clever trick. If you look at Figure 36.7 you can see that there is a knurled wheel on the side and three push buttons. These controls allow the operator to access the camera's menus fully, just as you can with the display and controls on the back of the camera (Figure 36.8).

As to the camera's menu logic, it is very intuitive and simple to understand, unlike many of the cameras I have reviewed in this book. You hardly need any instructions even if you have never used an HD camera. Give yourself an hour with someone from any competent camera supply house to guide you and I am sure you will feel confident in going out to shoot your first day with a RED One.

Just in case you are a confirmed film technician and feel all this HD nonsense is a little daunting, fix in your mind the last time you changed a lens on a film camera equipped with Arriflex accessories: how different would your view be from that in Figure 36.9? Other than a wire going to the viewfinder, I suggest it looks remarkably familiar. Believe me, it is!

The camera has the ability to accept several lens mounts. I imagine the Arriflex PL will be the most popular, but it can also be fitted with Mitchell BNC, Nikon still camera and Sony

Figure 36.6: The on-board monitor showing the same image as is available in the viewfinder

Figure 36.7: The RED on-board viewfinder showing the menu control wheel

Figure 36.8: The rear of the camera showing the easy to use menu control panel and the data card slot on its left

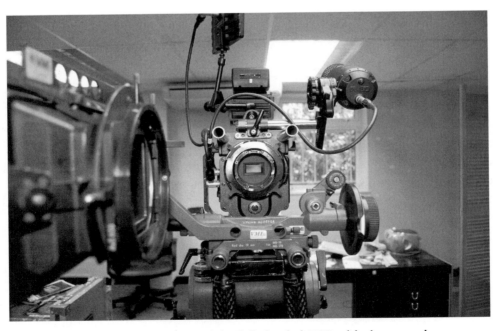

Figure 36.9: Looking down the throat of the fully loaded RED with the matte box swung aside ready for a lens change

Figure 36.10: A close-up of the throat of the camera showing the Mysterium™ sensor

B4 among others. In theory, these mounts are user interchangeable. In Figure 36.10 you can see a close-up of the throat of the camera when fitted with an Arriflex PL mount and the "Mysterium™" sensor looking for all the world like a film gate. How user friendly is that?

36.4 The Mysterium™ Sensor

I have to say, sitting on my side of the Atlantic when the RED One was first announced, the word Mysterium made me laugh, for it brought back memories of the kind of language used in my childhood space comics. I realize that RED did not, at that time, want to reveal the exact kind of sensor they were using and maybe it had more to do with my warped British sense of humor, but I found this the only doubtful part of their marketing strategy. The rest, as we all now know, was pretty faultless.

The sensor, RED have now admitted, is a CMOS device using Bayer patterning – a sensor capable of good images if downstream from it the images are handled carefully and with the full knowledge of what is needed in the image management processors that are going to look after it. I have been looking at RED One pictures since around build 10 of the software releases from RED and in the early days I was very concerned with the noise in the shadow areas of the image. I was, admittedly, not able to carry out very detailed examinations of what was going on at that time, but reducing the equivalent ISO speed of the camera seemed to improve things. Unfortunately, this defect is usually more relevant in low-key scenes where one is unlikely to welcome having to reduce the sensitivity of the camera by such a significant margin simply to obtain clean pictures.

RED have obviously been aware of this, as they have very honestly said, and the images I have described earlier in this chapter, which were shot using build 14 of the software, displayed little or no noise in the shadows, so they have clearly addressed this problem. The last camera I was able to look at before the publication deadline for this edition had build 16 installed and at least on the professional monitor on which I could view images and at full sensitivity I could see no residual problem with image noise.

36.5 Shooting Costs

At the time of writing, a RED One camera body will cost you $17,500. I am not going to quote any other currency here, as presently it can only be ordered in US dollars. It must be understood that this figure really does only cover the basic camera body. My rough calculations off the RED price list suggest that a camera with a single 18–50 mm zoom and the least in the way of accessories that you will need to go shooting will come to roughly $33,000 – a bit more than the cheap camera as advertised. If you look back at Figure 36.4 the camera James is looking through also has Arriflex follow focus and matte box on board. Arri accessories do not come cheap. Admittedly, other manufacturers' accessories are available but if you want a truly professional motion picture camera these are the kind of sums you are looking at. If you want a really good lens set, and this would very much be my personal choice, try the Cooke S4/i kit comprising a 15–40 mm T 2 zoom, with 50, 75 and 100 mm S4/1 primes, again all T 2. Rumor has it that that lens set will set you back something over $100,000. So we are not looking at quite as economical a package as first might be thought.

On the other hand, it must be remembered that, at the time of writing, a basic Sony HDW 750 HDCAM camcorder body will cost around $70,000, a Sony F23 around $150,000 and a Sony F35 around $250,000, and remember none of those prices is for anything more than the camera body. Suddenly the RED One is looking remarkably good value again!

36.6 RED Marketing

Perhaps even more revolutionary than the RED One camera has been the way it has been marketed. As I said at the beginning of this chapter, I was initially sceptical of all things RED but the marketing and after-sales attitude of the company have been refreshingly honest and clear. Right from the start of shipping the first cameras, RED promised that this camera could, in the main, be updated via the Net and those updates would be free to purchasers.

This promise has been kept. Indeed, as they have just announced that some time in the not too distant future they will be bringing out a 5K camera called the RED Epic they have also simultaneously announced that anyone purchasing a RED One after the announcement of the RED Epic will be able to return their camera and have it replaced with an Epic at a reasonable cost, still to be announced at the time of writing. That seems very fair to me.

In order to support their 4K format RED chose to use an entirely new codec to file the RAW images, which would have made it very difficult to import those images into currently available edit suites. RED put RED Cine, an image handling and conversion program, onto the Net and, again, this computer program is downloadable entirely free of charge. That also seems very fair to me.

36.7 Design Philosophy

RED play it very close to their chest, and why not, but like a couple of other HD cameras – the Dalsa comes to mind – RED seem to have approached the problem of creating high-quality images from the starting point of a computer rather than a camera. There is no problem with that so long as you get it right. Another premise seems to have been that you try to do the minimum amount of image processing in the camera and transfer as much of it as possible to the post-production arena, thereby reducing the cost of the camera, and its power consumption and possibly its weight, so that much of that processing happens in a relatively low-cost computer with high computing power that is run off the mains supply. Once again, no problem if you get it right.

36.8 Recording Media

If you look back at Figure 36.8, just to the left of the menu display you can see a Compact Flash card in the on-board card slot. Currently 8 and 16 gigabyte (GB) cards are available and, I believe, 32 GB cards are now becoming available. The simplest way to record your picture data, and probably the highest quality, is to record it in RED RAW files. The recording time on any data medium is dictated by the amount of data you are trying to store and this is, again, dictated by the size of the file that the image format you have chosen demands for each frame of picture.

If you have chosen to shoot with the RED One at its highest picture quality, 4K RAW at 24 frames per second (fps), then an 8 GB Compact Flash card will store around 4 minutes of screen time. A couple of 8 GB Compact Flash cards are shown in Figure 36.11. Equally, a 16 GB card will store around 7 minutes of screen time. If you choose to record your images on a 320 GB RED Drive as shown loaded on the camera in Figure 36.3, then you can record 180 minutes of screen time. I am sure you will not have much difficulty in working out how long

Figure 36.11: Compact Flash memory cards

your chosen media will last with the camera running – it is roughly 2 GB per minute. I suggest you make this a conservative estimate.

Running the camera at lower resolution will allow longer recording times on any drive and I am not going to go into this in detail here, as it is very well covered on the RED website and freely downloadable.

36.9 Which Drive to Choose?

Easy question, difficult answer. Unfortunately, at present it is not possible to record on both a Compact Flash card and an on-board hard drive at the same time. If a Flash card is inserted into the camera, the camera defaults to using this as the recording media. You have to answer this one for yourself and the decision breaks down into two primary questions: are you happy to put at least a whole day's work into one data box and trust it will be successfully stored and backed up at the end of that day, or are you prepared to pay for a Data Wrangler to make those precious copies from smaller segments of the day's work several times during the day? The latter path, assuming a horrid disaster, would mean you only lost a small proportion of the day's work. Coming from a film background I would favor the smaller storage capacity downloaded more often. It also makes for a lighter camera. On the other hand, one small box containing a day's work is attractively convenient. As I said, it's your choice.

36.10 Basic Camera Specification

36.10.1 The Mysterium™ Sensor

The Mysterium™ sensor can run at any frame rate between 1 and 60 fps, has a native color balance of 5000 K, and may electronically compensate for any color temperature between 1700 and 10,000 K. There are preset white balances for 3200 and 5600 K to match the conventional values used for motion picture film.

RED claim that the Mysterium™ sensor includes 12-bit analog-to-digital conversion for each pixel and is capable of delivering a 66 dB dynamic range, equivalent to 11 stops, when operating at the equivalent to 320 ISO.

36.10.2 Image Processing

Images from the sensor are, say RED, formatted as pixel defect corrected, but not color processed, 12-bit RAW data, which is similar to the way data are handled in a high-end digital still camera. The Progressive scan RAW images are compressed in-camera using wavelet-based RED Code and the compressed image data are stored on the in-camera Compact Flash (CF) card or on external e-SATA-based digital media such as the RED Drive or a RED Flash magazine.

The RAW sensor data are also converted to a white balanced 10-bit RGB 4:4:4 monitor video with SMPTE REC 709 color gamut that provides a program High Definition Serial Digital Interface (HDSDI) output for external video monitoring and recording via HDSDI and HDMI sockets on the side of the camera.

36.11 Conclusions

Much against my initial perception of the RED One, I find myself curiously attracted to the camera. There are a number of things I would like improved, but as we are still in an extended development stage for the software perhaps these matters are soon to be sorted. I would like to have seen more detail in the shadows. I would like to be able to record simultaneously on a Compact Flash card and on the on-board hard drive. I would like to be able to work in 2K files from the whole of the sensor, thus giving me smaller files, more than adequate for many applications, but still using the whole of the sensor area. At present, if you wish to work in 2K you only use a part of the sensor equivalent to the same area as a Super 16 mm film gate, thus losing the desirable lack of depth of field associated with a 35 mm image. I would like a viewfinder that does not stutter when I pan the camera.

To be fair, many of my requests I would make of some of the other cameras reviewed here, all of which cost more!

CHAPTER 37

The Sony HDW F790, F750 and F730 HD Cameras

In the year 2000 Sony transformed the professional camcorder market with the introduction of the HDW F900, later replaced with the F900R, which utilized three 1920 × 1080 pixel chips and recorded on a 1/2-inch tape in what was another step up for portable video tape recording, and which used a recording format they named HDCAM. This pixel array and recording format quickly became an international norm. This camera was firmly aimed at being able to replace 35 mm film, as well as starting the television High Definition (HD) revolution.

In 2002 Sony brought out three additional cameras, the HDW F750, F750P and F730; these still used the international HD pixel standard of 1920 × 1080 and the HDCAM recording format. Whereas the F900 utilized a 12-bit analog-to-digital processor, the F750/F730 cameras use a 10-bit processor. Despite this, the images from these cameras look every bit as good as those from the F900 when shown on television, which is the intended market for these cameras. I think most viewers seeing the images from an F750 on television would think they had been recorded on 35 mm film. These remarkable cameras are easily capable of a camera/recording stock costs below, sometimes significantly below, that of Super 16 mm film and yet deliver a superb picture quality comparable to 35 mm film.

A couple of years after the introduction of the F750 Sony brought out the F790, which looks exactly the same as the other 700 range cameras but moves up to a 12-bit processor as used in the F900R.

37.1 Frame Rates

There are two models of the 790, one which has the choice of either a 1080 59.94i or a 50i frame rate and the other, known as the 790P, which has the choice of either a 1080 50i frame rate or a 25 progressive segmented field (PSF) frame rate.

There are two models of the 750 designed for the NTSC environment, both of which record in the 60i (interlace) format, or more accurately 59.94i. These are the HDW F730 and the HDW F750. The F790 and the F750 use exactly the same picture head block and imaging chips as the earlier F900: three 2/3-inch FIT chips. The F730 uses three 2/3-inch IT chips. Though there is only a small reduction in overall picture quality when changing from an FIT chip to an IT chip, this change, combined with a simplification of the camera controls and facilities, provides a significant reduction in cost. The F730 is aimed at the more cost-conscious end of the market and the F790 and F750 at the quality-conscious customer.

There is a second model of the F750, intended for the PAL environment and known as the F750P, which is switchable between 25 frames Progressive scan and a 50 interlace format.

All the cameras record onto HDCAM tape exactly as with the original HDW F900.

37.2 The Camera Body

All the HDW 700 series cameras share the same camera body and their switches and controls are identical. The body is a few inches shorter front to back than the F900 and around 7 pounds lighter, but the same size and weight as the F790R; in fact, all the 700 series cameras are smaller and lighter than a conventional Digi Beta camera. There are none of the multiple frame rates available as with the F900R, only those discussed above. Figure 37.1 shows an F750P fitted with a 20 mm Zeiss Digi Prime lens and a Crosziel matte box. At the rear of the camera can be seen two aerials, which are attached to the slot-in radio receiver, thus allowing the sound recordist to feed back a mixed output to the tracks on the video tape without the use of a cable. This unit can be more clearly seen in Figure 37.2, which shows the back of the camera.

Figure 37.1: The Sony HDW 750P HD camera

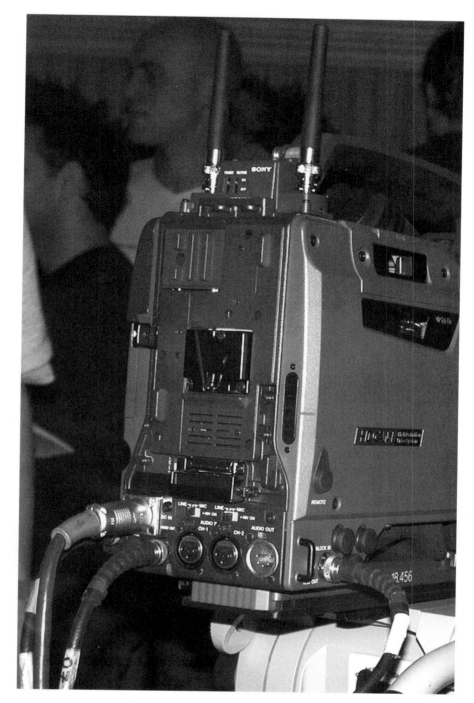

Figure 37.2: The rear of the HDW 750

The switch block that controls most of the camera functions and the menus has been somewhat redesigned from the ones on the F900 and the Digi Beta cameras, which are similar to each other. In Figure 37.3 you can see the new layout. The most significant change is the moving of the rotary encoder wheel from the front plate of the camera to the end of the camera control switch block, where it is more easily accessed. Also in Figure 37.3 you can see that, just below the filter code plate, there are now two assignable switches whose functions can be selected from within the menus.

The lens center to base plate height has been significantly reduced, thus lowering the center of gravity, which makes the camera even more suitable for hand holding.

37.3 Add-in Boards, etc.

There are a couple of potentially very useful add-in boards for the camera, one of which operates as a built-in down-converter that can output Standard Definition Serial Digital Interface (SDSDI) or an analog composite signal, the choice being selectable within the menu system. This board will be a great attraction to users in the television industry, for without

Figure 37.3: The HDW 750 switch block

any additional kit they can now view the camera's output on conventional broadcast monitors. As can be seen in Figure 37.2, there is no external change when the down-converter board is fitted; both High Definition Serial Digital Interface (HDSDI) and the SDSDI or composite BNC sockets are conveniently placed at the back of the camera on the operator side. The cannon plug in this illustration is providing an external DC supply.

The second add-in board is a picture cache, which allows several minutes of recording to be continually recorded without the video tape recorder (VTR) being switched on. Once the VTR is activated the cache starts to dump down its contents while still taking in new images; when the VTR run/stop control is hit the tape runs on for the chosen cache time to complete the recording.

In the 60i versions of the camera, cache times of 0, 1, 2, 3, 4, 5, 6 or 7 seconds may be selected and in the 25P/50i version 0, 1, 2, 3, 4, 5, 6 or 8 seconds may be chosen. There are no moving parts to this board as it utilizes solid-state memory and therefore should prove very reliable.

As we have seen, a radio receiver can be slotted into the back of the camera. Also, a GPS unit can be fitted on the top of the viewfinder and the position of the camera recorded either on the tape itself or onto the set-up memory card which, as in the F900, is a Sony memory stick.

37.4 Image Control via the Menus

Most of the image controls are accessible via the menus that one would expect on an F900 or, indeed, a Digi Beta camera; some have changed and there are a few new ones. The most interesting, and possibly unfamiliar, F790, F750 and F730 menus are the following.

37.4.1 Multi Matrix

Multi matrix allows for selective color enhancement or alteration. Any particular color can be selected or "grabbed" and have its hue changed over a range of approximately 22.5 degrees. This allows for secondary color correction, normally only possible in post-production, and is performed at full bit depth.

37.4.2 Auto Tracing White Balance

If the auto tracing white balance function is deployed, the camera will continuously monitor the ambient light color temperature and adjust the camera's settings accordingly. Therefore if you have this function switched on and take a shot where, with the camera running, you go from an outdoor environment lit by daylight and move to an interior scene lit with tungsten light the camera will automatically adjust the colorimetry to make both environments look color correct. A lot of the time this function works surprisingly well.

37.4.3 Color Temperature Control

There is a page in the menu called preset white where you can simply add overall blue or overall red to the scene, thus giving either a cooler or warmer look. This works simply and well.

37.4.4 Selectable Gamma Curves

The camera allows for multiple points in the gamma curve where it can be adjusted or modified, thus achieving a contrast range appropriate to the scene. Within the menu system there are also a number of preset gamma curves, which are:

Gamma calculating pattern A
- No. 1: SMPTE 240M standard, which sets an initial gain of 4.0
- No. 2: ITU-R.BT709 standard, which sets an initial gain of 4.5
- No. 3: BBC gamma setting, which gives an initial gain of 5.0.

Gamma calculating pattern B
- No. 1: Sensitivity is equivalent to 50 ISO
- No. 2: Sensitivity is equivalent to 100 ISO
- No. 3: Sensitivity is equivalent to 200 ISO.

I would not necessarily advise deploying any of these settings if there is any chance of your material going out to film, but for a purely television presentation they can be very useful. This holds true for all the gamma settings as well as black stretch.

37.4.5 RGB Gamma Balance

This adjustment alters the color balance of the midtones without affecting black or white.

37.4.6 Variable Black Gamma Range

This function makes possible fine adjustment of the tonal reproduction on the darker parts of the scene without affecting the midtones; while doing this it maintains the absolute black level. The variable range is Low, Mid and High.

37.4.7 Black Stretch

When variable black gamma range is performed it can be limited to picture luminance without affecting any other factors of the video signal. This can be very helpful in a dark scene when you wish to bring out more detail in the darker parts of the scene but wish the absolute black to stay black.

37.4.8 Adaptive Highlight Control (Auto Knee Mode)

With this function switched to "on" the camera's ADPS system will monitor the whole of the picture and adapt the knee point/slope settings for optimum reproduction of the scene. For instance, if you are shooting an interior with a bright window in shot, switching this function on should bring down the exposure just within the image contained by the window.

37.4.9 Knee Saturation Function

Sony refer to their TrueEye processor, which basically controls the highlights in a high-contrast scene. For instance, if knee correction is applied only via the RGB channels, skin tone when very brightly lit will occasionally look yellow and Sony claim applying this function should bring it back to a clear color. It does seem to work.

37.4.10 The Triple Skin Tone Detail Control

In addition to the usual single skin tone detail and color control found on most current Sony cameras, there are now three separate settings and the range of adjustment allows for modification to far more colors than just skin tone. Within each setting it is possible to grab a single color and substantially modify it, and this can be done to three individual colors. It works well and allows you to do far more than you might with a red enhancement filter; for a start it works on all colors.

37.4.11 Level Depend Detail

This function provides detail enhancement in extreme highlights; it automatically limits the amplitude of edge signals in high-contrast areas. Detail aliasing in these areas can be dramatically reduced.

37.5 Metadata Handling

The camera can record a unique material identifier (UMID) signal, which is standardized as SMPTE 330M. The purpose of this is to record information on the tape at every shot change. These data can include a universal label, an instance number, a material number, the time and date, spatial coordinates, the country, the origin and a user identifier code.

37.6 The Sony Tele-File System

The Sony Tele-File storage system allows information such as shot data, shot marks, etc. to be recorded onto an optional cassette label with a built-in memory integrated circuit so that all this information can travel with the cassette for the rest of its working life. This can significantly speed up the post-production process if used carefully.

37.7 The Optional HDSDI Adapter

Although a single HDSDI source comes out of the back of the camera there are occasions when more sources might be required and also access to all four of the on-tape soundtracks may be needed. The optional HDSDI adapter allows for all of this.

37.8 An Overview

The HDW F700 range of cameras is a very significant step forward in the move to a worldwide common standard of HD acquisition in the television industry. The 750 middle-of-the-range camera has a lower price tag than a Digi Beta camera had at its introduction 10 years previously and we all know how popular that camera became.

The HDW F730 is such an economical camera to purchase that it is hard to conceive how the take-up will not be at least as successful as was Digi Beta – this time the cost is less and the leap in quality of much greater significance.

The HDW F790P and F750P with their 25 fps Progressive scan capability are tailor-made for the European, and particularly UK, single camera television drama market, where they offer all the convenience of Digi Beta and a significant reduction in costs compared with the traditional acquisition medium, Super 16, and bring picture quality up to that usually expected of 35 mm origination.

CHAPTER 38

The Sony HDW F900R

38.1 The Camera

The Sony HDW F900R is the third generation of Sony's HDCAM camcorder range and is very much a derivative of both their original F900 and the later 700P cameras. Sony have listened to their clients and worked hard to bring together in the HDW F900R camera all the good points of both the previous cameras. Essentially they have packaged all but two, hardly used, facilities originally found in the F900 inside the casing of an HDW 750P, as can be seen in Figure 38.1, here fitted with a Zeiss Digi Prime lens and a production matte box. Remarkably they have also found space to incorporate internal converter boards from the 700P so that two High Definition Serial Digital Interface (HDSDI) outputs are standard and by adding an extra board inside the camera it is possible to replace one of the HDSDI outputs with a Standard Definition Serial Digital Interface (SDSDI) output. The only noticeable difference is the casing, which, though identical to the 750P, is now a much darker gray. In Figure 38.2 you can see the F900R ready for hand-held use and fitted with a broadcast-style zoom lens and a lightweight sun shade.

Compared with the old 900 the 900R is 10 percent shorter, 20 percent smaller by volume and 2.6 kilograms lighter. Sony say that the 900R fitted with a viewfinder, battery, cassette, microphone and a small zoom or prime lens weighs in at 5.4 kilograms, or 12 pounds. The power consumption has also been significantly reduced, thus allowing smaller and lighter batteries to be used. Having had one on my shoulder I am prepared to believe Sony; it's a much more operator-friendly camera than the original F900.

The camera can be switched between several frame rates. For Progressive scan use the available frame rates are 23.98, 24, 25 and 29.97. In interlace mode 50 and 59.94 are available. About the only facilities that were available on the original 900 and have been dropped on the F900R are the frame rates of 30 Progressive and 60 interlace for these were, in practice, found to have very little use.

The available shutter speeds on this model are: Off, 1/32, 1/48, 1/50, 1/60, 1/96, 1/125, 1/250, 1/500 and 1/1000.

Figure 38.1: Sony HDW F900R

The filter wheels contain, on the color correction wheel, A: 5600 K; B: 3200 K; C: 4300 K; and D: 6300 K. The neutral density (ND) wheel contains 1: Clear; 2: 1/4 ND; 3: 1/16 ND; and 4: 1/64 ND. While it is nice to see the almost worthless star filter replaced with the motion picture standard color correction filter of 5600 K, I feel it is a pity Sony have not seen fit to represent the ND filters also in the traditional motion picture way of expressing them as the true measurement of their density, which would be 1: Zero; 2: 0.6 ND; 3: 1.2 ND; and 4: 1.8 ND.

Sony claim that with the camera set at 24P and with 1/48 set as the shutter speed, the sensitivity of the camera will be approximately the equivalent of ISO 300.

38.2 The Chips

The chips and the beam splitter block are the same as for all the Sony HDW cameras in that they contain three 2/3-inch chips, with Red, Green and Blue portions of the image being

Figure 38.2: The Sony HDW F900R in handheld broadcast mode

separated optically as described in greater detail elsewhere in this book. Each FIT charge-coupled device (CCD) chip has a full 1920 × 1080 pixel array, again just as before.

38.3 The Processor

As with the original 900, the F900R utilizes a 12-bit processor while the video tape recorder (VTR) uses the same 4.4:1 compression algorithm, thus outputting to tape a video data rate of 140 MB/s when working in 59.94i mode.

38.4 Additional Facilities

It is also possible to add a picture cache board, which allows up to 8 seconds of buffered recording without the VTR running. Also available is a slow shutter/inverter board and a 2:3 pull-down converter board.

The camera control panel on the front of the camera is much the same as before but with the addition of a microphone level adjustment knob, as can be seen in Figure 38.3.

38.5 Menus

The F900R utilizes a menu system very like the original F900 camera, both in its Sony and Panavision forms.

Figure 38.3: The Sony HDW F900R front control panel

38.6 Overall Impressions

For television work, within most of Europe, the HDW 750P camera seemed to me to be as ideal as was possible with modern technology and a three-chip configuration. It is light and simple to use while giving exceptionally good pictures. The original HDW F900, on the other hand, had the advantages of 24P and a 12-bit processor, both facilities making it ideal when shooting for the cinema but it was unwieldy, especially with the HDSDI converter box on the back, and is heavy and somewhat cumbersome in use, which I can confirm having spent a morning shooting with an F900 on my shoulder fitted with the converter box, a sizeable battery, a Panavision 4.5:1 zoom and a full matte box.

The F900R combines the best of both cameras, being a lighter version than the F900 and having more facilities than the 750. Not surprisingly it does come with a cost premium when compared with the 750P, but is less expensive than the F900 was at the time of its introduction. I, for one, will make the HDW F900R very welcome indeed.

CHAPTER 39

The Sony F23 and F35

39.1 Some Background

At the time of writing, the F23 has been around a relatively short time and details of the F35 were only released very recently. As far as I could discern, hardly any F23s had made it to the UK and no F35s; these cameras are therefore two of only three I review here that I have not actually handled. Nevertheless, it is relatively easy to work out what they do from Sony-released information and their remarkable similarity to the Panavision Genesis. Indeed, it seems almost certain that they are the result of the Joint Venture agreements between Panavision and Sony and I am told that there was a mutual understanding that Sony would not release their versions until at least 2 years after Panavision had released the Genesis.

39.2 Basic Specifications

Both cameras share an almost identical body and both accept the Sony SRW-1 HDCAM-SR video tape recorder (VTR) mountable on top of the camera or on the rear of the camera body, again exactly as with the Genesis. Both cameras utilize a 14-bit analog-to-digital converter. The F35 has a variable frame rate from 1 to 50 frames per second and the F23 has preset steps of 23.98P, 24P, 29.97P, 50P, 59.94P, 50i and 59.94i.

The great difference between the two cameras lies right at the front of the camera bodies. The F23 has a hardened Sony B4 lens mount, behind which is Sony's usual High Definition (HD) optical splitter block with three 2/3-inch image sensors, while the F35 has an Arriflex PL lens mount, behind which is a single charge-coupled device (CCD) sensor the same size as a motion picture Super 35 mm frame, which appears to be the same, or very similar, sensor to the one fitted to the Genesis.

Both the camera bodies are similar though not exactly the same as the Genesis, for Sony have built them to accept standard Arriflex 19 mm bars and film accessories, so all the follow focus devices and matte boxes familiar to film technicians who have used Arri cameras will fit and work in exactly the same way.

Both cameras, together with the VTR, will output and record a full 4:4:4 1920 by 1080 16 × 9 image.

Currently quoted prices suggest that the F23 will retail at around $150,000 and the F35 at around $250,000. Neither camera is therefore aimed at the economy end of the market.

39.3 Why Introduce These Cameras?

From where I sit in the UK, that is not at all an easy question to answer. The F23 echoes the 900R but offers an even higher bit rate and enhanced image manipulation, but I look forward to seeing who will want to spend that much money in order to process the output from most B4 mounted broadcast lenses. Maybe that is the answer: somewhere in the broadcast market there is the demand for such a high-end camera. Time will surely tell.

The F35, on the other hand, despite its cost, does look as if it might have a place in the world currently occupied mainly by 35 mm film. Two of the most popular high-end HD cameras, the Arriflex D-21 and the Panavision Genesis, can currently only be rented from their respective manufacturers and there may well be a lot of camera rental houses currently offering 35 mm film equipment who are looking for just such an HD camera body to extend their footprint in the market and this camera, with its complete compatibility with Arri accessories and the 35 mm lenses they will already have on the shelf, might look a very attractive way to go, particularly if it offers Genesis-type picture quality. This option could greatly open up the progress of HD across the film acquisition world.

CHAPTER 40

The Thomson Viper

Since I wrote the second edition of this book the Thomson Viper has somewhat changed its place in the market. In the UK a few major suppliers have moved away from it, but some very dedicated alternative suppliers have recognized the camera's ability to produce very fine pictures and have dedicated themselves to offering a service that, if taken in its totality, removes some of the downside elements of the camera, notably in the recording formats needed and in post-production.

Thomson has taken a different approach to most other 2/3-inch three-chip camera manufacturers: its primary design parameter was that there should not be any data compression within the camera. This would be described as a 4:4:4 signal. This means that the data stream coming out of the back of the camera is so large that it takes two BNC cables to transfer it to some form of recording format. Thomson has named the form in which the data leave the camera FilmStream. With the current state of data recording technology there is no tape format that can cope with this much information and, if no compression is to be used, it must be fed to a server or some form of hard-disk or solid-state recording format. At its introduction the camera could not be used as a camcorder so the purity and amount of the data coming from it was both its main advantage and its greatest drawback, as recordings could only be made on rather unwieldy equipment and not on any commercially available unit utilizing tape.

40.1 The Camera Body

Figure 40.1 shows the operator side of the camera, which is fitted with a Zeiss 6–27 mm zoom lens. Figure 40.2 shows the other side of the camera. Some film technicians who have seen the camera have taken to its appearance, for it is not dissimilar in shape to the camera body of several current 35 mm film cameras, particularly so if you look at the front of the camera body in Figure 40.2, where you can see the housing for the mechanical shutter that is needed with the Thomson system.

Figure 40.1: The Thomson Viper fitted with a Zeiss 6–27 mm zoom Lens

Figure 40.2: The non-operate side of the Viper

40.2 Outputs from the Camera

At the rear of the camera there are three BNC plugs, the left hand of which is sending High Definition Serial Digital Interface (HDSDI) to a straightforward monitor; the right-hand two are, together, taking the FilmStream signal away for storage.

It is also possible to fit an alternative back to the camera, which will add a third output giving a down-converted PAL signal using a single BNC cable.

40.3 The Hard Drive Recorder

Figure 40.3 shows the DMAG hard-disk recording unit used by Motion FX, who have specialized in offering not only the Viper and a full range of Zeiss lenses to film producers, but have, in house, all the necessary downstream facilities to take the production right through to the finished product for exhibition in a cinema.

40.4 The Beam Splitter

The Thomson camera uses a beam splitter in the same way as all 2/3-inch three-chip cameras. If you refer to Chapter 13, you will find a full explanation of how this works.

40.5 The Viper's CCD Array

The Viper is primarily designed to produce the standard High Definition (HD) format image using 1920 pixels horizontally with 1080 pixels vertically, giving a total of 2,073,600 pixels for the complete image, this being the current international HD standard. The Thomson HD-DPM chip is a little cleverer than this, for while it has 1920 pixels horizontally it has four times as many subpixels vertically, which can be grouped in various ways to give some interesting imagery. If every four vertical subpixels are grouped together, then the standard 1080-line HD image is recorded. If every three pixels are grouped together then very nearly the equivalent of a cinemascope aspect ratio can be recorded, still with a full 1080-line vertical resolution. The actual aspect ratio formed using three-pixel grouping will be 2.37:1. Alternatively, if every five pixels are grouped together then an HD 16 × 9 image will be output in the 720-line format. This ability to switch between formats using subpixels to make up various vertical pixel groupings gives the camera a distinct advantage over cameras with a fixed 1080 vertical pixel array, especially when shooting in the equivalent of an anamorphic format, for then a conventional chip will only have a vertical resolution of a little over 800 lines.

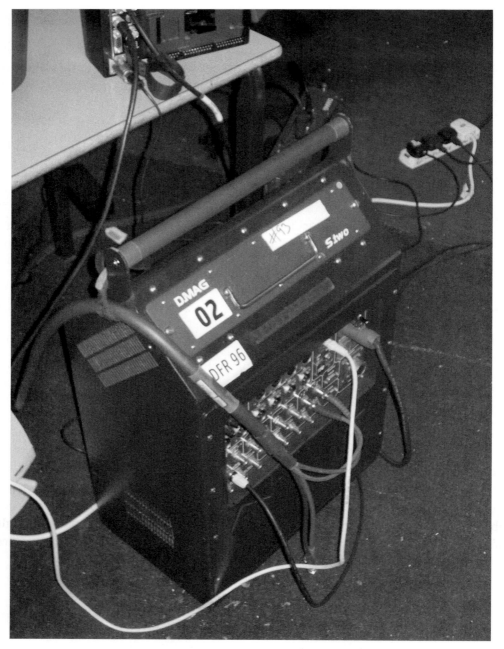

Figure 40.3: The DMAG hard drive recorder

40.6 The Mechanical Shutter

All charge-coupled device (CCD) imaging is sensitive to light at all times, though it can be electronically switched either to convert photons into electrons or to dump the electrons, which effectively switches the pixels off and is commonly known as an electronic shutter. If the Thomson chips are left on all the time there will be some image blur or streaking of moving highlights evident in the image. The Viper therefore uses a mechanical shutter to provide a brief period in every frame cycle during which the imaging chip will not have light reaching it and in this period the information is dumped to a playout-only chip, which is kept continually in the dark, and this releases the imaging chip for the next frame.

The Viper can be set with the mechanical shutter permanently open but the streaking and blur described above will be evident; there may be some occasions where for artistic reasons this is an advantage.

The mechanical shutter has an opening of 312 degrees. The exposure time can be further reduced electronically down to one-thousandth of a second.

40.7 Frame Rates

The Viper can be set to record in a large number of format combinations. It will work in a 1080-line Progressive scan mode both in a 16×9 format and a 2.37:1 format; it will also work in a 1080 interlace format and a 720-line Progressive scan format. Figure 40.4 shows which frame rates are available at the different vertical resolutions in both the available Progressive scan and interlace settings.

40.8 Resolution

Although the Thomson camera has 4320 vertical subpixels, it always groups them into a configuration of 1080 vertical master pixels. It would be wrong to think that the subpixels contribute to a greater resolution, for it is the combined subpixels that are output as a single unit of pixel information and therefore this is the resolution of the data that leave the camera.

40.9 The Camera's Processor Configuration

Figure 40.5 shows a block diagram of the processor stages within the camera. The analog signals from the three-color dedicated CCDs are converted to a 12-bit digital signal immediately behind the chips. If the camera is being used in the higher information FilmStream mode, the signal is then converted from the line 12-bit signal to a logarithmic 10-bit signal and is then sent to some recording device that can handle this information. Additionally, the add-on camera back can convert the RGB digital signal to an HDSDI or PAL

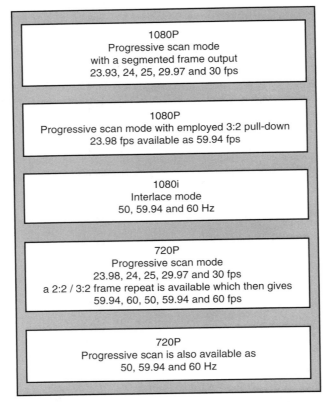

1080P
Progressive scan mode
with a segmented frame output
23.93, 24, 25, 29.97 and 30 fps

1080P
Progressive scan mode with employed 3:2 pull-down
23.98 fps available as 59.94 fps

1080i
Interlace mode
50, 59.94 and 60 Hz

720P
Progressive scan mode
23.98, 24, 25, 29.97 and 30 fps
a 2:2 / 3:2 frame repeat is available which then gives
59.94, 60, 50, 59.94 and 60 fps

720P
Progressive scan is also available as
50, 59.94 and 60 Hz

Figure 40.4: Frame rates available on the Thomson Viper camera

viewing signal. If no viewing facility is required, the add-on converter can be dispensed with and the camera can be set to output a pure FilmStream signal, an RGB signal or a YUV signal.

40.10 The Camera Back

If any viewing facilities are required from the camera a relatively small back can be attached to the camera to convert the signals to more convenient formats. The block diagram of the basic back is shown in Figure 40.6, where the RAW output from the camera is converted from a parallel FilmStream mode to a serial FilmStream mode and four other processors are used to output a conventional HDSDI output.

40.11 The Arguments for a Logarithmic Recording Format

Thomson put forward a strong argument for first converting the output from the imaging chips to a binary digital signal and then translating this signal to a logarithmic digital signal.

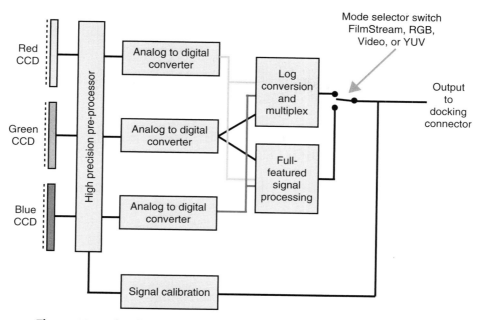

Figure 40.5: Simplified block diagram of the Viper camera's processors

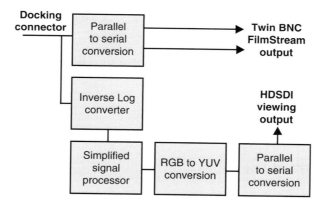

Figure 40.6: Simplified block diagram of the processors in the camera back

The argument is mainly based on two suppositions. First, that the human eye, and film, both respond to light in a logarithmic way and storing the data in a logarithmic form makes these data much more compatible to the image a human being would expect to see. Secondly, the human eye sees much more color and the brain is much more aware of the densities in the darker parts of an image. A logarithmic interpretation of a picture will provide much smaller steps between values in the darker parts of an image than it will for the lighter parts so, again, it is conforming itself to a more human response.

Thomson further claim that a linear 12-bit information stream will contain no more information than a 10-bit logarithmic data stream as the greater information in the shadows is so much better catered for in the logarithmic version that the gross data contained within it is higher than the same picture stored in a linear format.

Things have moved on and now they are far from the only camera manufacturer embracing logarithmic processing.

40.12 Lenses for the Viper

There is no question that the Viper camera is capable of full HD resolution and that outputting a full 4:4:4 signal at least theoretically provides a fuller digital interpretation of that image. The 4:4:4 signal is also arguably more robust, particularly if considerable post-production work is envisaged. Given the above, it would be a waste if the optical image provided to the imaging chips were not able to resolve a circle of confusion much better than one covering two pixels. In my opinion very near a one-pixel resolution must be achieved before the advantages of the Thomson approach will be seen on the screen, especially on a cinema screen.

40.13 Monitors for the Viper

As the Viper can easily deliver a standard HDSDI signal, exactly the same monitors are available as with most HD cameras. Unless you can afford the newer Progressive scan monitors when you pan the camera you will see horizontal stuttering, again exactly as with Sony and many other cameras, and this is not recorded but is simply a monitor problem.

40.14 Camera Accessories

The Viper is totally compatible with Arriflex camera accessories, and the base plate can be supplied to conform with the normal positioning of Arriflex lens support bars; therefore all lens control and matte boxes you would expect to order with a film camera are available with the Viper.

It is probably best to use the same kinds of tripod and tripod leg as you would use with a 35 mm camera, though the more robust ones that you might choose to use with 16 mm equipment should work more than adequately.

40.15 Shipping the Viper

The Viper is a robust camera but as with all sophisticated equipment it must be treated with respect. Standard motion picture precautions will more than suffice.

40.16 Conclusions

The Viper is beginning to look a little dated and because of its dedication to a 4:4:4 output has never been the easiest of cameras to use on location. That said, if you go to a supply company such as Motion FX who have put a huge amount of effort into supplying a service that will take you from shooting right through post-production to the cinema screen then it is, particularly with the Zeiss lenses, a system capable of very good results and can still be economically attractive.

Part 7
Star Gazing

CHAPTER 41

Where Do We Go From Here?

To be honest I haven't a clue! There are so many options with High Definition (HD) and all its higher-end derivatives it would, I suggest, be a foolish person who gave you an absolute answer to the above question. But then by getting to the end of this book you will have, I hope, gathered that I am nothing if not brave.

HD as we know it started in the year 2000 and quickly proved, to those who would listen, that it was a very viable medium which, in many ways, could contest the supremacy of 35 mm film. Many, many people did not want to believe this could possibly happen, but most of them have by now embraced it, or at least accepted it, as a worthy recording format for theatrical and high-end television productions. Ask yourself how long you think it will be before most television broadcasts in the developed world are originated and most often transmitted in HD – not long, I suggest.

41.1 HD Cameras

There are a couple of developments or changes that are starting to come through that, I believe, will seriously alter what will be accepted as the norm for a professional HD camera.

41.1.1 *Broadcast Cameras*

In the broadcast arena there are very significant advantages to using a three-chip camera where the three primary colors are separated by an optical block of three pieces of glass, two of them prisms, and including two dichroic mirrors. This configuration, though far from optically pure, has the significant advantage that there is one chip optically dedicated to providing a signal for each of the primary colors, Red, Green and Blue. This is what television needs and wants – so let TV have it, no problem.

But that optical block has some significant drawbacks if you are trying to make a movie for theatrical release. It severely degrades the optical quality of the image. Inevitably, putting the picture from a lens through all that extra glass does it no good. Also, having to calculate a lens that will refocus the image on the image plane quite a lot behind where it wants to, in order that the image can still focus on the chips after traveling through all that glass, again degrades the purity of the image.

Let us say three-chip cameras are fine within a television environment but get a little stretched when asked to provide the quality required of my arbiter – the Odeon Leicester Square. They can certainly do it on a film with little CGI but their images tend to fall apart a bit if put under post-production pressure.

41.1.2 Cameras That Really Emulate 35 mm Film

The current trend seems to be to produce high-end cameras that can use all the lenses that were so familiar to those who used to work with 35 mm film or those who loved the kind of picture they grew up with in the cinema of their youth. Marvelous, why shouldn't they?

To obtain this "look" an awful lot of cameras recently designed and brought to market now take the approach of utilizing a single sensor, somewhere around the size of the old 35 mm frame. I have to say I like this approach.

The interesting thing about some of these newer single-sensor cameras is that many of them would not be economically viable if the world of digital still cameras had not progressed so far and so fast. Since Oskar Barnack designed what was to become the first Leica 35 mm still camera, that still camera frame has had dimensions of 24 mm × 36 mm, twice the size of the old 35 mm motion silent picture frame of 24 mm × 18 mm. So? This is very significant, believe me.

Early on in the development of digital still cameras designed to replace 35 mm single lens reflex cameras, the designers became aware that unlike a film camera, where image size dictates the number of silver grains available to record that image, a silver grain's size being somewhat finite, the only thing limiting picture quality in a digital camera, at least as far as absolute resolution was concerned, was the number of pixels on the chip, not the size of the chip.

With this in mind it soon became apparent to many digital still camera manufacturers that if they halved the chip size, and most of them chose the 18 mm × 24 mm old silent movie frame size known in the stills world as half frame, a significant number of advantages would accrue provided there were still enough pixels on the chip. Cameras could be smaller, lighter and probably cheaper. More importantly, to cover the same field of view lenses only needed to be less than half the focal length and, again, would become smaller, lighter and cheaper. This was particularly important in many fields of still photography; think of the poor sports photographer working for a newspaper having to use a 600 mm lens on a 35 mm film to get that shot of, say, the goalkeeper. Now a lens no longer than 300 mm would be needed. Not only would this be lighter in the hand, but it would also encounter far less camera shake in the heat of the action.

How does this relate to motion picture cameras? The most significant contribution is that if these 18 mm × 24 mm sensors could be used in a moving picture camera then virtually all the lenses film motion picture crews were used to would give them the same image size, the same field of view and the same depth of field. Suddenly a digital movie camera would start to give images that looked very familiar, at least within these parameters.

The only problem was that early digital still cameras using an 18 mm × 24 mm sensor took some time to process the data from the chip. One solution was to buffer the data so that you could take a rapid sequence of perhaps five shots and you then had to wait several seconds for those data to be processed and written to the memory chip. This approach was not going to work with a camera that had to take at least 24 pictures a second and might very well be asked to shoot for at least 10 minutes before stopping and allowing the buffered pictures to be downloaded.

So, simplistically, what camera manufacturers did was put one hell of a big computer chip in the camera so that they could use the still camera sensors and feed the data into something very like Photoshop, but the size of the processor would allow Photoshop to process 24 pictures per second.

Job done? Not quite. The time taken for a still camera to process the image before storing it allowed the processor to undertake considerable noise reduction programs and, if a complementary metal-oxide semiconductor (CMOS) sensor with Bayer patterning was used, apply some sophisticated data processing to get rid of the excess of green, etc.

As I write, data processors are becoming able to handle huge amounts of data, enabling very sophisticated picture processing to happen at least 24 times a second, and several cameras can work very happily at 50 frames per second or even faster.

So my prediction for cameras? Very soon we will see cameras able to process images at significantly higher frame rates; they will have high resolution and far less noise in the shadows than many show at present. This will require bigger and faster processors, so how big and heavy the camera battery will be remains to be seen.

41.2 Recording Formats

It looks like the movie world is heading for solid-state recording, with all that entails. It does allow much higher data transfer rates but, with the present cards etc., the workflow on set to be able to safely reuse these storage media can be a bit of a nightmare. As the perceived notion is that every 2 years storage capabilities multiply by a factor of 10 and the new 10 times bigger storage costs about the same, I can only imagine that this will free up camera manufacturers to do even more wonderful things. Let's hope so.

41.3 Entertaining our Audience

None of the above is really going to help our audience very much. I am sorry to disappoint you.

At the end of the day all our audience wants is a good story well told and without anything to come between that story and their suspension of disbelief in the storytelling process.

Let's hear it for good scripts!

And that seems to me to be an appropriate place to end this book.

Thank you for reading. Hopefully we will meet again for the next edition – when things will certainly be very different!

Index